sixth edition

Phonics They Use
Words for Reading and Writing

Patricia M. Cunningham
Wake Forest University

PEARSON

Boston • Columbus • Indianapolis • New York • San Francisco • Upper Saddle River
Amsterdam • Cape Town • Dubai • London • Madrid • Milan • Munich • Paris • Montréal • Toronto
Delhi • Mexico City • São Paulo • Sydney • Hong Kong • Seoul • Singapore • Taipei • Tokyo

Vice President, Editor-in-Chief: Aurora Martínez Ramos
Associate Sponsoring Editor: Barbara Strickland
Editorial Assistant: Katherine Wiley
Senior Marketing Manager: Christine Gatchell
Executive Marketing Manager: Krista Clark
Production Manager: Maggie Brobeck
Editorial Production and Composition Service: Jouve India
Interior Design: Denise Hoffman
Cover Design: Karen Noferi

Credits and acknowledgments borrowed from other sources and reproduced, with permission, in this textbook appear on appropriate page within text.

Cover image: Getty Images/Digital Vision

Photo of author on back cover by Dorothy P. Hall
Photos in text by Patricia M. Cunningham unless otherwise indicated.

Many of the designations by manufacturers and sellers to distinguish their products are claimed as trademarks. Where those designations appear in this book, and the publisher was aware of a trademark claim, the designations have been printed in initial caps or all caps.

10 9 8 7 6 5 4 3 2 1

ISBN 10: 0-13-294409-X
ISBN 13: 978-0-13-294409-0

brief contents

contents

part two
Fluency   **75**

part four
Research and Terminology   *223*

introduction

When this book first appeared in 1991, very few reading gurus—my best friends included—gave it much of a chance. Phonics was not something you talked about, and most people believed (or pretended to believe) that teachers had stopped doing it! Somehow the first edition sold enough copies to allow it to be revised, and the second edition appeared just as people were beginning once again to talk about phonics. As this sixth edition appears, my concerns about phonics have done a complete about-face! Underemphasized in 1991, for the last decade it has dominated the curriculum in many schools. I think of the old Beatles song, "All You Need Is Love!" When people talk about teaching children to read, they are often saying, "All You Need Is Phonics!" Phonics is an important part of any complete reading program—but it is only one part. It is necessary, but not sufficient! Children need to be reading and writing, to be read to, and to be taught how to comprehend what they read. A complete reading program includes all the necessary components to turn children into avid, thoughtful readers and writers. In this edition of *Phonics They Use*, I have redoubled my efforts to remind you that what matters is not how much phonics they know—but what they actually use when they need it for decoding a new word while reading and spelling a new word while writing.

The biggest change in this edition is the addition of three chapters on assessment. Assessment now plays a huge role in literacy instruction. Teachers at all grade levels spend a lot of their precious instructional time giving assessments, scoring assessments, reporting assessments, and preparing students to take the assessments. In many schools, assessment has become the "tail that is wagging the dog." Assessment is an important part of instruction. Good, valid assessments lead us to make wise decisions about who needs what kind of instruction. But that instruction is why assessment matters. If assessment is taking the lion's share of the time, little time is left for the instruction that assessment was intended to inform. All three assessment chapters provide ways teachers can incorporate assessment into their daily literacy routines. Chapter 5 provides a checklist of early reading concepts and ways teachers can observe their children in daily literacy activities to determine how well each child is developing these concepts. Chapter 8 describes how the fluency measures can be expanded to also give you information about a reader's word-identification accuracy, expression, and comprehension. In Chapter 13, you will find phonics assessments that help you determine which decoding strategies students are actually using as they read and write, not just which letter-sounds they know.

Schools all over the country are experiencing a huge increase in the number of English language learners in classrooms at all grade levels. In this edition of *Phonics They Use*, I have included suggestions for making phonics and spelling instruction more successful for children facing the daunting task of learning a new language as they learn to read and write. "For English Language Learners" boxes appear throughout the chapters and include a variety of ways teachers have adapted the *Phonics They Use* activities to include their students who are learning English.

Relevant new research is included in the research summary in Chapter 14. All the previous chapters have been updated and contain some of the best activities from prior editions along with some new ideas and activities.

Part One has five chapters that together will help you establish a firm foundation for all children to learn to read. Chapter 1 defines five critical understandings children must develop to start their journey down the literacy road: the functions of print and the desire to learn to read, print concepts, phonological and phonemic awareness, concrete words, and letter names and sounds. Four activities—shared reading of predictable books, predictable charts, writing, and "Getting to Know You"—are included to help you build these early reading concepts.

Phonological and phonemic awareness are the focus of Chapter 2. Children develop their phonological awareness as they learn to count words and clap syllables. Their phonemic awareness is expanded as they participate in the activities designed to develop the concept of rhyme and teach blending and segmenting. Activities are also included using the children's names to build phonological and phonemic awareness.

Chapter 3 contains activities to build children's store of concrete words and to teach letter names and sounds. Activities in this chapter include focusing on the names of letters, using alphabet books, learning foods and actions to solidify letter sounds, establishing key words for sounds, and enjoying two very popular activities, "Changing a Hen to a Fox" and "Guess the Covered Word."

Making Words is a popular, multilevel phonics activity enjoyed by teachers and students. In Chapter 4, you will find the kindergarten version of Making Words. Instead of manipulating little letter cards, which many five-year-olds find to be a difficult eye-hand coordination task, children become the letters and arrange themselves to spell the words.

Chapter 5 is one of the new assessment chapters. Here you will find a checklist of early reading concepts and ways to determine who is learning what by observing their interactions during the activities described in the previous chapters. Chapter 5 also includes suggestions for differentiating instruction based on your observation and analysis of your students' responses.

Part Two has three chapters that provide activities for helping children learn to read and write fluently. Chapter 6 suggests classroom-tested ways to develop fluency. Children become fluent readers as they engage in easy reading, observe models of expressive reading, and engage in meaningful, enjoyable repeated reading activities.

Chapter 7 describes activities for teaching high-frequency words. In English, a little over 100 words account for every other word we read and write. Most of these words are abstract, meaningless, connecting words. Many of them have irregular spellings and pronunciations. Chapter 7 describes ways to build meaning for these words and explains how to use a word wall so that children learn to automatically and rapidly identify them while reading and spell them while writing.

Chapter 8 includes ways to expand the pervasive Words Correct per Minute (WCPM) fluency, which only measures reading speed, to measure the other essential components of fluency—accuracy, expression, and comprehension. Chapter 8 also includes some fluency interventions that have been shown to be effective in improving both fluency and reading achievement.

Part Three contains activities that will help your students use rhyming and morphemic patterns to decode and spell words. In Chapter 9, you will learn how Making Words can help all levels of children move forward in their decoding and spelling abilities. Chapter 10 focuses on rhyming patterns with a variety of activities you can use to teach children to decode and spell using patterns. Chapter 11 includes activities to help your students learn to decode and spell using roots, prefixes, and suffixes—the building blocks of many polysyllabic words in English. In Chapter 12 you will discover how you can use the Making Words format with older children to teach them the morphemic patterns we use to decode and spell big words. Chapter 13 includes assessments you can use to determine not just what your students know about phonics but what decoding and spelling strategies they actually use when they read and write. Chapter 13 also includes coaching strategies for students who know phonics skills but don't use them when they are reading and writing, as well as activities that older struggling readers who still need phonics instruction find engaging and from which they can learn decoding strategies that most children master in the early grades.

Part Four includes a chapter on the theory and research underlying the instruction in *Phonics They Use* and a chapter on phonics terminology. Everything in *Phonics They Use* is grounded in the research literature, and the pertinent research is summarized in Chapter 14. The last chapter summarizes some of the major terminology teachers are expected to know. The chapter cautions you not to use too much of this jargon with your students because it may confuse them and take their attention away from what you are really trying to teach them. Since teachers are expected to know this terminology, however, Chapter 15 provides you with a handy reference.

New to This Edition

A new chapter on assessment and differentiation of early reading concepts (**Chapter 5**) includes a checklist of early reading concepts and ways to determine who is learning what by observing their interactions during the activities described in the previous chapters. Chapter 5 also includes suggestions for differentiating instruction based on your observation and analysis of your students' responses.

A new chapter on fluency assessment and interventions (**Chapter 8**) includes ways to expand the pervasive Words Correct per Minute (WCPM) fluency, which only measures reading speed, to measure the other essential components of fluency—accuracy, expression, and comprehension. Chapter 8 also includes some fluency interventions that have been shown to be effective in improving both fluency and reading achievement.

A new chapter on phonics assessment, coaching, and interventions (**Chapter 13**) includes assessments you can use to determine not just what your students know about phonics but what decoding and spelling strategies they actually use when they read and write. Chapter 13 also includes ways to coach students who know phonics skills but don't use them and phonics interventions for older struggling readers.

More suggestions and adaptations for English language learners, scattered throughout the chapters, will help make phonics and spelling instruction more successful for English language learners as they learn to read and write. These "For English Language Learners" boxes contain valuable information on ways to include students who are learning English.

Phonics interventions for older struggling readers: Some older students who struggle with reading have not learned basic phonics skills. Using activities such as Brand Name Phonics, The Wheel, and Mystery Word Match, older students can learn to use patterns from words they know to decode and spell other words, including big words.

Updated research, materials, and technology tips

New! CourseSmart eTextbook Available

CourseSmart is an exciting choice for purchasing this book. As an alternative to purchasing the printed book, you may purchase an electronic version of the same content via CourseSmart for a PC or Mac and for Android devices, or an iPad, iPhone, and iPod Touch with CourseSmart Apps. With a CourseSmart eBook, you can read the text, search through it, make notes online, and bookmark important passages for later review. For more information or to purchase access to the CourseSmart eBook for this text, visit **www.coursesmart.com**.

Look for availability of alternative eBook platforms and accessibility for a variety of devices on **www.mypearsonstore.com** by inserting the ISBN of this text and searching for access codes that will allow you to choose your most convenient online usage.

Acknowledgments

I am indebted to all the wonderful teachers who have shared their ideas and adaptations of ideas for making phonics instruction both informative and engaging. I hope this new edition of *Phonics They Use* will continue to support you in providing the best, most multilevel, and transfer-oriented phonics instruction possible. In addition, I would like to thank the reviewers for this edition: JaneMarie Dewailly, Arkansas State University; Christine M. Eaton, Little Learners Early Childhood Center, Inc., Olathe, KS; Christine Frazer, Henry P. Fieler Elementary School, Merrillville, IN; James E. Gentry, Tarleton State University, Stephenville, TX; Tracy Hendrix, Carnesville Elementary School, Carnesville, GA; Allison Wynhoff Olsen, The Ohio State University; Melissa Olson, Eau Claire Area School District, Eau Claire, WI; and Shayne B. Piasta, The Ohio State University.

part one

Building the Foundation for Phonics They Can Use

Part One has five chapters that together will help you establish a firm foundation for teaching all children to read. Chapter 1 defines five critical understandings children must develop to start their journey down the literacy road:

Functions of print and desire to learn to read

Print concepts

Phonological and phonemic awareness

Concrete words

Letter names and sounds

Four activities—shared reading of predictable books, predictable charts, writing, and "Getting to Know You"—are described to build these early reading concepts.

Phonological and phonemic awareness are the focus of Chapter 2. Children develop their phonological awareness as they learn to count words and clap syllables. Their phonemic awareness is expanded as they participate in the activities designed to develop the concept of rhyme and teach blending and segmenting. Activities are also included using the children's names to build phonological and phonemic awareness.

Chapter 3 contains activities to build children's store of concrete words and to teach letter names and sounds. Activities in this chapter include focusing on the names of letters, using alphabet books, learning foods and actions to solidify letter sounds, establishing key words for sounds, and enjoying two very popular activities, "Changing a Hen to a Fox" and "Guess the Covered Word." Chapter 4 presents sample lessons for Making Words in kindergarten. Chapter 5 describes assessments you can use to determine how your students are developing the early reading concepts and ways to differentiate instruction.

chapter 1

Early Reading and Writing Activities

Before we begin helping children learn letter–sound relationships they can use— we must be sure our students know what they are trying to learn and how it is useful to them. There is a tremendous amount of research, usually included under the term *emergent literacy* (Teale & Sulzby, 1991), that shows us what happens in the homes of children where literacy is a priority. We know that children born into homes where someone spends time with them in reading and writing activities will walk into our schools with an incredible foundation on which our instruction can easily build. These children experience an average of over 1,000 hours of quality one-on-one reading and writing activities.

Parents (or parent substitutes including grandmothers, aunts, uncles, brothers, and sisters) read to children and talk with them about what they are reading. This reading is usually done in the lap position, where the child can see the pictures as well as the words used to tell about the pictures. Favorite books are read again and again, and eventually most children choose a book that they pretend-read—usually to a younger friend or a stuffed animal.

In addition to reading, these children are exposed to writing at an early age. They scribble and make up ways to spell words. They ask (and are told) how to spell favorite words. They make words with magnetic letters and copy favorite words from books. From the over 1,000 hours of reading and writing experiences, these children learn some incredibly important concepts. These concepts include:

Functions of print and desire to learn to read

Print concepts

Phonological and phonemic awareness

Concrete words

Letter names and sounds

Early Reading Concepts

❋ Functions of Print and Desire to Learn to Read

Imagine you are visiting in a kindergarten classroom. You have a chance to talk with several children, and you ask them, "Why are you learning to read and write?" Some children answer, "You have to learn to read and write." When pushed, they can name all kinds of "real-world" things as reasons for reading and writing—books, newspapers, magazines, recipes, and maps. Other children respond to the why-learn-to-read-and-write question with answers such as "to do your workbook," "to read in reading group," and "to go to second grade." Children who give "school-world" answers to this critical question demonstrate that they don't see reading and writing as part of their real world. Children who don't know what reading is for in the real world do not have the same drive and motivation as children for whom reading and writing, like eating and sleeping, are things everyone does. In addition, children who pretend-read a memorized book and "write" a letter to Grandma want to learn to read and write and are confident that they can!

❋ Print Concepts

Print is what you read and write. Print includes all the funny little marks—letters, punctuation, space between words and paragraphs—that translate into familiar spoken language. In English, you read across the page in a left-to-right fashion. Because your eyes can see only a few words during each stop (called a fixation), you must actually move your eyes several times to read one line of print. When you finish that line, you make a return sweep and start all over again, left to right. If there are sentences at the top of a page and a picture in the middle and more sentences at the bottom, you read the top first and then the bottom. You start at the front of a book and go toward the back. These arbitrary rules about how we proceed through print are called *conventions*.

Jargon refers to all the words we use to talk about reading and writing. Jargon includes such terms as *word, letter, sentence,* and *sound.* We use this jargon constantly as we try to teach beginners to read:

> "Look at the *first word* in the *second sentence.* How does that *word begin*? What *letter* has that *sound*?"

Using some jargon is essential to talking with children about reading and writing, but children who don't come from rich literacy backgrounds are often very confused by this jargon. Although all children speak in words, they don't know words exist as separate entities until they are put in the presence of reading and writing. To many children, letters are what you get in the mailbox, sounds are horns and bells and doors slamming, and sentences are what you have to serve if you get caught committing a crime! These children are unable to follow our "simple" instructions because we are using words for which they have no meaning or an entirely different meaning.

Many children, however, come to school knowing these print concepts. From being read to in the lap position, they have noticed how the eyes "jump" across the lines of print as someone is reading. They have watched people write grocery lists and thank-you notes to Grandma and have observed the top–bottom, left–right movement. Often, they have typed on the computer and observed these print conventions. Because they have had someone to talk with them about reading and writing, they have learned much of the jargon.

While writing down a dictated thank-you note to Grandma, Dad may say, "Say your sentence one word at a time if you want me to write it. I can't write as fast as you can talk." When the child asks how to spell **birthday,** he may be told, "It starts with the letter **b,** just like your dog Buddy's name. **Birthday** and **Buddy** start with the same sound and the same letter."

Children with reading and writing experiences know how to look at print and what teachers are talking about as they give them information about print. All children need to develop these critical understandings in order to learn to read and write.

✳ Phonological and Phonemic Awareness

Phonological awareness and *phonemic awareness* are terms that refer to children's understandings about words and sounds in words. *Phonological awareness* is the broader term and includes the ability to separate sentences into words and words into syllables. Phonemic awareness includes the ability to recognize that words are made up of a discrete set of sounds and to manipulate sounds. Phonemic awareness is important because children's levels of phonemic awareness are highly correlated with their success in beginning reading (Ehri & Nunes, 2002; National Reading Panel, 2000). Phonological awareness develops through a series of stages during which children first become aware that language is made up of individual words, that words are made up of syllables, and that syllables are made up of phonemes. It is important to note here that it is not the "jargon" children learn. Five-year-olds cannot tell you there are three syllables in **dinosaur** and one syllable in **Rex**. What they can do is clap out the three beats in **dinosaur** and the one beat in **Rex**. Likewise, they cannot tell you that the first phoneme in **mice** is "**mmm,**" but they can tell you what you would have if you took the **mmm** off **mice—ice.** Children develop this phonemic awareness as a result of the oral and written language they are exposed to. Nursery rhymes, chants, and Dr. Seuss books usually play a large role in this development.

Phonemic awareness is an oral ability. You hear the words that rhyme. You hear that **baby** and **book** begin the same. You hear the three sounds in **bat** and can say these sounds separately. Only when children realize that words can be changed and how changing a sound changes the word are they able to profit from instruction in letter–sound relationships.

Children also develop a sense of sounds and words as they try to write. In the beginning, many children let a single letter stand for an entire word. Later, they use more letters and often say the word they want to write, dragging out its sounds to hear what letters they might use. Children who are allowed and encouraged to "invent-spell" develop an early and strong sense of phonemic awareness.

❋ Concrete Words

If you sit down with kindergartners on the first day of school and try to determine if they can read by giving them a new book to read or testing them on some common words such as **the, and, of,** or **with,** you would probably conclude that most kindergartners can't read yet. But many kindergartners can read and write some words. Here are some words a boy named David could read when he went to kindergarten:

> David
>
> Mama
>
> Daddy
>
> Bear Bear (his favorite stuffed animal)
>
> Carolina (his favorite basketball team)
>
> Pizza Hut
>
> I love you (written on notes on good days)
>
> I hate you (written on notes on bad days)

Most children who have had reading and writing experiences will have learned 10 to 15 words before entering school. The words they learn are usually concrete words that are important to them. Being able to read these words matters, not because they can read much with these few words, but because children who come to school already able to read or write some concrete words have accomplished an important and difficult task. They have learned how to learn words.

❋ Letter Names and Sounds

Finally, many children have learned some letter names and sounds. They may not be able to recognize all 26 letters in both upper- and lowercase, and they often don't know the sounds of **w** or **v,** but they have learned the names and sounds for the most common letters. Usually, the letter names and sounds children know are based on those concrete words they can read and write.

❋ The Foundation

From the research on emergent literacy, we know that many preschoolers have hundreds of hours of literacy interactions during which they develop understandings critical to their success in beginning reading. We must now structure our school programs to try to provide for all children what some children have had. This will not be an easy task. We don't have 1,000 hours, and we don't have the luxury of doing it with one child at a time, and when the child is interested in doing it! But we must do all we can, and we must do it in ways that are as close to the home experiences as possible. In the remainder of this chapter, you will find activities successfully used by kindergarten and first-grade teachers who are committed to putting all children in the presence of reading and writing and allowing all children to learn:

Functions of print and desire to learn to read

Print concepts

Phonological and phonemic awareness

Concrete words

Letter names and sounds

For older children just acquiring English, these understandings are also critical for them to develop the foundation on which reading and writing can grow.

Shared Reading of Predictable Books

Teachers of young children have always recognized the importance of reading a variety of books to children. There is one particular kind of book and one particular kind of reading, however, that has special benefits for building the reading and writing foundations—shared reading with predictable Big Books.

Shared reading is a term used to describe the process in which the teacher and the children read a book together. The book is read and reread many times. On the first several readings, the teacher usually does all of the reading. As the children become more familiar with the book, they join in and "share" the reading. In order to share in the reading, your children must be able to see the words as well as the pictures. There are many wonderful Big Books and if you have access to a document camera or can scan the pages and project them on your smart board, you can enlarge the print in smaller books. News magazines for primary children, including *Time for Kids, Scholastic News,* and *Weekly Reader,* often include a "big picture" edition. You can use this enlarged edition for shared reading, and then students can read the normal-size edition with friends or in centers, or they can take it home to share with families.

Predictable books are the best kind of books to use with shared reading. Predictable books are books in which repeated patterns, refrains, pictures, and rhyme allow children to "pretend-read" a book that has been read to them several times. Pretend reading is a stage most children go through with a favorite book that some patient adult has read and reread to them. Perhaps you remember pretend reading with such popular predictable books as *Goodnight Moon, Are You My Mother?,* or *Brown Bear, Brown Bear.* Shared reading of predictable books allows all children to experience this pretend reading. From this pretend reading, they learn what reading is, and they develop the confidence that they will be able to do it. They also develop print concepts and begin to understand how letters, sounds, and words work.

In choosing something for shared reading, consider three criteria. First, the text must be very predictable. The most important goal for shared reading is that even children with little experience with books and stories will be able to pretend-read the book after several readings and develop the confidence that goes along with that accomplishment. Thus, you want a book without too much print and one in which the sentence patterns are very repetitive and the pictures support those sentence patterns.

Second, you want a book that will be very appealing to the children. Since the whole class of children will work with the same book, and since the book will be read and reread, you should try to choose a book that many children will fall in love with.

Finally, the book should take you someplace conceptually. Many teachers choose books to fit their units or build units around the books.

Shared reading is called "shared" because the children join in the reading. There are many ways to encourage children to join in. Many teachers read the book to the children the first time and then just invite the children to join in when they can on subsequent reading. You might also want to "echo read" the book, with you reading each line and then the children being your echo and reading it again. Some teachers like to read the book with the children several times and then make an audio recording in which the teacher reads some parts and the whole class or groups of children read the other parts. Children delight in going to the listening center and listening to themselves reading the book!

In addition to books, many teachers write favorite poems, chants, songs, and finger-plays on long sheets of paper or on the smart board. These become some of the first things children can actually read. Most teachers teach the poem, chant, song, or finger-play to the children first. Once the children have learned to say, chant, or sing it, they then are shown what the words look like. The progression to reading is a natural one, and children soon develop the critical "of course, I can read" self-confidence. Once children can read the piece, many teachers copy it and send it home so that each child can read it to parents and other family members. They also place copies in centers and around the room so that children can read these favorite pieces as they do center reading and read the room.

After the book has been read, enjoyed, and reread in a variety of ways, most children will be able to read (or pretend-read) most of the book. This early "I can read" confidence is critical to emerging readers, and the shared book experience as described is a wonderful way to foster this. When engaging in shared reading with predictable books, try to simulate what would happen in the home with a child who delights in having a favorite book read again and again. First, you focus on the book itself, on enjoying it, rereading it, talking about it, and often acting it out. As you do this, you develop concepts and oral language. When most of the children can pretend-read the book, you focus their attention on the print. Provide writing activities related to the book and help children learn print conventions, jargon, and concrete words. When children know some concrete words, you use these words to begin to build phonemic awareness and letter–sound knowledge.

❊ Children Understand What Reading Is for and Develop the Desire to Learn to Read as They Engage in Shared Reading

As children join in the shared reading of a predictable book, they experience what reading is. They know what it feels like and sounds like and, most importantly, they develop the confidence and desire to learn to read. Think of shared reading experiences as the training wheels on a bike. Training wheels allow a child to get the feel of the bike, to steer and stop, to ride faster and slower, without also having to concentrate on keeping the bike upright. Once the child develops confidence in bike riding and some bike riding skills, the training wheels are removed and the child rides without them—but often with a parent running alongside the bike! Soon, the child will ride the bike completely on his or her own. Shared reading allows children to experience reading before they have all the print tracking and decoding skills to read on their own. As they develop these skills, they will move toward being independent readers and will no longer need the training wheels support provided by shared reading.

❊ Children Develop Print Concepts as They Engage in Shared Reading

Once you and the children have read and reread a favorite predictable book, poem, song, or chant, you can use that text to help them develop print concepts, including some important jargon such as *word* and *sentence* and *tracking print from left to right*. The most concrete activity you can use to build these print concepts is called Sentence Builders. In Sentence Builders, you write all the words and punctuation marks from a portion of the text on separate index cards. The cards are distributed to various children and these children build a sentence by matching their card to the words and punctuation marks in the text.

Here is how the words for the Sentence Builder activity for *Brown Bear, Brown Bear* might get done. The teacher and children reread the first page of *Brown Bear, Brown Bear,* and the teacher asks the children to tell her what words and punctuation marks to write on the cards. Directed by the children, she prints one to a card these words:

The teacher places these words in order along the chalk ledge or in a pocket chart and the children read the sentence chorally.

The teacher turns the page and tells the children that she wants to write all the words and punctuation marks needed to make the sentence on this page but not write again any words already written. The children decide that she needs a card for:

But not for *see,* which is already written; cards are needed for:

This sentence is then constructed taking the *see* out of the first sentence.

The process speeds up as the children realize that just a few words need to be written for each of the remaining pages. The words not already written from previous sentences are written as needed, and each sentence is built along the chalk ledge or in the pocket chart. Each sentence is also read chorally as one child points to the words to be read.

Once the book is completed, you have all the words and punctuation marks needed to do Sentence Builders for each sentence in *Brown Bear, Brown Bear*. Distribute all the cards to all the children, giving several words to some children if necessary. Go back to the beginning of the book and have the class read the sentence chorally as the children who have cards with words or punctuation marks in that sentence come to the front of the room and build that sentence. Children love being the words and making the sentences. Equally important, since they become the words, they are interacting with the text to learn left-to-right sequence and the difference between a word and a sentence.

After doing this sentence-building activity as a class, put the book and the cards in a center so that your children can manipulate the words and re-create the text.

❋ Children Learn Some Words as They Engage in Shared Reading

Imagine that you have read and reread *Brown Bear, Brown Bear* or any of the many favorite predictable books with your students. You have written the words on cards and let the children match the words to sentences in the book and build the sentences. You have done the Sentence Builder activity several different times, allowing different children to be different words. Children are going to learn some of the words. Many children will learn the concrete words that name the animals, such as **bear, bird,** and **duck.** They might also learn some of the color words, such as **brown, red,** and **yellow.** Because words are repeated in all the sentences, some children will learn some of the abstract connecting words, such as **what, do, you, see, I,** and **at.**

As noted at the beginning of this chapter, children from literate homes have often experienced 1,000 hours of reading and writing before coming to school. Many of the books read to young children are predictable books that they insist on having read over and over and from which they learn some of the words. Shared reading simulates this experience and gives everyone the opportunity to encounter what reading feels like, to understand print concepts, and to learn to read some words.

Predictable Charts

Just as children enjoy reading predictable books together, they also like to write and read predictable charts. A predictable chart is created by the teacher and children. What makes it predictable is that all the sentences begin with the same stem. Each child's response completes the sentence. The first predictable chart made in Mrs. C's classroom simply included the names of all the class members.

The teacher always begins the chart, modeling the sentence pattern she wants children to use.

My name is Mrs. C.

figure 1.1   **The first predictable chart made in Mrs. C's classroom**

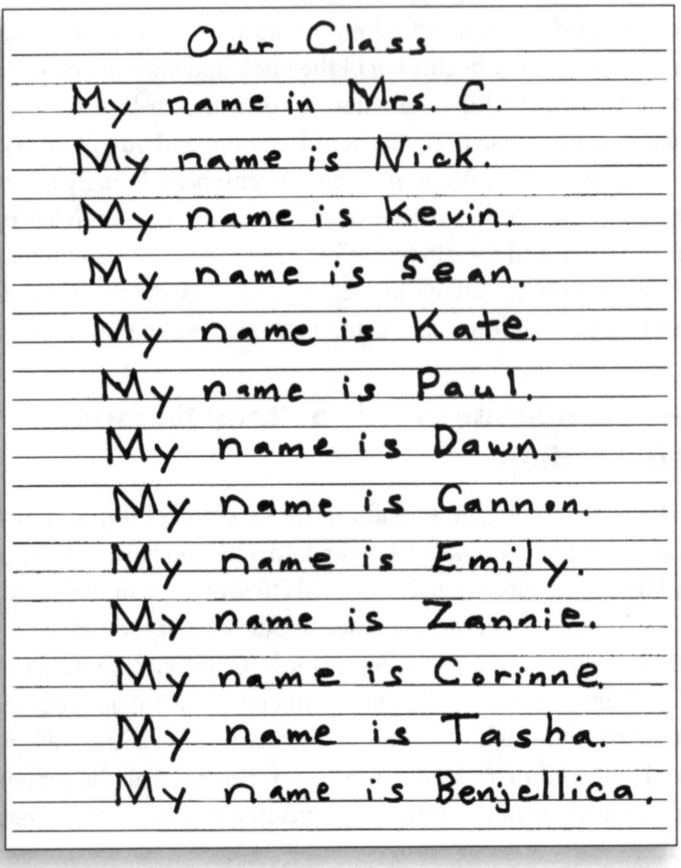

> Our Class
> My name in Mrs. C.
> My name is Nick.
> My name is Kevin.
> My name is Sean.
> My name is Kate.
> My name is Paul.
> My name is Dawn.
> My name is Cannon.
> My name is Emily.
> My name is Zannie.
> My name is Corinne.
> My name is Tasha.
> My name is Benjellica.

Next, the teacher calls on each child to tell his or her name. The teacher writes each sentence on the chart and leads all the children to all read each sentence. Once the chart is written, each child comes and reads his or her sentence pointing to each word as the word is read.

For the second predictable chart, Mrs. C chose to focus on colors.

After a discussion of favorite colors, Mrs. C began a chart on Colors by saying and writing the first sentence. She put her name in parentheses after the sentence so that everyone would know it was her sentence.

I like green. (Mrs. C)

Next she called on Kevin to tell his favorite color.

I like red. (Kevin)

Maria and Sean were called next.

I like pink. (Maria)
I like red. (Sean)

figure 1.2　**The Colors predictable chart**

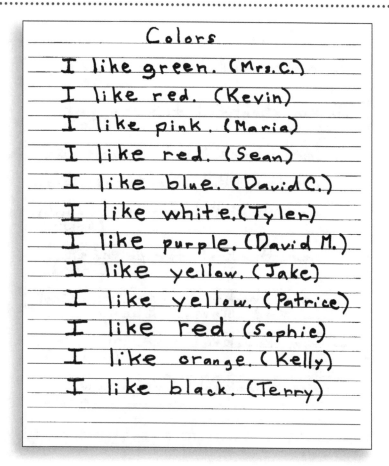

As Thanksgiving approached, Mrs. C and her children made a chart telling what they were thankful for.

In Mrs. C's classroom, there are many children who have limited early reading experiences and several English language learners. She does a new chart each week and uses the chart to teach print concepts, to teach concrete and function words, and to be sure every child knows what reading and writing are for and is developing the confidence to become a reader and a writer. Here is how the predictable chart activities proceed in a typical week.

Monday　Half the class meets with Mrs. C, and she begins the chart with their sentences. After each sentence is written, all the children read that sentence as the child whose sentence it is points to the words.

Tuesday　The other half of the class meets with Mrs. C. Their sentences are added to the chart and read by all the students.

Wednesday　On Wednesday, the whole class gathers and chorally reads the whole chart. Next the teacher asks children to come up to the chart and point out

figure 1.3   **The Thanksgiving predictable chart**

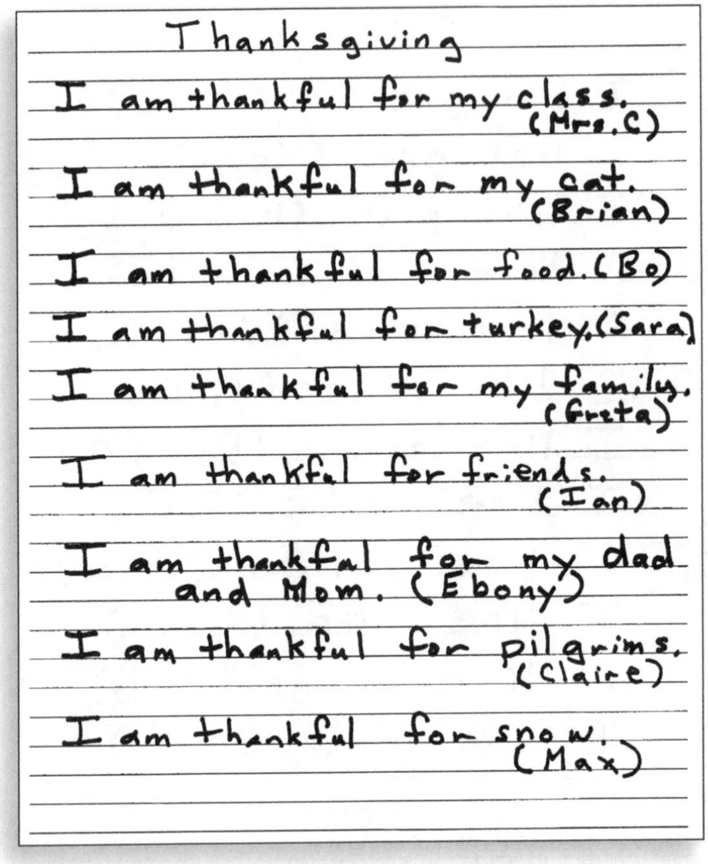

```
Thanksgiving
I am thankful for my class.
                        (Mrs. C)
I am thankful for my cat.
                       (Brian)
I am thankful for food. (Bo)
I am thankful for turkey. (Sara)
I am thankful for my family.
                        (Greta)
I am thankful for friends.
                        (Ian)
I am thankful for my dad
    and Mom. (Ebony)
I am thankful for pilgrims.
                      (Claire)
I am thankful for snow.
                    (Max)
```

anything they notice. The children notice a variety of things depending on what they know about letters, sounds, words, and reading. These may include:

"All sentences begin with **I Like**."

"**Pink** and **purple** begin with the same letter."

"**Kevin's** and **Kelly's** names start with a capital **K**."

"**I** is at the beginning of every sentence!"

"**I** is always a capital (or big) letter."

"**Benjellica** has the longest name."

"**Bo** has the shortest name."

"All sentences have this [pointing to all the periods] at the end."

When the children have "noticed" all kinds of important concepts about print and words on the chart, Mrs. C tells them that she needs their help to make the word cards needed to create all the sentences on the chart. Mrs. C leads the class to read the first sentence on the chart:

I am thankful for my class. (Mrs. C)

The children tell her what the words are and she writes these words on index cards.

figure 1.4   Words in the first sentence written on index cards

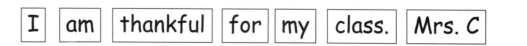

Together, they read the second sentence:

I am thankful for my cat. (Brian)

The class decides that two new words are needed to create Brian's sentence. The teacher writes these on index cards. To make Brian's sentence, the class decides that they need to remove the word *class* and Mrs. C's name and replace these with the word *cat* and Brian's name. Brian does the honors.

figure 1.5   Brian's sentence with the words written on index cards

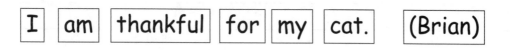

The lesson proceeds more quickly as the children realize that cards need to be created just for the last words and each student's name. Cards are created and the child whose sentence is being made replaces the words from the previous sentence to create the new sentence.

figure 1.6   Ebony's sentence

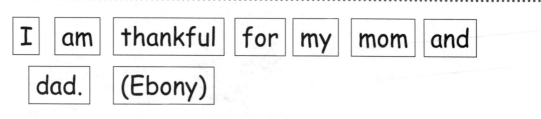

Thursday   The word cards made on the previous day are used to do a sentence builder activity similar to that described for *Brown Bear, Brown Bear*. The word cards are distributed to all the children. Each child gets his or her own name and one or two other cards. The class reads each sentence, and children who

figure 1.7 Some pages from the class book on Colors

figure 1.7 continued

have the words in that sentence come up and arrange themselves to build the sentences. For this chart, the children with the words *I, am, thankful,* and *for* stay in place and other words join them to form the sentences. (When the sentences of the children holding the cards that are in every sentence are being built, these children get to choose a "sub" to hold their card while they go to the end of the sentence so they can hold up their name.)

Friday   On Friday, the whole class participates in making a class book based on the predictable chart. To prepare for Friday's lesson, Mrs. C copies each child's sentence on a sentence strip. Each child cuts his or her sentence into words and pastes these words in the correct order on the bottom of a large piece of drawing paper. Then the child illustrates the page. (Although usually the children draw the illustration, for the class book on colors Mrs. C used a free clip art site to let children find pictures of objects beginning with the chosen color. The children printed these out and cut and pasted them on their pages.) When completed, the class books are put in the "Reading Center." By Thanksgiving, the children will have made 10 class books. These are perennial favorites for independent reading time. The children never tire of reading about themselves and their friends!

✳ Children Learn Print Functions, Print Concepts, and Words from Their Predictable Charts

Just as children learn print functions, print concepts, and words from the shared reading of predictable text, they also develop these early reading concepts as they participate in making the predictable charts and class books. They learn that reading and writing are for telling about yourself and learning about your classmates. They track print from left to right and proceed in that order as they build the sentences and when they paste them on their page of the class book.

All children learn some words from the charts and books. Most children learn to read their names and the names of many of their classmates, which are written at the end of every sentence. They learn some concrete words—**cat, football,** and **pizza,** for example—as they write and read about their favorite animals, sports, and foods. Children who come to school with many of the early reading concepts in place often learn the abstract connecting words—such as *for, like,* and *is*—that are repeated again and again on the charts. Predictable charts provide many opportunities to learn both interesting, concrete words and high-frequency abstract words.

Writing

Just as children from literacy-oriented homes read before they can read by pretend-reading a memorized book, they write before they can write! Their writing is usually not readable by anyone besides themselves, and sometimes they read the same scribbling different ways. They write with pens, markers, crayons, paint, chalk, and normal-size pencils with erasers on the ends! They write on chalkboards, magic slates, walls, drawing paper, and lined notebook paper. (They just ignore the lines!)

They write in scribbles, which first go anywhere and then show a definite left-to-right orientation. They make letterlike forms. They underline certain letters to show word boundaries. As they learn more about words and letters, they let single letters stand for entire words. They draw pictures and intersperse letters with the pictures. They make grocery lists by copying words off packages. They copy favorite words from books. They write love notes (e.g., "I love you, Mama").

Emergent literacy research has shown that the ability of children to learn is not ruined by being allowed to write before they can write. Rather, they learn many important concepts and develop the confidence that they can write (Sulzby, Teale, & Kamberelis, 1989). Here are some activities that promote writing for all.

✢ Provide a Print-Rich Classroom

Classrooms in which children write contain lots of print in them. In addition to books, there are magazines and newspapers. Charts of recipes and directions for building things hang as reminders. Environmental print boards contain labels from favorite foods—Cheerios, peanut butter, yogurt—and advertisements from local restaurants and stores—Walmart, Taco Bell, Food Lion. Children's names are on their desks and on many different objects. There are class books, bulletin boards with labeled pictures of animals under study, and labels on almost everything. Children's drawings and all kinds of writing are displayed. In these classrooms, children see that all types of writing are valued. Equally important, children who want to write "the grown-up way" can find lots of words to make their own.

✢ Let Children Watch You Write

As children watch you write, they observe that you always start in a certain place, go in certain directions, and leave space between words. In addition to these print conventions, they observe that writing is "talk written down." There are numerous opportunities in every classroom for the teacher to write as the children watch—and sometimes help—with suggestions of what to write.

In many classrooms, the teacher begins the day by writing a morning message on the board. The teacher writes this short message as the children watch.

Dear Class,

Today is Friday. We will go to music at 10:00. After lunch, we will make our 14th class book telling where we like to shop.

I love you,

Mrs. C

The teacher then reads the message, pointing to each word, and invites the children to join in on any words they know. Sometimes teachers take a few minutes to point out some things students might notice from the morning message:

"How many sentences did I write today?"

"How can we tell how many there are?"

"What do we call this mark I put after *I love you*?"

"Do we have any words that begin with the same letters?"

"Which is the longest word?"

These and similar questions help children learn print tracking and jargon and focus their attention on words and letters.

❋ Include Interactive Writing

Interactive writing is "sharing the pen." This notion of not only letting children tell you what to write but also letting them "share the pen" is what makes interactive writing different from watching the teacher write and what makes it important to include as another writing format.

To do interactive writing, you gather the children up close to you at a chart or the board and with the children you think of something you want to write. For beginning lessons, what you write should be quite short—no more than a sentence or two. Perhaps you and the children decide that you should write about Brad's birthday and that the sentences should say:

Today is Brad's birthday. He is six years old.

You then might ask children to look around the room and see if they can find the word **today** anywhere. When a child finds the word **today,** that child is given the pen and comes up and writes **Today**—the first word in the sentence.

The writing continues as the teacher asks if anyone can come up and write **is**. Brad comes and writes his name. The teacher adds the apostrophe and Brad adds the **s.** Together the teacher and children stretch out **birthday**. Different children come and write the letters they can hear and the teacher fills in the other letters to get **birthday** spelled correctly. Another child volunteers to put the period to show that they have finished the first sentence. The same procedure is continued with the second sentence. Children who can spell **he** and **is** come and write those words. **Six** is found on the number chart and someone comes and writes **six. Years** and **old** are stretched out with volunteers writing letters they can hear and the teacher filling in missing letters. Finally, a child adds the period at the end of the second sentence. Children love "sharing the pen" and they pay much more attention to the writing when they are a part of it. Regular, short interactive writing sessions should be a part of every young child's day.

❋ Let Them Write and Accept Whatever Kind of Writing They Do

Accepting a variety of writing—from scribbling to one-letter representations, to invented spellings, to copied words—is the key to having young children write before they can write. Sometimes it is the children and not the teacher who reject beginning attempts. If more advanced children give the less advanced children a hard time about their "scribbling," the teacher must intervene and firmly state a policy, such as:

> "There are many different ways to communicate through writing. We use pictures and letters and words. Sometimes we just scribble, but the scribbling helps us remember what we are thinking. We use all these different ways in this classroom!"

Without this attitude of acceptance, the very children who most need to explore language through writing will be afraid to write.

Writing is the most "visible" way to develop print concepts. As children watch you write the morning message or sentences on a chart, they see print tracking in operation. You can make these concepts more obvious by being intentional and "thinking aloud" about what you are doing as you are doing it. Here are some of the common "think-alouds" done by teachers that help children pay attention to print concepts as they watch the teacher write. (Jargon and concepts are bolded and should be emphasized as you say them.)

> "Today I am going to write two **sentences** to tell you about what will happen at 10:00.
>
> "I start the first **word** of my **sentence** with a capital **letter**."

The teacher writes *We,* saying "We" as she writes it.

> "I need a **space** before my next **word**."

The teacher puts a "finger space" and then writes *will.* Each word is read by the teacher as she writes it.

> "Another finger **space** and I can write the third **word** of my **sentence**."

The teacher writes *have.*

> "This **word** is also a **letter** and takes only one **letter** to spell it."

The teacher writes *a.*

> "The next word is a **long word** and takes **seven letters** to spell it."

The teacher writes *special*.

"The **last word** in my **sentence** is . . ."

The teacher writes and says "*treat*."

"I am at the **end** of my **first sentence** so I will put a **period** here to show that.

We will have a special treat.

I have one more **sentence** to write. I will write it on this **second line** and **start back on the left** again."

The teacher writes:

Bobby's mom is bringing cupcakes for his birthday!

As she writes, she talks about what she is doing as she did for the first sentence.

As the year goes on, instead of telling the children what she is doing, she asks them what she should do, with questions such as:

"I am writing the **first word** in my **sentence**. What kind of **letter** do I need?"

"I have finished my **first word**. What do I need to leave **between the first word and the next word**?" "I am at the **end of my sentence**. What should I put here to show that?"

"I am going to write another **sentence. Where should I start** writing it?"

Because children can actually watch you write and see the message go down one letter and word at a time, many people believe that modeling writing for children is one of the most effective ways to teach print concepts.

Letting the children write—in whatever way they can—is another powerful way to teach print concepts. As the children write, the teacher circulates and encourages children—coaching them with gentle prompts:

"I will put a little dot here on the **left side** to help you start your sentence in the right place."

"You have the word **I** written. Tell me the rest of your sentence."

The child says the sentence, "I like my cat." The teacher says,

"Good. Put a finger space here and then write your second word, **like**. Can you find **like** in the room to spell it, or should we stretch it out?"

"Is that the end of your sentence? What do you need to put at the end of your sentence?"

"Are you going to write another sentence? Where will you begin it?"

Some teachers hesitate to let children write before they know much about reading and writing because the writing is far from perfect. It helps many teachers to remember that when young children are writing, it doesn't matter what it looks like when they finish. What matters are all the understandings they are developing as they go through the process. Writing provides the "teachable moment" to teach print concepts, and all young children should be encouraged and applauded for their early writing efforts.

❋ Children Learn Print Concepts, Words, Phonemic Awareness, and Some Letter Names and Sounds as They Write

Encouraging young children to write has many benefits. As children write, they learn the print concepts of left to right and leaving spaces between words. (Even when children are scribbling, they usually scribble from left to right and stop occasionally to write a new scribble.) Children often write about themselves and each other, copying names of favorite foods, restaurants, and other places from the print in the classroom. From these writing opportunities, they learn concrete, important-to-them words. As they stretch out words to "put down the sounds they hear," they are developing phonemic awareness. People of all ages are more apt to remember things they actually use; children are no exception. As they use what they are learning about letters and sounds to try to spell words, they are applying their phonics knowledge. Writing is perhaps the best opportunity for developing young children's print concepts, concrete words, phonemic awareness, and knowledge of letters and sounds. Because they are writing what they want to tell, children become perfectly clear about what reading and writing are for.

Getting to Know You

Most teachers begin their year with some get-acquainted activities. As part of these activities, they often designate a special child each day. In addition to learning about each child, the teacher can focus attention on the special child's name and use the name to develop some important understandings about words and letters.

To prepare for this activity, write all the children's first names (with initials for last names if two names are the same) with a permanent marker on sentence strips. Cut the strips so that long names have long strips and short names have short strips. Let the children watch you write their names and have them help you spell their names if they can. After writing each name, display it in a pocket chart or other board. As you put each name up, comment on letters shared by certain children or other common features:

"Rasheed's name starts with an R—just like Robert's."

"Bo's name takes only two letters to write. He has the shortest name, but he is one of the tallest boys."

"We have two Ashleys, so I will have to put the first letter of her last name—M—so that we will know which Ashley this is."

The children will watch and think as the names are being written, and probably all will pay close attention because they are so egocentric—interested in themselves and in each other. Their attention for anything, however, diminishes after 15 to 20 minutes, so if you have a large class, you may want to write the names in two different sessions.

Once you have all the names written and displayed, ask volunteers to come and find a name they can read. Many children will read their own, and almost everyone will remember Bo!

Tell the children that each day one of them will be the special child and that in order to make it fair—because some children will have to wait 20 or more days—you are going to put all the names in a box and shake up the box and, without looking, draw one of the names. Explain what the special child will get to do each day. Some teachers crown that child king or queen, let him or her lead the line, decide what game to play for P.E., sit in a special chair to greet visitors, pass things out, take messages to the office, and so on. Do keep in mind that whatever you do for the first, you must do for all the rest, so make sure you can sustain whatever you start. (Remember the "Don't do anything the first month of marriage you don't want to do the whole rest of your married life" advice most of us got but ignored!) Each day, reach into the box and draw out a name. This child becomes the special child and the focus of many literacy activities. For our example, we will assume that David is the first name pulled from the box.

✳ Interviewing and Shared Writing

Have David come to the front of the room and sit in a special chair. Appoint the rest of the children as class reporters. Their job is to interview David and find out what he likes to eat, play, and do after school. Does he have brothers? Sisters? Cats? Dogs? Mice? Decide on a certain number of questions (five to seven) and call on different children to ask the questions.

After the interview, write your "newspaper article" on this special child using a shared writing format in which the children give suggestions and you and they decide what to say first, last, and so on. Record this on a chart while the children watch. The chart should not be more than five or six sentences long and the sentences should not be too complex because these news articles about each VIP will form some of the first material most children will be able to read. The interview and the writing of the chart should be completed within the children's 20-minute attention span and can be if the teacher limits the number of questions and takes the lead in the writing of the article. This first activity for each child—interviewing and shared writing of the article—develops crucial oral language skills and helps children see how writing and reading occur.

figure 1.8 **Sample pages from All About Us Class Book**

David Cunningham is 5 years old. He does not have any brothers or sisters. He has a pet cat named Harriet. He has 3 cousins, Jon, Sarah, and Kevin. David likes to eat pizza. He likes to play basketball. His favorite team is the Boston Red Sox.

Kathleen Gallagher is 5 years old. She has a brother named Ryan. She has a pet cat named Squeaky. She likes to eat chocolate ice cream. She likes to skate. Her favorite holiday is Halloween.

❋ Shared Reading of the Charts

The second activity is the reading of David's chart. This takes place later in the day and, again, does not take more than 20 minutes. On the first day, you will have only one chart to read. Lead the children to read it chorally several times and let volunteers come and read each sentence. Guide their hands so that they are tracking print as they read. Most teachers display each chart for five days and then let the child take the chart home with instructions to display it on the child's bedroom door. That way, there are only five charts in the room at any one time but every chart gets read and reread on five different days.

Many teachers also write (or type) the article from the chart and, after all the children have had their special days and have been interviewed, compile a class book containing each article (often along with a picture of each child). Each child then has one night to take the book home so that each child's family can get to know the whole class.

❋ Children Learn What Reading and Writing Are For, Print Concepts, and Some Words through Getting to Know You Activities

Getting to Know You is another opportunity for children to become clear about the functions of reading and writing. Children pay very close attention as each child is being interviewed and as the chart about each child is written. They love to reread the charts and class book (a compilation of these charts) over and over. The "hook" in Getting to Know You is that the reading and writing are centered on the most important people in the world—the children themselves! Writing is for telling important things and reading is for learning and enjoying, and

For English Language Learners

The activities included in this chapter are important for helping launch all children successfully on their literacy journey; they are especially crucial for English language learners. Children who are learning to speak and understand English as they are learning to read and write need the language support and the confidence boost endemic to these activities. Predictable books and predictable charts have repeated sentence patterns that allow children learning English to feel successful in reading as they add these simple sentences to their English spoken language. Providing a print-rich classroom, letting children watch you write, and supporting children's fledgling attempts at writing allows your English language learners to feel successful at writing when their—like everyone else's—efforts are less than perfect. English language learners, along with their English-speaking classmates, delight in the Getting to Know You charts both when they are the subject of these charts and when they are learning and reading about their friends. The jump-start to literacy activities included in this chapter have been successful with children learning English—young children and older children alike.

children who emerge into literacy through Getting to Know You activities have no doubt about how important and satisfying reading and writing are. Just as in shared reading and predictable charts, children are put into a very comfortable, supportive environment through which they learn significant print concepts and begin to add words to their reading and writing vocabularies.

Summary

In order to make sense of phonics instruction, children must develop some basic concepts. They must know why people read and write and develop an "I can't wait 'til I can do it too" attitude. They must learn how to track print and understand the print-related jargon used to talk about print. Children also need to develop a basic level of phonological and phonemic awareness, learn some important-to-them words and learn some letter names and sounds. This chapter has suggested four activities—shared reading of predictable text, predictable charts, writing, and Getting to Know You—that will help children begin to develop these basic concepts. The remaining chapters in Part One will focus specifically on phonological and phonemic awareness and learning some words as well as letter names and sounds.

chapter 2

Phonological and Phonemic Awareness

As described in Chapter 1, phonological and phonemic awareness refers to children's understandings about words and sounds in words. *Phonological awareness* includes the ability to separate sentences into words and words into syllables. *Phonemic awareness* includes the ability to recognize that words are made up of a discrete set of sounds and to manipulate sounds. Many children come to school with well-developed phonemic awareness abilities, and these children usually come from homes in which rhyming chants, jingles, and songs are part of their daily experience. These same chants, jingles, and songs should be a part of every young child's day in the classroom. Children also develop a sense of sounds and words as they try to write. Children who are allowed and encouraged to "invent-spell" develop an early and strong sense of phonemic awareness.

Many of the activities discussed in Chapter 1 help children develop phonemic awareness. As children participate in shared reading and writing, they become aware of words as separate entities. Sentence Builders help children understand what words are. Encouraging invented spelling during writing is one of the main ways teachers have of helping children develop their understanding of how phonemes make up words. As children try to spell words, they say them slowly, listening to themselves saying the sounds and thinking about what they are learning about letters and sounds. Following are other activities you can use to promote phonological and phonemic awareness.

Developing Phonological Awareness

Phonological awareness includes the ability to separate sentences into words and words into syllables. Two activities, Counting Words and Clapping Syllables, help develop children's phonological awareness.

❊ Counting Words

To count words, all children should have 10 counters in a paper cup. (Anything manipulable is fine. Some teachers use edibles such as raisins, grapes, or small crackers and let the children eat their counters at the end of the lesson. This makes cleanup quick and easy.) Begin by counting some familiar objects in the room (windows, doors, trash cans), having all children place one of their counters on their desks as each object is pointed to. Children should return counters to the cup before beginning to count the next object.

Tell the children that they can also count words by putting down a counter for each word you say. Explain that you will say a sentence in the normal way and then repeat the sentence, pausing after each word. The children should put down counters as you slowly say the words in the sentence and then count the counters and decide how many words you said. As usual, children's attention is better if you make sentences about them. ("Carol has a big smile." "Paul is back at school today." "I saw Jack at the grocery store.") Once the children catch on to the activity, let them say some sentences, first in the normal way, then one word at a time. Listen carefully as they say their sentences the first time because they will often need help saying them one word at a time. Children enjoy this activity, and not only are they learning to separate out words in speech, but they are also practicing counting skills.

❊ Clapping Syllables

Once children can automatically separate the speech stream into words, they are ready to begin thinking about separating words into some components. The first division most children learn to make is that of syllables. Clapping seems the easiest way to get every child involved, and the children's names (what else?) are the naturally appealing words to clap. Say the first name of one child. Say the name again, and this time, clap the syllables. Continue saying first names and then clapping the syllables as you say them the second time and invite the children to join in clapping with you. As children catch on, say some middle or last names. The term *syllables* is a little jargony and foreign to most young children, so you may want to refer to the syllables as beats. Children should realize by clapping that **Paul** is a one-beat word, **Miguel** is a two-beat word, and **Madeira** is a three-beat word.

When the children can clap syllables and decide how many beats a given word has, help them to see that one-beat words are usually shorter than three-beat words—that is, they take fewer letters to write. To do this, write on sentence strips some words children cannot read and cut the strips into words so that short words have short strips and long words have long strips. Have some of the words begin with the same letters but be different lengths so that children will need to think about word length to decide which word is which.

For the category "animals," you might write **horse** and **hippopotamus**; **dog** and **donkey**; **kid** and **kangaroo**; and **rat**, **rabbit**, and **rhinoceros**. Tell the children that you are going to say the names of animals and they should clap to show how many beats the word has. (Do not show them the words yet!) Say the first pair, one at a time (**horse**, **hippopotamus**) and then have the children say them. Help the children decide that **horse** is a one-beat word and **hippopotamus** takes a lot more claps and is a five-beat word. Now, show them the two words and say, "One of these words is **horse** and the other is **hippopotamus**. Who thinks they can figure out which one is **horse** and which one is **hippopotamus**?" Help the children by explaining that because **hippopotamus** takes so many beats to say, it will probably take more letters to write. Continue with other pairs—and finally with a triplet—**rat**, **rabbit**, **rhinoceros**—to make the activity more multilevel.

Developing the Concept of Rhyme

Recognizing and producing rhyming words is an essential part of phonemic awareness. To develop the concept of rhyme, teachers can use nursery and other rhymes and take advantage of all the wonderful rhyming books.

✻ Do Nursery Rhymes

One of the best indicators of how well children will learn to read is their ability to recite nursery rhymes when they enter kindergarten. Since this is such a reliable indicator, and since rhymes are so naturally appealing to children at this age, kindergarten classrooms should be filled with rhymes. Children should learn to recite these rhymes, sing the rhymes, clap to the rhymes, act out the rhymes, and pantomime the rhymes. In some kindergarten classrooms, they develop "raps" for the rhymes.

Once the children can recite many rhymes, nursery rhymes can be used to teach the concept of rhyme. The class can be divided into two halves—one half says the rhyme but stops when they get to the last rhyming word. The other half waits to shout the rhyme at the appropriate moment:

First half:	There was an old woman who lived in a shoe.
	She had so many children, she didn't know what to
Second half:	do.
First half:	She gave them some broth without any bread,
	and spanked them all soundly and put them to
Second half:	bed.

Nursery and other rhymes have been a part of our oral heritage for generations. Now we know that the rhythm and rhyme inherent in nursery rhymes are important vehicles for the beginning development of phonemic awareness. They should play a large role in any kindergarten curriculum.

✳ Do Rhymes and Riddles

Young children are terribly egocentric, and they are very "body oriented." In doing rhymes and riddles, therefore, have children point to different body parts to show rhyming words. Tell children that you are going to say some words that rhyme with **head** or **feet**. After you say each word, have the children repeat the word with you and decide if the word rhymes with **head** or **feet**. If the word you say rhymes with **head**, they should point to their head. If it rhymes with **feet**, they should point to their feet. As children point, be sure to respond, acknowledging a correct response by saying something like, "Carl is pointing to his head because **bread** rhymes with **head**." You may want to use some of these words:

meet	bread	led	sleet	seat	red	sheet	fed
bed	beat	sled	thread	dead	greet	heat	shed

Now, ask the children to say the missing word in the following riddles (the answers all rhyme with **head**):

On a sandwich, we put something in between the . . .

When something is not living anymore, it is . . .

To sew, you need a needle and . . .

The color of blood is . . .

We can ride down snowy hills on a . . .

Here are other riddles, the answers to which rhyme with **feet**:

Steak and pork chops are different kinds of . . .

On a crowded bus, it is hard to get a . . .

You make your bed with a . . .

When you are cold, you turn on the . . .

If children like this activity, do it again, but this time have them listen for words that rhyme with **hand** or **knee**. If the word you say rhymes with **hand**, they should point to their hand. If it rhymes with **knee**, they should point to their knee. Some words to use are:

sand	band	land	see	me	bee	stand
grand	we	free	brand	tea	tree	and

Here are some riddles for **hand**:

At the beach, you dig in the . . .

To build a house, you must first buy a piece of . . .

The musicians who march and play in a parade are called a . . .

You can sit or you can . . .

And here are some more that rhyme with **knee**:

You use your eyes to . . .

You could get stung by a . . .

If something doesn't cost anything, we say it is . . .

You can climb up into a . . .

To challenge your class, have them make up riddles and point for words that rhyme with **feet**, **knee**, **hand**, or **head**. As each child gives a riddle, have the riddle giver point to the body part that rhymes with the answer. Model this for the children by doing a few to show them how.

✻ Sing Rhymes and Read Lots of Rhyming Books

There are many wonderful rhyming books, but because of its potential to develop phonemic awareness, one deserves special mention. Along with other great rhyming books, Dr. Seuss wrote *There's a Wocket in My Pocket*. In this book, all kinds of Seussian creatures are found in various places. In addition to the wocket in the pocket, there is a vug under the rug, a nureau in the bureau, and a yottle in the bottle! After several readings, children delight in chiming in to provide the nonsensical word and scary creature that lurks in harmless-looking places. After reading the book a few times, it is fun to decide what creatures might be lurking in your classroom. Let children make up the creatures, and accept whatever they say as long as it rhymes with their object:

"There's a pock on our clock!"

"There's a zindow looking in our window!"

"There's a zencil on my pencil!"

Once you have found some wonderful books with lots of rhymes, follow these steps to assure your children are learning to recognize and produce rhymes:

1. Pick a book with lots of rhymes that you think your children will "fall in love with." Read, enjoy, and talk about the content of the book, and let children become thoroughly comfortable and familiar with the book. Remember that children who are lucky enough to own books want books read to them again and again.

2. After the children are very familiar with the book, reread it again, and tell them that the author of this book made it "fun to say" by including lots of

rhymes. Read the book, stopping after each rhyme, and have children identify the rhyming words and say them with you.

3. For the next reading, tell the children that you are going to stop and have them fill in the rhyming word. Read the whole book, stopping each time and asking the children to supply the rhyming word.

4. The activities in steps 2 and 3 have helped children identify rhymes. We also want children to produce rhymes. Depending on the book, find a way to have your students make up similar rhymes. Producing rhymes was what children were doing when they made up rhyming items such as "the zencil on the pencil."

Recognizing and producing rhymes is one of the critical components of phonemic awareness. Children who engage in these kinds of activities with wonderful rhyming books will develop the concept of rhyme.

Teaching Blending and Segmenting

Blending is the ability to put sounds back together to form words. *Segmenting* is the ability to separate a word into its component sounds. Blending and segmenting are difficult concepts for many children, but they can develop them if you use a lot of blending and segmenting games, tongue twisters, and sound boxes.

✳ Play Blending and Segmenting Games

In addition to hearing and producing rhyme, the ability to put sounds together to make a word—blending—and the ability to separate out the sounds in a word—segmenting—are critical components of phonemic awareness. Blending and segmenting are not easy for many children. In general, it is easier for them to segment off the beginning letters (the *onset*) from the rest of the word (the *rime*) than it is to separate all the sounds. In other words, children can usually separate **bat** into **b/at** before they can produce the three sounds **b-a-t**. The same is true for blending. Most children can blend **S/am** to produce the name **Sam** before they can blend **S-a-m**. Most teachers begin by having children blend and segment the onset from the rime and then move to blending and segmenting individual letters.

There are lots of games children enjoy that can help them learn to blend and segment. The most versatile is a simple riddle guessing game. The teacher begins the game by naming the category and giving the clue:

"I'm thinking of an animal that lives in the water and is a **f/ish**."
(or **f/i/sh**, depending on what level of blending you are working on)

The child who correctly guesses **fish** gives the next riddle:

"I'm thinking of an animal that goes quack and is a **d/uck.**" (or **d/u/ck**)

This sounds simplistic, but children love it, and you can use different categories to go along with units you are studying.

A wonderful variation on this guessing game is to put objects in a bag and let children reach in the bag to choose one. Then they stretch out the name of the object and call on someone to guess "What is it?" Choose small common objects you find in the room—a cap, a ball, chalk, a book. Let the children watch you load the bag and help you stretch out the words for practice as you put them in.

Children also like to talk like "ghosts." One child chooses an object in the room to say as a ghost would, stretching the word out very slowly: "dddoooorrr." The child who correctly guesses "door" gets to ghost talk another object: "bbbooookkk." The ghost-talk game and the guessing game provide practice in segmenting and blending as children segment words by stretching them out and other children blend the words together to guess them.

❋ Tongue Twisters and Books with Lots of Alliteration

In addition to concepts of rhyme, blending, and segmenting, children must learn what it means that words "start the same." This understanding must be in place before children can make sense of the notion that particular letters make particular sounds. Children often confuse the concept of words beginning or starting with the same sound with the concept of rhyme, so many teachers like to wait until most of their students have a firm grasp of the concept of rhyme before focusing on whether words begin with the same sound. Just as with rhyme, teachers can help children understand the concept of words that start the same by using wonderful books such as *All about Arthur—An Absolutely Absurd Ape* by Eric Carle. Arthur, an ape who plays the accordion, travels around the country meeting lots of other musicians—including, in Baltimore, a bear who plays a banjo, and a yak in Yonkers. *Dr. Seuss's ABC,* in which each individual letter of the alphabet appears throughout a sentence, such as in the sentence beginning "Many mumbling mice . . . ," is another excellent example of an appealing book that helps children understand what it means to "start the same." Activities using alliterative books should follow the same steps as those for rhyming books:

1. Read and enjoy the book several times.
2. Point out that the author used some "start the same" words to make the book fun to say and identify these words.
3. Let the children say the "start the same" words with you as you read the book again.
4. Have the children come up with other words that "start the same" that the author could have used on that page.

Tongue-Twister Books

Here are some wonderful tongue-twister books:

All about Arthur—An Absolutely Absurd Ape (Eric Carle, Simon & Schuster, 1974)

Alphabet Annie Announces an All-American Album (Susan Purviance & Marcia O'Shell, Houghton Mifflin, 1988)

Animalia (Graeme Base, Abrams, 1987)

The Biggest Tongue Twister Book in the World (Gyles Brandeth, Sterling, 1978)

Dr. Seuss's ABC (Dr. Seuss, Random House, 1963)

Faint Frogs Feeling Feverish and Other Terrifically Tantalizing Tongue Twisters (Lillian Obligada, Viking, 1983)

Six Sick Sheep (Jan Cole, Morrow, 1993)

A Twister of Twists, A Tangler of Tongues and Busy Buzzing Bumblebees and Other Tongue Twisters (Alvin Schwartz, HarperCollins, 1972)

Once you have read and enjoyed several tongue-twister books, why not create a tongue-twister book for your class? Let the children help you make up the tongue twisters and add two or three each day. Turn the tongue twisters into posters or bind them into a class book and ask the children to read them with you several times—as slowly as they can and as fast as they can. Help the children understand that what makes tongue twisters hard to say fast is that the words all start the same and you keep having to get your mouth and tongue into the same place. The same first sound repeated over and over is also what makes them so much fun to say. Here are some to get you started. You and your students can surely make up better ones. Be sure to use children's names from your class when they have the right letters and sounds!

Billy's baby brother bopped Betty.

Carol can catch caterpillars.

David dozed during dinner.

Fred's father fell fifty feet.

Gorgeous Gloria gets good grades.

Hungry Harry hates hamburgers.

Jack juggled Jill's jewelry.

Kevin's kangaroo kicked Karen.

Louie likes licking lemon lollipops.

Mike's mom makes marvelous meatballs.

Naughty Nellie never napped nicely.

Patty picked pink pencils.

Roger Rabbit runs relays.

Susie's sister sipped seven sodas.

Tom took ten turtles to town.

Veronica visited very vicious volcanoes.

Wild Willy went west.

Yippy yanked Yolanda's yellow yoyo.

Zany Zeb zapped Zeke's zebra.

As you work with books with lots of words that begin the same and with tongue twisters, begin by emphasizing the words that start the same. This is the phonemic awareness understanding that underlies phonics knowledge. When your students can tell you whether words start with the same sound and can come up with other words that start that way, shift your instruction to which letter makes which sound. You can use the very same books and tongue twisters again, this time emphasizing the sound of the letter. Books with alliteration and tongue twisters can help children develop the "starts the same" component of phonemic awareness and can help them learn some letter sounds.

✳ Sound Boxes

Some children find it very difficult to segment words into sounds. Many teachers have found success using a technique called Sound Boxes (Elkonin, 1973), in which children push chips, pennies, or other objects into boxes as they hear the sounds. In the first lessons, children have a drawing of three boxes.

The teacher says familiar words composed of three sounds, such as **cat**, **sun**, **dog**, and **pan**. Often children are shown pictures of these objects. After naming each object, the teacher and children "stretch out" the three sounds, distorting the word as little as possible: "sssuuunnn." Children push a chip into each box as they say that part of the word. It is important to note here that the boxes represent sounds—phonemes—not letters. **Cake**, **bike**, and **duck** have three sounds but four letters. These words would be segmented into three sound boxes. After the children get good at segmenting words with three sounds, they are given a drawing with four boxes and they stretch out some four-phoneme words such as **truck**, **crash**, and **nest**. Sound Boxes are used extensively to develop phonemic awareness in children in Reading Recovery (Clay, 1985), a highly successful one-on-one tutoring program that works with first-graders who are in the bottom 20 percent of the class.

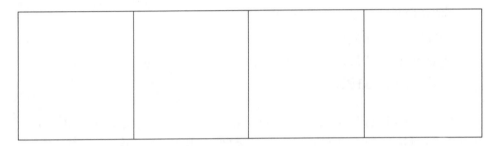

Once the children can push the chips to represent sounds, they can push letter cards into boxes. From the letters **m**, **b**, **s**, **t**, and **a**, the teacher could ask the children to push these letters to spell words such as **sat**, **bat**, **mat**, **bam**, **Sam**, **tab**, **bats**, **mats**, **tabs**, and **stab**. Children should not work with letters in the sound boxes until they have developed some phonemic awareness and are working on learning letter names and letter sounds. Later on, children can actually write the letters in the boxes as they are attempting to spell words they are writing.

Using Names to Build Phonological and Phonemic Awareness

You can use your children's names to build phonological and phonemic awareness.

Clap Syllables   The first way that children learn to pull apart words is into syllables. Say each child's name and have the children clap the beats in that name as they say it with you. Help children to see that Tran and Pat are one-beat names, Manuel and Patrick, two beats, and so on. Once children begin to understand, clap the beats and have all the children whose names have that number of beats stand up and say their names as they clap the beats with you.

Matching Beginning Sounds   Say a sound—not a letter name—and have all the children whose names begin with that sound come forward. Stretch out the sound as you make it: "ssss." For the "sss" sound, Samantha, Susie, Steve, and Cynthia should all come forward. Have everyone stretch out the "sss" as they say the names. If anyone points out that Cynthia starts with a **c** or that Sharon starts with an **s**, explain that he or she is correct about the letters but that now you are listening for sounds.

For English Language Learners

All children—those learning English as well as those whose native language is English—need to develop phonological and phonemic awareness to be successful readers. In 2006, the National Literacy Panel (August & Shanahan, 2006) concluded that there was a great deal of variation in the levels of phonemic awareness among English language learners and that this variability was related to age, language and literacy experiences, and level of language proficiency in both languages. The organization also concluded that difficulties in phonemic awareness are not causing more difficulties for English language learners in learning to read when compared with native speakers. Phonemic awareness skills developed in the first language seem to predict and be instrumental in phonemic awareness development in the second language. For teachers, the comforting news appears to be that phonemic awareness development activities such as those described in this chapter are appropriate for both native speakers and English language learners.

Hear Rhyming Words   Choose the children whose names have lots of rhyming words to come forward. Say a word that rhymes with one of the names and have the children say the word along with the name of the rhyming child.

Segment Words into Sounds   Call children to line up by stretching out their names, emphasizing each letter. As each child lines up, have the class stretch out the name with you.

Summary

Phonological and phonemic awareness is an essential part of the foundation for learning to read. Children need to understand how sounds go together in words. They need to be able to manipulate words in their heads. The activities in this chapter mimic activities children from literacy-rich homes do before coming to school. If schools provide young children with a variety of activities such as those suggested here, all children can develop phonological and phonemic awareness and greatly increase the possibility that they will become fluent readers and writers.

chapter 3

Concrete Words, Letter Names, and Sounds

In addition to print concepts and phonological and phonemic awareness, the foundation for success in learning to read and write requires that children learn some concrete words, letter names, and sounds. If they have been engaging in the activities described in the previous two chapters, most children will have already begun developing these skills. Activities in this chapter build on and extend the activities from previous chapters to help all children learn some concrete words, letter names, and sounds.

Children's Names

In Chapter 1, you learned how to do the Getting to Know You activity to help children get off to a successful start in reading and to build print concepts. In addition to writing and reading charts about each child, most teachers also focus activities on each child's name. As described in Chapter 1, children need to learn some concrete words—interesting, important-to-them words. Names are often the first words many children learn to read, and they are immensely interested in their name and the names of their friends.

To use names to teach words, letters, and sounds, many teachers create a name word wall on which to display the names, often with photos, of each child. Each day a name is pulled and everyone's attention is focused on that name. After doing the activities with each child's name, the name is added to the name board. Here are some of the activities you can do with the names.

✳ The First Name

Reach into your container and pull out a name. Assume that David is the first name to come out. Point to the word **David** on the sentence strip and develop children's understanding of jargon by pointing out that this word is David's name.

Tell them that it takes many letters to write the word **David** and let them help you count the letters. Say the letters in **David—D-a-v-i-d**—and have the children chant them with you cheerleader style. (We call this cheering for David, and he loves it!) Point out that the word **David** begins and ends with the same letter. Explain that the **d** looks different because one is a capital **D** and the other is a small **d**—or uppercase and lowercase—whatever jargon you use.

Take another sentence strip and have the children watch as you write **David**. Have them chant the spelling of the letters with you. Cut the letters apart and mix them up. Let several children come and arrange the letters in just the right order so that they spell **David**. Have the other children chant to check that the order is correct. Add David's name to your name board. Include a photo of David if possible.

✳ The Next Names

Imagine that it is the next day and the name pulled from the box is Catherine. Hold up the sentence strip and have the children say the letters in **Catherine** with you. Next, have the children chant the letters—cheering for Catherine. Help the children count the letters and decide which letter is first, last, and so on. Point out that **Catherine** has two **e**'s and they look exactly the same because they are both small (lowercase) **e**'s. Write **Catherine** on another sentence strip and cut it into letters. Have children arrange the letters to spell **Catherine**, using the first sentence strip name as their model.

Put **Catherine** on the name board and compare the two names. Which has the most letters? How many more letters are in the word **Catherine** than in the word **David**? Does **Catherine** have any of the same letters as **David**?

The next name to come out is **Robert**. Do all the same activities for Robert. Say and count the letters. Cheer for Robert by chanting the letters in his name. Write his name again, cutting it into letters and rearranging the letters to spell his name. Be sure to note the two **r**'s and talk about why they look different.

As you put **Robert** on the name board, compare it to both **David** and **Catherine**. **Robert** has an **e** and **Catherine** has two **e**'s. **Robert** and **Catherine** both have a **t**. **Robert** doesn't have any of the same letters that **David** has. Robert's name has six letters—more than **David** but less than **Catherine**.

Mike comes out next. When you have a one-syllable name with which there are many rhymes (**Pat**, **Tran**, **Joe**, **Sue**, etc.), seize the opportunity to help the children listen for words that rhyme with that name. Say pairs of words—some of which rhyme with Mike:

Mike/ball   Mike/bike   Mike/hike   Mike/cook   Mike/like

If the pairs rhyme, everyone should point at Mike and whisper, "Mike." If not, they should shake their heads and frown.

Cindy comes out. **Catherine** and **Cindy** both begin with the letter **c** but begin with different sounds. Have Catherine and Cindy stand on opposite sides of you. Write their names above them on the chalkboard. Have the children say **Catherine** and **Cindy** several times—drawing out the first sound. Help them to understand that some letters can have more than one sound and that the names **Catherine** and **Cindy**

show us that. Tell the class that you are going to say some words, all of which begin with the letter **c**. Some of these words sound like **Catherine** at the beginning and some of them sound like **Cindy**. Say some words and have the children say them with you:

    cat   celery   candy   cookies   city   cereal   cut

For each word, have them point to Catherine or Cindy to show which sound they hear. Once they have decided, write each word under **Catherine** or **Cindy**.

Continue to pull names each day, and as you add each to your board or wall, help the children notice whatever they can about letter–sound relationships. The names your children have will determine what you will help the children to notice. If you don't have names such as **Catherine** and **Cindy**, you would not point out the two sounds of **c** this early in the year, but, if you do, you have to help the children understand that some letters have more than one sound or they will get confused. Children do notice things you don't point out, and if you teach **c** as having just the sound in **Catherine**, **cat**, and **candy**, Cindy may be looking at her nametag and wondering why she can't hear the sound! English is not a one-letter, one-sound language. There are relationships, but they are complex. Teachers must help children see how letters represent sounds, but if teachers make it simpler than it really is, some children are apt to notice the contradiction and get confused and maybe come to the dangerous conclusion that "there isn't any system and pattern to these letters and sounds."

So, if you have a **Joseph** and a **Julio** or a **Sheila** and a **Sam**, use the preceding procedure when the second name goes up. Point out that it is the **sh** in **Sheila** that gives **s** its different sound. Most of the children who are just beginning to learn about how letters and sounds are related would not need to know this. But those who were already reading when they came to school probably know the single-letter sounds and are ready to realize that some letter combinations have different sounds.

As you get to about the halfway point in adding the names, let the children take charge of noticing the similarities and differences between the names. Instead of pointing out as you add **Rasheed** that his name starts with the same letter and sound as **Robert** and he has two **e**'s and his name ends with a **d** like **David**, ask the children:

> "What do you notice about the letters and sounds in Rasheed's name and the other names on the board?"

There are systems and patterns to the way letters in English represent sounds. Our instruction should point out these patterns. Children who see a new word and ask themselves how that new word is like the other words they know can discover many patterns on their own.

✳ When All the Names Are Displayed

Once all the names are displayed and most children have learned most of the names, you can begin to solidify some of that letter–name sound knowledge. Imagine that the names of the children displayed on the word wall or name board are:

David	Rasheed	Robert	Catherine	Cindy
Mike	Sheila	Sam	Joseph	Julio
Amber T.	Matt	Erin	Shawonda	Bianca
Erica	Kevin	Adam	Delano	Brittany
Bo	Tara	Amber M.	Octavius	Kelsie

Begin with a letter that many children have in their names and that usually has its expected sound. With this class you might begin with the letter **r**. Ask all children whose names have an **r** in them to come to the front of the class and have each child hold a card with his or her name on it. First count all the **r**'s. There are nine **r**'s in all. Next have the children whose name contains an **r** divide themselves into those whose names begin with an **r**—Robert and Rasheed; those whose names end with an **r**—Amber T. and Amber M.; and those with an **r** that is not the first or the last letter—Brittany, Erica, Tara, Erin, and Catherine. Finally, say each name slowly—stretching out the letters—and decide if you can hear the usual sound of that letter. For **r**, you can hear them all.

Now choose another letter and let all those children come to the front of the room and display their name cards. Count the number of times that letter occurs and then have the children divide themselves into groups according to whether the letter is first, last, or in between. Finally, say the names stretching them out and decide if you can hear the usual sound that letter makes. **D** would be a good second choice. You would have David and Delano beginning with **d**; David and Rasheed ending with **d**; and Cindy, Shawonda, and Adam having a **d** that is not first or last. Again, you can hear the usual sound of **d** in all these names.

Continue picking letters and having children come up with their name cards until you have sorted for some of the letters represented by their names. When doing the letters **s**, **c**, **t**, and **j**, be sure to point out that they can have two sounds and that the **th** in **Catherine** and the **sh** in **Sheila**, **Shawonda**, and **Rasheed** have their own special sounds. You probably wouldn't sort out the names with an **h** because although **Shawonda**, **Sheila**, **Rasheed**, **Catherine**, and **Joseph** have an **h**, the **h** sound is not represented by any of these. The same would go for the **p**, which only occurs in **Joseph**. When you have the children come down for the vowels, **a**, **e**, **i**, **o**, and **u**, count and then sort the children according to first, last, and in between, but do not try to listen for the sounds. Explain that vowels have many different sounds and that the children will learn more about the vowels and their sounds throughout the year.

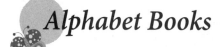

Alphabet Books

"The Alphabet Song" has been sung by generations of children. Children enjoy it, and it does seem to give them a sense of all the letters and a framework in which to put new letters as they learn them. Many children come to school already able to sing "The Alphabet Song." Let them sing it and let them teach it to everyone else. Once the children can sing the song, you may want to point to alphabet cards (usually found above the chalkboard) as they sing. Children enjoy "being the alphabet" as they line up to go somewhere. Simply pass out laminated alphabet cards—one to each child, leftovers to the teacher—and let the children sing the song slowly as each child lines up. Be sure to hand out the cards randomly so that no one gets to be the *A* and lead the line or has to be the *Z* and bring up the rear every day!

There are also lots of wonderful alphabet books to read and enjoy. Many of these fit into your themes or units. Simple books with not too many words on a page and with pictures that most of the children recognize are the most helpful to children in building their letter–sound and letter–name knowledge. Once the book has been read and reread several times, children will enjoy reading it during their self-selected reading time. It is very important that children have time to choose and read books each day. Simple alphabet books that have been read to the class provide books that children can read on their own before they can read books with more text.

Once you and the children have read several alphabet books, you might want to make a class alphabet book and/or have each child make one. Work on a few pages each day and use all your resources—alphabet books you read to them, things in the room, places children like to eat—to brainstorm a huge list of the

Alphabet Books

Here are a few alphabet books that meet our "not too many words, familiar pictures, kids love to read them" criteria:

A Is for Astronaut (Stan Tucker, Simon & Schuster, 1995)

The Accidental Zucchini (Max Grover, Harcourt, 1993)

Alphababies (Kim Golding, DK Publishing, 1998)

The Alphabet Tale (Jan Garten, Random House, 1964)

By the Sea: An Alphabet Book (Ann Blades, Kids Can Press, 1985)

Dr. Seuss's ABC (Dr. Seuss, Random House, 1963)

Eating the Alphabet (Lois Ehlert, Harcourt, 1989)

It Begins with an A (Stephanie Calmenson, Hyperion, 1993)

John Burmingham's ABC (John Burmingham, Crown, 1993)

The Monster Book of ABC Sounds (Alan Snow, Puffin, 1994)

Paddington's ABC (Michael Bond, Puffin Books, 1996)

Q Is for Duck (Mary Elting, Michael Folsom, & Jack Kent, Clarion, 2005)

Summer Stinks (Marty Kelly, Zeno Press, 2001)

Thomas' ABC Book (Wilbert Awdry, Golden Books, 1998)

Tomorrow's Alphabet (George Shannon & Donald Crews, Greenwillow, 1999)

possible words for each page. Depending on your class, you may want to put just one word and picture on each page or several words and pictures for each letter. If children are making individual books, let them choose the order in which they will select the letters for the books as well as the words for their pages. They will most often choose the letters they know best first. Knowing what they choose can help teachers identify what it is that children know.

Letter Actions and Foods

Eating and actions are important activities to young children. Teaching children actions for the consonant letters and having them associate these letters with foods help many children remember their sounds. For each action, write the letter on one side of a large index card and the action on the other. The first time you teach each letter, make a big deal of it. March around the classroom to marching music when you study **m**. Go out on the playground and jump rope and do jumping jacks when you introduce **j**. Play hopscotch and pretend to hop like bunnies when you introduce **h**.

Once the children have learned actions for several letters, there are many activities you can do right in the classroom without any props. Have all the children stand by their desks and wait until you show them a letter. They should do the action associated with the letter until you hide the letter behind your back. When they have all stopped and you have their attention again, show them another letter and have them do that action. Continue this with as many letters as you have time to fill. Be sure to make comments, such as, "Yes, I see everyone marching because **m** is our marching letter."

In another activity, you pass out the letters for which children have learned actions to individual children. Each child gets up and does the action required and calls on someone to guess which letter that child was given.

In Follow the Letter Leader, the leader picks a letter card and does that action. Everyone else follows the leader doing the same action. The leader then selects another card, and the game continues.

Teachers have different favorite actions, and you will have your own favorites. Try to choose actions with which everyone is familiar and that are called by only one name. Here is a list of actions I like. The action for **s** is my particular favorite. You can use it to end the game. Children say, "It is not an action at all," but they remember that "**s** is the sitting letter":

bounce	hop	nod	vacuum
catch	jump	paint	walk
dance	kick	run	yawn
fall	laugh	sit	zip
gallop	march	talk	

Letter Action Picture Cards

This set of 24 picture cards from Really Good Stuff contains pictures of children doing actions with all the common beginning consonants and the digraphs **ch**, **sh**, **th**, and **wh**.

jump

Photos © 2011 Really Good Stuff®

Children remember what they do and what they eat. Many teachers like to feature a food for each letter. Ask the children to help prepare the food and then eat it. Try to choose nutritious foods that children like, and consider any food allergies. Choose foods with a clear single sound to represent each letter. **Bananas** is better than **bread** because **bread** begins with **br** and many young children have trouble separating these two sounds. Here are some possible foods:

bananas	hamburgers	noodles	vegetables
cookies	Jell-O	popcorn	watermelon
donuts	Kool-Aid	raisins	yogurt
fish	lemonade	soup	zucchini bread
gum	milk	toast	

Key Words for Sounds

Once your students are moving along in their phonemic awareness, have learned many of the letter names, and are beginning to learn some of the sounds, you can help them consolidate this knowledge by deciding with them on one key word to represent each sound. Many publishing companies and reading series include some key words for the common letter sounds, but often children call the word something other than what is intended ("puppy" for **dog** or "bunny" for **rabbit**, for example), and the key words can confuse rather than support their learning of letter sounds. Many teachers work with their classes to come up with a key word that works for them. Let all the children have a say in this and spend some time discussing which word would be most helpful and which word they like best. Remember that "liking something" is very important to young children! You may want to use some of the wonderful examples from alphabet books, some of the names of your children when they are clear examples for the sound, and some favorite foods and favorite places familiar to all the children. For the vowels, you might want two examples, one for each of the common sounds. Try to use "pure" sounds—a word with just **f**, not **fr** or **fl**—since separating these blended sounds is difficult for children in the beginning. Here are the key words one class decided they liked. The names are all names of children in the class or of famous people. Use this as an example of the kind of chart your children might help construct, but remember this works only if the children have ownership in choosing the words and if they like their choices.

A a	apple, ape	N n	nose
B b	boys	O o	octopus, Oprah
C c	cookies	P p	Pizza Hut
D d	dinosaur	Q q	quarter
E e	elephant, Ethan	R r	red
F f	fun	S s	soup
G g	girls	T t	Taco Bell
H h	Harry	U u	underwear, unicorn
I i	insect, ice cream	V v	Vicki
J j	Jessica	W w	Wendy's
K k	Kmart	X x	x-ray
L l	Latecia	Y y	yellow
M m	McDonald's	Z z	zoo

Alphabet Picture Cards

Alphabet Starters (published by Rigby in 1996) provides little books for each letter of the alphabet. Each book contains seven key words with wonderfully clear pictures. The *g* book has words and pictures for *gate, girls, goats, garage, garden, goggles,* and *guitar*. The *r* book has *rabbit, red, road, river, rainbow, ring,* and *rope*. Books for the vowels have pictures and words for both the long and short sounds. The *i* book has *insects, invitation, igloo, ice cream,* and *iron*. Young children love reading these simple but engaging books, and the books help them learn letter sounds along with the important phonemic awareness concept of "starts the same."

For English Language Learners

Alphabet books, letter foods and actions, and key words for sounds help all children learn letter names and sounds. For English language learners who may not know the meaning of many of the words, providing a picture cue along with the key words will help them access meaning and add to their English vocabularies. Alphabet books, of course, have pictures that accompany the words and thus are one of the very best tools for developing alphabet name and sound knowledge. By adding pictures to your display of letter actions, foods, and key words, you will provide the meaning link needed by English language learners to profit from the concrete connections.

Changing a Hen to a Fox

Children love to pretend, and in this activity they pretend they can change one animal, a hen, into a fox. They do this by changing one letter at a time. As they change that letter, they listen for where they hear the changing letter and review all the single consonants. To begin this activity, write the names of five animals on the board—each of which has a different vowel sound:

cat   hen   pig   fox   bug

The teacher and the children say these words together, stretching out each word and talking about the beginning, middle, and ending sounds. Particular attention is given to the middle sound—the vowel sound—in each of these words. Next, the teacher asks the children,

"Can you change a hen into a fox?"

He tells the children that if they follow his directions and think about letters and sounds, they will be able to do this. The children all take a sheet of paper and these directions are given.

"Write **hen**." (The teacher points to the word **hen** on the board and everyone copies it onto their papers.)

"Now change the **hen** to **pen**." (The teacher and children decide they have to change just the first letter from an **h** to a **p** and write **pen** under **hen**.)

"Now change your **pen** into a **pet**." (Children decide they have to change the last letter from an **n** to a **t** and write **pet**.)

More Hen to Fox Lessons

Here are seven other Changing a Hen to a Fox lessons.

pig	bug	pig	cat	fox	bug	cat
rig	dug	big	bat	box	hug	hat
rid	dig	wig	hat	bop	dug	rat
rib	pig	win	rat	top	dig	rag
rob	pin	fin	pat	mop	big	bag
Bob	pen	fit	pet	map	bag	big
box	ten	fat	pen	mat	bat	dig
fox	en	cat	hen	cat	cat	pig

"Can you change **pet** to **pit**?" (The teacher helps them stretch out **pit** and decide it is the vowel they need to change and this vowel has the same sound as **insect**.)

"Now change **pit** to **sit**."

"Next change **sit** to **six**."

"Then change **six** to **fix**."

"Finally, change **fix** to **fox**."

Children love changing the letters and the animals, and they are using what they are learning about letters and sounds to spell lots of other words. In addition, children develop crucial phonemic awareness skills as they listen to the words and decide what part of the word is being changed. (Many teachers initiate this activity by reading Mem Fox's *Hattie and the Fox* to the children.)

Guess the Covered Word

Most short words are made up of two patterns, the beginning letters and the vowel and letters that follow it. The beginning letters (also called *onsets*, which include single *consonants, digraphs,* and *blends*) are all the letters up to the vowel. Children need to learn the sounds for these letters—which are quite consistent and reliable. Unfortunately, although many children "learn" these sounds—they can circle pictures that begin with them and tell you what letter makes a particular sound if you ask them—they don't use them when they read and write. When writing and trying to figure out the spelling of a word such as **smelly**, they might begin it just with an **s** or an **sl** instead of an **sm**. Faced with an unfamiliar word in their reading, they often guess a word that makes sense but does not begin with the right letters or guess a word with only the correct first letter, ignoring the other letters. All of the activities in this chapter stress learning and using all the beginning letters. Guess the Covered Word lessons teach these beginning letter sounds systematically and teach them in the context of reading. Children learn that guessing just based on beginning letters—or just based on making sense—is not a very good strategy. But when they use all the beginning letters and the sense of the sentence and consider the length of the word, they can make very good guesses at new words.

Guess the Covered Word lessons help students learn to cross-check—to simultaneously think about what would make sense and about letters and sounds. To prepare for a Guess the Covered Word activity, write five to seven sentences and cover one word in each sentence. Use sticky notes to cover the words and cover them in such a way that, after three or four guesses are made with no letters showing, you can uncover all the letters up to the vowel. (If you have a smart board, you can create the lessons for it using black rectangles to cover the words.) For your first lessons, include in your covered words only words that begin with a single initial consonant and that are the last words in the sentence.

Kevin wants a pet **hamster**.

Mike wants a pet **turtle**.

Paola wants a pet **goldfish**.

Tracy wants a pet **pony**.

Jasmine wants a pet **kitten**.

Begin the activity by having students read the first sentence and asking students to guess the covered word. Write three or four guesses next to the sentence. Pointing out to the children that "it sure can be a lot of words when you can't see any letters," uncover all the letters up to the vowel (which in these first lessons is only one). Erase guesses that don't begin with that letter. Have students suggest possible words that make sense and begin with the correct letter and write these responses. When all the guesses that begin correctly and make sense are written, uncover the whole word and go on to the next sentence.

You can use Guess the Covered Word activities to teach and review all the beginning sounds. As the children begin to understand the strategy they need to use, include some covered words that are not the last word in the sentence. Have them read the whole sentence, skipping the covered word and then coming back to it to make guesses. Use

Ashley likes to ▮ at home.
Tyler has a new ▮ in his closet.
Maddy, will you go ▮ with me?
Jose found a ▮ in the forest.
Tristan heard the ▮ ring.

This chart is ready for a Guess the Covered Word Lesson.

the common single consonants—**b c d f g h j k l m n p r s t v w y z**—in your first lessons.

You can also use the Guess the Covered Word lesson format to teach the digraphs **sh**, **ch**, **th**, and **wh**. Follow the same procedure of getting three or four guesses with no letters showing and then uncovering all the letters up to the vowel. Here are some example sentences you might use when you are focusing on the digraphs **sh**, **ch**, and **th**. Be sure to include some words that begin with just **s**, **c**, and **t**.

Corinda likes to eat **chicken**.

Michaela likes **turkey** burgers.

Latoya ate **thirteen** waffles.

Sean likes orange **sherbet**.

Bob likes strawberry **shortcake**.

Chris bakes pies for **Thanksgiving**.

Carol likes carrot **cake**.

Chelsea likes **chocolate** cake.

For English Language Learners

Learning to read as you are learning a new language is difficult for students of any age. Learning how to decode and spell words is more difficult for English language learners because English has many sounds that do not exist in other languages. In Spanish and some other languages, the five vowels have one and only one sound, and this sound is often different from the sound represented by these letters in English words. When you are reading Spanish, the vowel **a** has the sound it has in **father**. The vowel **e** is similar to what we call a long **a** sound and is similar to the sound **e** has in **egg**. The vowel **i** has the sound **i** has in **police**—which we would call a long **e** sound. **O** has a sound that is like the long **o** sound in **vote**. The sound for **u** is like the **u** sound in **tutor**. Many vowel sounds we hear in English words, including all five short vowel sounds, and sounds for **ou**, **ow**, **au**, **aw**, **oo**, **ar**, **er**, and **or** do not exist in Spanish. Not as serious but still creating roadblocks for beginning readers are the differences in sounds for the consonants. In Spanish, the **h** is always silent and the **j** has the sound English gives to the **h**. In Spanish (and Japanese and Korean), **b** and **v** have the same sound. The combination **qu** in Spanish always has the **k** sound. The sounds for **w, z, sh, th,** and **wh** do not occur in Spanish.

When teaching phonics to children whose first language is Spanish, it is probably best to start with the letters that have the same sounds. The consonant letters **p, b, t, k, m, n, f, s, w,** and **y** have almost the same sound in both languages and would be a good place to begin. As children develop some confidence in their decoding ability, the sounds that don't exist in Spanish and letters that have different sounds in Spanish and English can be introduced.

When children have learned the common consonant and digraph sounds, you can use the Guess the Covered Word format to teach the common blends **bl**, **br**, **cl**, **cr**, **dr**, **fl**, **fr**, **gl**, **gr**, **pl**, **pr**, **sc**, **scr**, **sk**, **sl**, **sm**, **sn**, **sp**, **spr**, **st**, **str**, **sw**, and **tr**. Remember to include some words with single consonants so that your students continue to pay attention to all the letters up to the vowel.

We all love it when it **snows**.

Some people go **skiing**.

People ride in **snowmobiles**.

The **snowplow** is fun to ride on, too!

You can go down a hill fast in a **sled**.

Walking back up is hard if the snow is **slippery**.

The snow melts when the **sun** comes out.

Guess the Covered Word is a very versatile strategy. You can use it with a big book and cover a word or two on each page. Another possibility is to write paragraphs summarizing what the children have learned during a science or social studies unit and cover words in it.

Through Guess the Covered Word activities, children learn that just guessing words is not a good decoding strategy, but when they guess something that makes sense in the sentence, has all the right letters up to the vowel (not just the first letter), and is the right length, they can figure out many new words. They also learn to use the letter sounds they know to decode unfamiliar words with phonics patterns they have not yet learned.

Summary

Children from literate homes already know many words, letters, and sounds when they come to school. They can usually read their names and the names of their relatives and friends and other important-to-them words. They also know many letter names and sounds. By beginning the school year with activities such as those described in this chapter, you will level the playing field for children whose home environments did not or could not provide them with opportunities to develop the word and letter knowledge essential for success in beginning reading.

chapter 4

Making Words in Kindergarten

Making Words (Cunningham & Cunningham, 1992) is a multilevel phonics and spelling activity in which students are given a certain number of letters and guided to manipulate these letters to make some words. Making Words is an active, hands-on, manipulative activity in which children discover letter–sound relationships and learn how to look for patterns in words. Making Words was originally designed to help students in primary grades learn phonics and spelling. (Examples of primary grades lessons are included in Chapter 7.) Kindergarten teachers saw how effective Making Words was in helping children learn how to combine letters to read and spell words and wanted to apply the technique with their kindergartners. Because manipulating small letter cards was not developmentally appropriate for 4- and 5-year-olds, the Making Words strategy was adapted so that the children "wear" the letters and other children manipulate the "letter children" into words. Here is how Making Words kindergarten-style works.

Instead of individual children manipulating individual small letter cards, in kindergarten it is best to use a class set of large, "wearable" letter cards. The letter cards have capital letters on one side and lowercase letters on the other side with yarn attached to the top. Children wear these letter cards around their necks and become the letters as they make words using just one pattern or "word family."

Because you want your fledgling readers to connect the Making Words activity to reading, begin each kindergarten Making Words lesson by rereading a book that contains examples of the rhyming pattern you are working on. As you read the book, stop each time you come to a word with that pattern and have the children say the word and identify the pattern. After reading the book, give the pattern cards to two or three children, who become the letter cards for your pattern. Next, distribute other letter cards that will make words with that pattern. All the letter children come to the front of the room. The children making the pattern hold hands. The other children stand to the side. To give

Making Letter Cards

On 9'' × 12'' white construction paper or tagboard, type or paste large cut-out black letters, capitals on one side and lowercase on the other side. Next, laminate these letter cards so you can reuse them. Finally, punch holes at the top on each side and then thread enough yarn through the holes to make it possible to put the letter cards comfortably around your students' necks. Make sure the letter cards have lowercase letters on one side and capital letters on the other side because you will need capital letters to make names. Make two of the most common letters (**e, b, l, n, p, r, s,** and **t**) because some words and patterns require these.

your students lots of practice decoding and spelling rhyming words, use two different activities in which the beginning letters combine with the pattern letters to create rhyming words. In the first activity, ask specific letter people to come join the pattern.

"I need letter person **c** to come stand next to **a-t**."

When the **c** is standing next to **a-t**, the whole class blends the beginning sound with the pattern to decode the word **cat**. You then call each of the other beginning letter people to join the pattern and the class blends the letters to decode the various words.

For the second activity, you say one of the words previously made. The children who are not letter people today point to the letter who needs to join the pattern to make the word. Here is an example lesson for the **at** pattern.

A Sample Making Words Kindergarten Lesson

After reading the rhyming book *The Cat in the Hat* and identifying the **a-t** words in this book, the teacher chooses two children to be the pattern letters today. These children put on the yarned letter cards and become the letters **a** and **t**.

Next, the teacher passes out other yarned letter cards (**b, c, f, h, m, p, r,** and **s**) to other children in the class. All these cards have consonants on them that will make words with the **at** pattern. The letters **a** and **t** join hands to show that they are the pattern and will stay together throughout the lesson. The teacher, along with the students, blend these two letter sounds together and say **a/t, at**.

The teacher asks the **c** to join **a** and **t** and then asks the children what word they have just made. The teacher and the class blend together the letter sounds **c/a/t** and say **cat**. Then the teacher uses the word **cat** in a sentence: "I once had a big, fat, gray **cat**."

Next, the teacher calls on another letter child (**b**) to stand in front of the letters **a** and **t** and asks, "Who can read the word I just made?" Together, the teacher and the class blend the three letter sounds to make the word **b/a/t, bat**. Again, the teacher uses the word in a sentence: "I hit the ball with a **bat**."

The teacher continues calling letters to join **a-t**, helping children to blend and pronounce the words and putting the words in sentences.

"**f/a/t, fat**	The vet put my dog on a diet because he was getting **fat**."
"**h/a/t, hat**	In winter, I wear a **hat** to keep my ears from freezing."
"**r/a/t, rat**	A **rat** is a big rodent."
"**s/a/t, sat**	We **sat** in the front row at the game."
"**m/a/t, mat**	After lunch, we each get out our **mat** for rest time."

When the teacher calls for **p** to join **a-t**, she has **p** first show the lowercase side and then the capital side and reminds children that names are always spelled with capital letters.

"**p/a/t pat**	Sometimes I give you a **pat** on the back when you have done a very good job."
"**P/a/t pat**	With the capital letter, **P/a/t** spells the name **Pat**. Do you know anyone named **Pat**?"

Next, the children do another round of Making Words using the letter cards, this time not only blending and segmenting sounds but also listening for

This class is ready for a Making Words Kindergarten lesson.

what letter they need to make or spell a word. For this second round, the teacher distributes the same letters to different children. Once again, the teacher has the letters **a** and **t** stand together and hold hands. The teacher and students blend these two letter sounds together again and pronounce **at**. The teacher then says a word that can be made by adding a letter to **at**, **fat**. The teacher asks all the children in the class to point to the letter that is needed in front of **at** to make the word **fat**. The children point to **f** and the teacher asks **f** to come and stand with **at** and leads the class to say **f/at**, **fat**. The letter **f** leaves (segmenting) and **at** is left standing alone. They continue to use this **at** pattern to spell other words. The teacher asks, "What letter do we need to spell **bat**? **cat**? **mat**? **rat**? **sat**? **Pat**? For each word, the class points to and names the letter that should stand next to **at** to spell the word. The children wearing the needed letter join the two children with **at**—holding their letter cards (**c**, **h**, **b**, **f**, **h**, **m**, **r**, **s**, or **p**) in front of **at** to spell or make each of the words. All the children blend and pronounce the word. If the letters make a name, the teacher talks about names and the letter children turn their letter cards around to the capital letter side.

At the end of the activity, the teacher gives the lesson more scope by having two children come up together and blend these two beginning letter sounds, and read and spell words that begin with two beginning letters, such as **brat** and **flat**.

When the children have made words with the **at** pattern and have read and spelled the words with the teacher, she or he then collects the letter cards by asking, "Will the person who has the **a** bring it to me? Will the person with the letter **t** bring it to me?" As each person hands the teacher the letter, the teacher asks the whole class to say the common sound made by that letter. The teacher continues to call each letter and have everyone say the sound of that letter until all letters are collected. Collecting the letters in this way provides everyone some additional practice with letter names and sounds.

Rhyming Patterns for Making Words Kindergarten Lessons

Begin your Making Words lessons with easy two-letter patterns, such as **a-t** and **i-n**. Later in the year, do some lessons with three-letter patterns, such as **a-c-k** and **u-n-k**. At the end of the year, include some lessons with silent letters and vowel teams, such as **a-t-e** and **e-a-t**. Here is a list in alphabetical order of the patterns you might want to teach and some common words kindergartners might read and spell with those patterns. Uncommon words such as **vat** or **glut** are not included. If some of these words are not in the listening vocabulary of your students, do not include them in the lesson. It is important for kindergarten children that when they blend letters to make a word, they can match that word to a word in their oral language store.

- **ack** will help you read and spell **back, Jack, Mack, pack, rack, sack, tack, Zack, black, smack,** and **track**
- **ad** will help you read and spell **bad, Dad, had, lad, mad, pad, sad, Tad, glad,** and **Brad**
- **ake** will help you read and spell **bake, cake, fake, Jake, rake, lake, make, take, wake, Blake, flake,** and **brake**
- **all** will help you read and spell **ball, call, fall, hall, mall, tall, wall, small,** and **stall**
- **am** will help you read and spell **bam, jam, ham, Pam, ram, Sam, clam,** and **slam**
- **ame** will help you read and spell **came, fame, game, name, same, tame, blame,** and **flame**
- **an** will help you read and spell **can, Dan, fan, man, pan, ran, tan, van, plan,** and **scan**
- **and** will help you read and spell **band, hand, land, sand, brand, grand,** and **stand**
- **ank** will help you read and spell **blank, Hank, rank, sank, blank,** and **drank**
- **ap** will help you read and spell **cap, lap, map, nap, rap, sap, clap, snap,** and **slap**
- **ar** will help you read and spell **bar, car, far, jar, scar,** and **star**
- **at** will help you read and spell **bat, cat, fat, hat, mat, Nat, pat, Pat, rat, sat, brat, flat,** and **scat**

- **ate** will help you read and spell **date, gate, hate, Kate, late, mate, Nate, rate, plate,** and **skate**
- **ay** will help you read and spell **day, hay, Jay, lay, may, Ray, say, way, play, clay,** and **stay** (**stray, spray**)
- **eat** will help you read and spell **beat, heat, meat, neat, seat,** and **treat**
- **ed** will help you read and spell **bed, fed, led, Ned, red, Ted, bled, Fred,** and **sled**
- **eep** will help you read and spell **beep, deep, keep, peep, weep, steep,** and **sweep**
- **ell** will help you read and spell **bell, fell, sell, well, yell, smell,** and **spell**
- **en** will help you read and spell **Ben, den, hen, Jen, men, pen, ten,** and **Glen**
- **end** will help you read and spell **bend, lend, mend, send, blend,** and **spend**
- **ent** will help you read and spell **bent, dent, tent, rent, sent, vent, went, Brent, spent,** and **Trent**
- **est** will help you read and spell **best, nest, pest, rest, test, west, vest,** and **Crest** (**toothpaste**)
- **et** will help you read and spell **bet, get, jet, met, net, pet, set, vet, wet,** and **yet**
- **ick** will help you read and spell **Dick, kick, lick, Nick, pick, Rick, sick, tick, trick,** and **stick**
- **ide** will help you read and spell **hide, ride, side, tide, wide, bride, glide,** and **slide**
- **ill** will help you read and spell **Bill, dill, fill, hill, kill, mill, pill, will, still,** and **spill**
- **in** will help you read and spell **bin, fin, kin, pin, sin, tin, win, twin,** and **spin**
- **ine** will help you read and spell **dine, fine, line, mine, nine, pine, spine,** and **twine**
- **ing** will help you read and spell **Bing, ding, king, ring, sing, wing, bring, sting,** and **swing** (**string, spring**)
- **ink** will help you read and spell **pink, link, mink, rink, sink, wink, blink, stink,** and **drink**
- **ip** will help you read and spell **dip, hip, lip, rip, sip, tip, zip, skip, slip, trip,** and **drip** (**strip**)
- **it** will help you read and spell **bit, fit, hit, kit, pit, sit, spit, slit,** and **skit**
- **ock** will help you read and spell **dock, lock, rock, sock, block, clock,** and **stock**
- **og** will help you read and spell **dog, fog, hog, jog, log, frog,** and **smog**
- **ook** will help you read and spell **cook, book, hook, look, took, brook,** and **crook**

- **op** will help you read and spell **bop, cop, hop, mop, pop, top, crop, drop,** and **stop**

- **ot** will help you read and spell **cot, dot, hot, got, lot, not, pot, rot, spot, slot,** and **plot**

- **ub** will help you read and spell **cub, rub, sub, tub, club,** and **stub**

Steps in a Making Words Kindergarten Lesson

1. Choose a book that contains the rhyming pattern you want to work on. Read the book at least once to your students and enjoy and talk about the book, without attention focusing on the pattern. Reread the pages of the book that contain your chosen pattern and have your students say and identify the rhyming words that have that pattern. Don't skip this step. Children need to see that the phonics patterns they are manipulating are real words that come from real books. Phonics is useless if students use it only during phonics time and don't make the transfer to reading and writing.

2. Choose children to be the pattern letter people. Have these children come to the front of the room, put on their letter cards, and join hands. Have everyone in the class blend the pattern letters to read the rhyming pattern.

3. Distribute the consonant cards that are needed to make words to other children and have them stand in a line alongside the pattern children.

4. Name a letter and ask that letter to come and stand right next to the pattern children. Have everyone in the class blend the letters and read the word. Use the word in a sentence after it is made. Continue to call letters and have letter people come and join the pattern and have everyone blend and read the name until all words are made. When a name is made, talk about how capital letters are needed and make sure the letter card is turned to its capital side. In this step, children are blending and segmenting sounds to read words.

5. After the children have read words, have them use the letters to spell words. Use the same letter cards and the same words but instead of asking a letter to come and join the pattern, say a word and let the class point to the letter that is needed to spell that word. (You may want to choose children who were not letter people for the first activity to be the letter people for the second activity so that more children have a chance to be the letters.)

6. To make the lesson more multilevel, include some words at the end that your students can spell by blending two beginning letters with the pattern (**bl, br, cl, cr, dr, fl, fr, gr, pl, pr, sc, sk, sl, sm, sn, sp, st, sw, tr,** and **tw**). If you like, include a word with a three-letter blend (**spr, str**).

7. Collect the letter cards by calling for the letters and having everyone say the sound for that letter. This provides a quick review of letter names and sounds for children who still need this practice.

- **ug** will help you read and spell **bug, dug, hug,** jug, **mug, rug, tug, slug, snug,** and **plug**
- **ump** will help you read and spell **bump, dump, hump, jump, lump, pump, plump, slump,** and **stump**
- **un** will help you read and spell **bun, fun, gun, run, sun, spun,** and **stun**
- **unk** will help you read and spell **bunk, dunk, hunk, junk, sunk, skunk, stunk,** and **trunk**
- **ut** will help you read and spell **but, cut, gut, hut, nut,** and **rut**

The sample lesson previously described comes from *Making Words Kindergarten: 50 Interactive Lessons That Build Phonemic Awareness, Phonics, and Spelling Skills* (Hall & Cunningham, 2009). Several other lessons are shown here.

Sample Lessons for Early, Middle, and Late Year

❊ Pattern: ent (early in the year)

Letters needed: e, n, t, b, d, p, t, r, s, v, and **w**

1. **Books to read**

   - *My Grandpa and I* by P. K. Hallinan (Candy Cane Press, 2002), ISBN 0-82494-219-1. Read the book; reread the page with the **ent** pattern and talk about the **ent** pattern in **tent** and **went**.
   - *The Night before Summer Vacation* by Natasha Wing (Grosset & Dunlap, 2002), ISBN 0-448-42830-X. Read the book; reread the pages with the **ent** pattern and talk about the **ent** pattern in **went** and **tent**.
   - *Hop on Pop* by Dr. Seuss (Random House, 1963, renewed 1991), ISBN: 0-394-80029-X. Read the book; reread page 53 and listen for the **ent** pattern in **went, sent,** and **tent**.

2. **Making Words: Blend and segment to read words**

   First, make the pattern **ent** with the letter card children. Lead the children to say the letter sounds and pattern **e/n/t, ent**. Then make and read a word using one of the other letter cards (**w**) and ask, "Who can read this word?" Together with the class, blend the letter sounds and say **w/e/n/t, went**. Use the word in a sentence: "I **went** to the store with my friend." Continue this way with the other letters to make and read **b/e/n/t, bent; d/e/n/t, dent; t/e/n/t, tent; r/e/n/t, rent; s/e/n/t, sent;** and **v/e/n/t, vent**. Use two letter sounds together with the pattern to make and read the words **Brent, spent,** and **Trent**. Remember to use and talk about the capital letter used for names.

3. **Making Words: Blend and segment to spell words**

   After making and reading words, use the same letter cards and lead the class to spell words. Ask the class to point to the letter to put in front of **ent** to make the word **went.** Continue to make and spell **bent, dent, tent, sent, rent, vent, Brent, spent,** and **Trent.**

4. **Collect the letter cards**

   Call for each letter to review the letter names.

✳ Pattern: ay (middle of the year)

Letters needed: **a, y, b, c, d, f, h, l, k, m, p, r, s, t,** and **w**

1. **Books to read**

   - *Annie Bananie* by Leah Komaiko (Scholastic, 1987), ISBN 0-590-42844-6. Read the book; reread pages 8 and 9 and talk about the **ay** pattern in **play** and **away.** On page 18 talk about the **ay** pattern in **away** and **birthday.**
   - *Miss Spider's Tea Party* by David Kirk (Scholastic, 1994), ISBN 0-590-47724-2. Read the book; reread page 4 and talk about the **ay** pattern in the words **May, day, stay,** and **away.**
   - *The Cat in the Hat* by Dr. Seuss (Random House, 1957, renewed 1985), ISBN 0-394-80001-X. Read the book; reread pages 1, 37, and 60 and point out the **ay** pattern in **play** and **day.**

2. **Making Words: Blend and segment to read words**

   First, make the pattern **ay** with the letter card children. Explain that you can't hear the **y** sound; you can hear only the letter **a** when you say its name. Have the children say the **ay** sound with you. Then, make and read a word using one of the other letter cards (**d**) and ask, "Who can read this word?" Together with the class, blend the letter sounds and say **d/ay, day.** Use the word in a sentence: "What a nice (rainy) **day.**" Continue this way with the other letters to make and read **h/ay, hay; F/ay, Fay; J/ay, Jay; K/ay, Kay; l/ay, lay; m/ay, may; R/ay, Ray; s/ay, say;** and **w/ay, way.** Remember to use and talk about the capital letters for names. Use two letter sounds together with the pattern to make and read the words **clay, play,** and **stay.**

3. **Making Words: Blend and segment to spell words**

   After making and reading words, use the same letter cards and lead the class to spell words. Ask the class to point to the letter to put in front of **ay** to make the word **day.** Continue to make and spell **hay, Fay, Jay, Kay, lay, may, Ray, say, way, clay, play,** and **stay.**

4. **Collect the letter cards**

   Call for each letter to review the letter names.

❋ Pattern: ate (late in the year)

Letters needed: **a, e, t, d, h, l, k, m, k, p, r,** and s

1. **Books to read**

    -   *The Wedding* by Eve Bunting (Charlesbridge, 2005), ISBN 1-58089-040-7. Read the book; reread page 8 and talk about the **ate** pattern in **gate**, **date**, and **late**.
    -   *The Library* by Sarah Stewart (Farrar, Straus, & Giroux, 1999), ISBN 0-37444-394-7. Read the book; reread the pages with the **ate** pattern and talk about the **ate** pattern in **skate**, **rate**, **date**, and **late**.
    -   *Counting Is for the Birds* by Frank Mazzola Jr. (Charlesbridge, 1997), ISBN 0-88106-950-7. Read the book; reread the page with the **ate** pattern and talk about the pattern in **mate** and **rate**.

2. **Making Words: Blend and segment letter sounds to read words**

    Using the letter card children, make **ate**. Explain that you can't hear the **e** sound; you can hear only the **a** when you say its name and **t** in this pattern. We call this a silent **e**. (Have the letter card child with the **e** put his or her hand over his or her mouth.) Have the children say the **ate** sound with you. Put the child with the letter card **d** in front of the three children wearing **ate**. Ask the children to read this word. Lead the class to say **d/ate**, **date**. Use the word in a sentence: "Today's **date** is the fifth of March." Then make and read some other words: **g/ate**, **gate**; **h/ate**, **hate**; **m/ate**, **mate**; **l/ate**, **late**; and **K/ate**, **Kate**. Remember the capital letter needed for **Kate**. Use two letter sounds together with the pattern to make and read the words **plate** and **skate**.

3. **Making Words: Blend and segment letter sounds to spell words**

    Using the three letter cards **ate**, ask the children to point to the letter needed to make the word **date**. When they point to the letter child **d**, have them say **d/ate**, **date**. Then follow the same procedure to make and spell **gate**, **hate**, **Kate**, **mate**, **late**, **plate**, and **skate**.

4. **Collect the letter cards**

    Call for each letter to review the letter names.

For English Language Learners

Your English language learners will enjoy being the letters and creating the words but they may need meaning support for some of the words. Fortunately, the meaning of many of the words being made—**cat, hat, car, jar, van, pan**—can be supported by pictures. Other words are action words—**ran, sat, clap, snap, slide**—that you can demonstrate and invite children to do with you. If you have English language learners in your classroom, consider which words in your Making Words lesson can be supported through pictures or actions. Clip art is readily available on many Internet sites and you can locate them through an image search on Google and other search engines.

Summary

The manipulation of letters and sounds to make new words is an important part of learning to read, and making words is a wonderful way to introduce your kindergarten class to how beginning letters are combined with rhyming patterns to read and spell words. Young children are concrete learners who learn best when they can see and do an activity. Wearing the letters and making words is an excellent way for young children to practice the phonemic awareness skills of rhyming, blending, and segmenting. Simultaneous with the development of these phonemic awareness skills, children are learning letter names and sounds and the most common rhyming patterns. In every lesson, the teacher leads the children through two activities. In the first activity, they blend beginning letters and rhyming patterns to read words. In the second activity, they decide which letters are needed to make a word and are thus learning to use letter sounds to spell words.

chapter 5

Early Reading Concepts: Assessment and Differentiation

Assessment is part of everything we do. Most of us make an assessment of the weather each morning to decide what to wear. We assess the food, service, and atmosphere as we dine at the new restaurant in town to decide whether to come back. We assess our new neighbors as we watch them interact with each other and move their furniture in. As we go through our daily routines, we are constantly assessing—usually by observing. "Sizing up the situation" lets us make wise decisions about how to proceed.

Sometimes, it is easier to define something by beginning with what it is not. Assessment is not grading—although assessment can help you determine and support the grades you give. Assessment is not standardized test scores—although these scores can give you some general idea of what children have achieved so far. Assessment is collecting and analyzing data to make decisions about how children are performing and growing. Caldwell (2009) describes four steps for assessment. First, identify what you want to assess. Second, collect evidence. Next, analyze that evidence. Finally, make a decision and act on that decision.

Assessment is an ongoing process for experienced teachers who are astute kid watchers. As the children respond to the various activities, teachers notice who can do what. They write down these observations or note them on a checklist. If you want to know if a child knows why we learn to read and write and desires to learn to read, watch that child as he or she engages in reading and writing activities. If you want to know if a child can track print, sit down with that child and ask her to point to words as you read them. If you want to know if a child can blend and segment words, say some words one letter at a time and see if the child can tell you what word you said, and then say some words and ask the child to say them slowly—one letter at a time.

Following Caldwell's assessment steps, the first thing you need to decide is what you want to assess. When assessing early reading strategies, you want to assess the foundational concepts described in this section of the book. Do your students know what reading and writing are for and do they readily engage in these activities? Do they know the conventions and jargon of print? Are they developing phonological and phonemic awareness? Are they accumulating some words they can read and spell? What is their level of alphabet awareness? Can they name most letters, tell you the common sounds for letters, and name some words that begin with these letters? This chapter will describe some quick assessments you can incorporate into your daily instruction to help you determine how well your students are developing the foundational skills.

To keep up with their observations, many teachers of young children record the results on a checklist such as the example shown here. Each day, they focus on two or three children and observe and talk with these children as they are engaged in reading and writing to determine how they are developing the critical understandings. Teachers often use a simple system of putting a minus (–) to indicate the child does not have that concept, a question mark (?) when it is unclear that the child has it, and a plus (+) to indicate the child does seem to have developed that concept. Two pluses on two different dates is a reliable indicator that the child has indeed learned the concept.

Beginning Reading Concepts Checklist

Name	Date Checked + ? –	Date Checked + ? –	Date Checked + ? –	Date Checked + ? –
Knows Functions of Print and Wants to Learn to Read				
Participates in shared reading				
Attempts to read favorite books				
Attempts to write				
Knows Print Concepts and Jargon				
Knows print, not pictures, is what we read				
Tracks print left to right, return sweep				
Points to each word as it is read				
Identifies one word, one letter, one sentence				
Identifies first and last letter in a word				
Demonstrates Phonological Awareness				
Counts words in oral sentence				
Claps syllables				

Continued

Name	Date Checked + ? –	Date Checked + ? –	Date Checked + ? –	Date Checked + ? –
Demonstrates Phonemic Awareness				
Stretches out words while writing				
Blends sounds to form words				
Segments words into sounds				
Recognizes rhyming words				
Recognizes words that begin alike				
Demonstrates Alphabet Awareness				
Names most letters				
Gives common sound for most letters				
Names words that begin with common letters				
Reads and Writes Some Words				
Some classmates' names				
Some concrete interesting words				
Some high-frequency function words				

Date _____ Comments

Date _____ Comments

Date _____ Comments

Date _____ Comments

Assessing Early Reading Concepts: Functions of Print

Knowing what reading and writing are for is one of the major concepts that motivate children to work at learning to read and write. Children who know that books contain stories that entertain you and make you laugh and that relate to things that happen in their lives are eager to try to learn to read. Children who know that some books are full of interesting facts—about animals and holidays and people—want to learn to read so that they can learn more "interesting stuff." Children who know that writing is a way to tell about yourself and things you care about and that you can write cards and letters and emails are eager to learn to write. To determine which of your children know the functions of print, observe them during shared reading of big books and shared writing of predictable charts. Do they participate eagerly even if their reading and writing skills are just beginning to develop? Observe them as they interact with favorite books. Do they "pretend read" these books and talk about what they see in the pictures? Observe them as they write. Do they know that writing is a way of telling about something? Can they read what they wrote—even if no one else can yet read their concoctions of scribbles and pictures along with some letters and words? Children who participate in shared reading and writing and who attempt to read and write demonstrate that they know what reading and writing are for and want to learn to read.

Knows Functions of Print
Participates in shared reading
Attempts to read favorite books
Attempts to write

Assessing Early Reading Concepts: Print Concepts

The most basic concept children must learn about print is that it is the print and not the pictures that you read. Children also need to learn to track print. Children who can track print can point to words, starting on the left and going from left to right. They then make a return sweep and track across the next line of print. They can match words to speech by pointing to each word as they read. Another important concept for learning to read is understanding the jargon of print. Do your students know the difference between a word, a sentence, and a letter? These print concepts are essential to successfully beginning the journey toward literacy and thus are some of the most important concepts to assess early in the school year.

To assess print concepts, sit down individually with each child during independent reading time. Have the child pick a favorite page from the book he or she is reading and say,

"I will read this page to you if you show me what to read."

The child who knows that the print, not the pictures, is what you read will point to the words.

If the child points to the picture, point to the words and say:

> "These are the words I am going to read. Your job is to point to the
> words as I read them. Point to the word I should start reading."

If the child points to the first word, ask the child to point to the words as you read them. If not, put the child's finger on the first word and read the first word.

> "This is the first word. Now point to all the words I should read."

Observe if the child points to each word as you read it going left to right and making a return sweep at the end of each line.

You also want to know if the child understands some of the particular jargon we use in talking about print. After reading the page to the child, ask the child to point to just one word and to just one letter; then ask the child to show you one sentence. Isolate a word on the page and ask the child to point to the first and last letter in that word.

Knows Print Concepts and Jargon
Knows print, not pictures, is what we read
Tracks print left to right, return sweep
Points to each word as it is read
Identifies one word, one letter, one sentence

Assessing Early Reading Concepts: Phonological and Phonemic Awareness

Children who have phonological awareness know what words are. They can tell you how many words are in a spoken sentence. They can clap syllables in words and know that the word **motorcycles** takes more claps than the word **car**. Children who have phonemic awareness can manipulate words. They can stretch out words and tell you what word you have said when you stretch out a word. They can tell you that **bike** rhymes with **Mike** and that **book** begins like **bike**. They can make up silly rhymes for objects in the classroom. They can segment words into their component sounds and blend sounds back together and identify the blended word.

You can assess your students' phonological and phonemic awareness by observing their ability to do these tasks as you are doing the activities described in Chapter 2. You can also do some quick checks with individual children whose class participation leaves you unsure about their understanding.

To determine which children can identify the separate words in a spoken sentence, observe them as they move the counters to show each word in a sentence you say (p. 28). If you are clapping the syllables in a word (p. 28), observe their responses. For children who appear to be just following the lead of the other children, do these activities with them individually to determine their understanding of phonological awareness.

Likewise, you can observe their responses in activities you are doing to develop phonemic awareness. If you are saying riddles, perhaps asking children what words rhyme with **feet**, **head**, **hand**, or **knee** (p. 30), observe how quickly they respond. If they seem to be just following the lead of the other children, take them aside and do some riddles with them individually.

To determine which children understand the concept of words beginning with the same sound, call children to line up by saying a word that begins like their names.

"If your name begins like **dog**, you can line up. Everyone point to the people who can get in line."
"If your name begins like **ship**, you can line up. Everyone point to the people who can get in line."

Observe how quickly they point to the correct people. Do a similar name/word matching activity individually with children whose responses do not clearly indicate they have the important concept of words beginning with the same sound.

Determine how well they can segment words by listening in on their attempts to stretch out words while writing or when they are using sound boxes to represent the separate sounds in words (p. 35). To determine their ability to blend sounds into words, call out the names of children to line up by saying the sounds in their names separately:

t/o/d   d/a/v/i/d   l/i/z/e

Have everyone point to the person whose name you said. Watch how quickly your students recognize whose name it is. Do this activity of stretching out the names of children individually with children whose blending ability you can not readily observe.

Phonemic awareness is not a single concept, and it is not an easy concept for many children. Most of the activities described in Chapter 2 are activities in which students are actively responding. By observing their responses, you can determine which children have developed the various phonemic awareness concepts. You can then do individual assessments with children whose group responses do not clearly indicate their understanding. Just as for print concepts, you should require two plusses on two different days before deciding that a child has developed the concept.

Demonstrates Phonological Awareness
Counts words in oral sentence
Claps syllables
Demonstrates Phonemic Awareness
Stretches out words while writing
Blends sounds to form words
Segments words into sounds
Recognizes rhyming words
Recognizes words that begin alike

Assessing Early Reading Concepts: Alphabet Awareness

Unlike determining whether children have grasped print and phonological and phonemic awareness concepts, you generally cannot tell which children are learning letter names and sound by observing their responses. In most classrooms, you will need to use a more formal process to assess this knowledge. The most efficient way to do this is to create a sheet containing all the letters. When you think many children have learned many of the letter names and sounds, sit down with two or three children each day and ask them to name the letters. Note the letters that the children correctly name along with the date on their record sheet in the Name column. Next, point to letters you expect them to know sounds for and ask:

"Can you tell me what sound this letter makes?"

If they give an appropriate sound, indicate this along with the date in the Sound column.

Finally, point to each letter (except **x**) and ask:

"Do you know any words that begin with this letter?"

Indicate letters they know a word for along with the date in the Word column.

❋ Alphabet Letter Knowledge Record Sheet

Show the child a sheet containing all the lowercase letters in random order and ask the child: "Name all the letters you know."

m	j	r	v	l	a
d	f	h	k	c	g
o	p	i	y	b	s
e	t	x	u	z	n
w	q				

Put the date for all letters correctly named in the Name column. Next, point to the letters you expect him or her to know sounds for and ask what sound that letter makes. Put the date for all correct sounds in the Sound column. Finally, point to each letter (except **x**) and ask the child to name a word that begins with that letter. Indicate beginning sounds for which a word is known, with the date, in the Word column. Recheck letters for which names, sounds, or words were not known and note the date they were correctly identified.

Child's Name			
Letter	**Name**	**Sound**	**Word**
f			
h			
d			
g			
k			
s			
l			
a			
j			
p			
w			
q			
o			
u			
r			
t			
y			
e			
i			

Continued

Child's Name			
Letter	**Name**	**Sound**	**Word**
m			
b			
n			
v			
x			
c			
z			

Demonstrates Alphabet Awareness
Names most letters
Gives common sound for most letters
Names words that begin with common letters

Assessing Early Reading Concepts: Word Learning

If you sit down with children on the first day of school and try to determine if they can read by giving them a simple book to read or testing them on some common words such as **the, and**, **of**, or **with**, you would probably conclude that most children can't read yet. But many children enter school with some known words. The words they know are usually "important-to-them" concrete words. Knowing 10 to 15 words is important not because the child can read much with these few words, but because in learning these first words, the child has learned how words are learned. Children who come to school already able to read or write some concrete words know how to learn the more difficult, abstract words.

All children should have learned some words from the reading and writing activities described in the previous chapters. To assess their word learning, you may want to check their ability to read the names of the children in the class, some of the most interesting words from favorite big books and predictable charts. You can also observe the words they are spelling correctly in their writing. For children who came to your class already knowing some concrete words, you may want to see if they have learned some of the high-frequency words—such as **like**, **is**, **in**, and **the**—often repeated in big books and predictable charts. The expectation should not be that everyone is learning all words (although your

> **tech tip**
>
> You can find some excellent tools for assessing print concepts, rhyme, blending and segmenting, and other early reading skills on the web at http://teams.lacoe.edu/reading/assessments/assessments.html. In addition to the assessment tools themselves, you can watch videos of teachers giving the assessments.

children who came to school already reading will astound you with how little repetition they require to learn a word!) but that everyone is adding some words to their store of words they can read.

Reads and Writes Some Words
Some classmates' names
Some concrete interesting words
Some high-frequency function words

Differentiating Instruction

As the saying goes, "Knowledge is power!" If you are regularly assessing how your students are progressing toward developing the essential early reading concepts, you will know who needs an additional nudge and maybe some one-on-one instruction. All the activities for building the foundation have "something for everyone." Regardless of where your students are in their early reading concepts, there are things they can learn from each lesson format. Also, every lesson format offers you opportunities to focus on particular children who you know need to work with particular skills.

Shared reading, predictable charts, morning message, and writing are activities that have a lot of scope. Children with little print experience learn what reading is and begin to develop concepts of print. They learn that each sentence starts at the left and goes to the right. They see the teacher start at the top and go the bottom. They hear the teacher talk about "words," "sentences," and "letters" and learn what this print-related jargon means. Most children learn a few words and begin to notice how words are the same and different. Children who come to school with these print concepts already established are not "spinning their wheels." These children actually learn many of the words in the books, messages, and charts. Often they can read these texts entirely on their own. Perhaps most important, all children develop the desire to learn to read and the confidence that they are learning to read!

As you assess your students' print concepts and jargon, pay particular attention to those children who are not developing these concepts. During shared reading, morning message, and work with predictable charts, let a child who is not automatically at tracking print hold the pointer and, with your help if needed, point to the words for everyone to read. As you dismiss children from the group, ask children who are still unclear about what a word and letter and sentence are to stay for a few extra minutes and use the shared reading, morning message, or predictable chart to review these concepts.

When making class books from predictable charts, seize the opportunity to work individually with each child who is not tracking print or who is unclear about print jargon. Give that child the sentence strip and connect the words **sentence**, **word**, and **letter** to that child's sentence.

> "Carl, here is the **sentence** you told me about what you are thankful for. Can you read it to me?"

Carl reads his sentence.

> "That was a great **sentence**. Can you count the number of **words** you used in your **sentence**?"

Carl points to and counts the words.

> "Super. Now I want you to cut your **sentence** into **words**. Let's draw some lines between the **words** so you can cut your **sentence** into **words**."

Carl cuts his sentence into words.

> "Great. Can you tell me which **word** is the longest? Can you count the number of **letters** in that **word**? Can you point to the **first letter** in that long **word**? Now, point to the **last letter** in that **word**."

Carl is able to do each of these tasks.

> "Super, now let's put your **words** in order on the bottom of this page to make your **sentence**. Then you can glue the **words** down and draw your picture and you will have created a wonderful page in our class book!"

When children are engaged in independent reading and writing, you can also provide one-on-one instruction to children who need to develop print concepts. To help them become automatic at print tracking, offer to read a page of their book to them and tell them their job is to point to the words. When you have finished reading the page, help them to use their fingers to frame one sentence, one word, and one letter. Help them find the first and the last word on the page and the first and last letter in the longest word.

When they are writing, ask them what they want to say. When they have told you their message, say their sentence one word at a time. Guide them to start at the left of the page, help them stretch out words, and accept whatever they write for each word. Show them how to put a "finger space" between words. When doing this, don't focus on handwriting or spelling. Remember what you are trying to help them develop: print concepts and jargon. You want them to learn the convention that print starts on the left and moves to the right. You want them to stretch out **words** and listen for the **sounds** of the **letters**. You want them to learn that their **sentence** is made up of individual **words** and that you put a space between the **words**.

All the activities with rhyme and with the alphabet also have a lot of scope. Children who come to school with well-developed phonemic and alphabet awareness have often spent time with family reading lots of books—including alphabet books and books with lots of rhyme. When you use lots of rhyming books and alphabet books in your classroom activities, children whose family literacy experiences have been limited can build their alphabet and phonemic awareness skills. The children who bring these skills with them to school learn to read many of the words in these books and may be able to read them independently.

If you have children who lag behind the others in their alphabet knowledge, consider having all your children create their own alphabet books. For each page in the book, brainstorm with your children all the words they know that begin with that letter. Return to all the alphabet books you have read and focus just on the letter you are working on that day. If you have used the letter actions and foods (p. 43) as well as the key words for sounds (p. 44) to teach the letter names and sounds, review these too. Look at the print in the room and find words displayed there. From all these sources, create a list of all the possible words for each letter.

Here is the list one class created for the letter **m**. Each child chose three of the words and drew pictures to go with them for the **m** page of their alphabet book.

march	milk	McDonalds	Michaela	Maria	Monday
month	math	Mrs. C	monkeys	mitten	map
money	moon	mouse	mask	man	mom
mop	music	mouth	macaroni	magnet	mug

When the alphabet books are complete, assess the children again whose letter name, sound, and word skills were not well developed. You will be amazed at the progress they can make when the instruction is personalized by letting them choose the words they want to represent each letter.

Guess the Covered Word is another lesson format with lots of scope. Look back at this section in Chapter 3 (p. 47). What opportunities do you see here for your struggling students to solidify their alphabet awareness skills? Will they be learning strategies for figuring out words, even if they don't yet have the necessary decoding skills? At the same time, will other students be getting additional practice with the sounds of beginning letters? What about your advanced students? What might students who already have well-established alphabet awareness learn from engaging in regular Guess the Covered Word lessons? Can you imagine that they would learn to read most of the words in the sentences and greatly increase the numbers of words they could read?

Look back at the MAKING WORDS kindergarten-style lessons described in Chapter 4. Do you have some children who would be learning letter names and sounds and the concept of rhyme and other children who would be learning the rhyming patterns and be able to read and spell many of the words you included in the lessons?

Summary

Differentiating instruction is essential if all children are going to make progress in their literacy journey. All the activities described in the previous four chapters present opportunities that have a lot of scope. By participating in these lessons, students can learn whatever they are ready to learn—whatever is in their zone of proximal development. When you determine what concepts and skills you want children to learn and then assess their progress toward meeting those goals, you can tailor your instruction during these activities to each child's particular needs. In most cases, children who struggle to learn what others are learning don't need different instruction. They just need you to assess their progress and then personalize the instruction for them.

part two

Fluency

Fluency is the ability to read most words in context quickly, accurately, automatically, and with appropriate expression. Fluency is critical to reading comprehension because of the attention factor. Part Two has three chapters that provide activities for helping children learn to read more fluently.

Chapter 6 defines fluency and suggests classroom-tested ways to develop fluency. Children become fluent readers as they engage in lots of easy reading, have daily opportunities to hear and participate in expressive oral reading, and participate in some repeated reading activities.

Chapter 7 describes activities for teaching high-frequency words. In English, a little over 100 words account for every other word people read and write. Most of these words are abstract, meaningless, connecting words. Many of them have irregular spellings and pronunciations.

Chapter 7 describes ways to build meaning for these words and explains how to use a word wall so that children learn to automatically and rapidly identify these words while reading and spell them while writing.

In Chapter 8 you will find ways to assess fluency that include more than just rate and accuracy. You will also find some ideas for fluency interventions.

chapter 6

Fluency Activities

Sometimes to understand what something is, you have to understand what it is not. To experience what it feels like to read without fluency, read this paragraph **aloud** WITHOUT first reading it to yourself. When you have finished reading it, cover it and summarize what you read.

FLUENCYISTHEABILITYTOREADMOSTWORDSINCONTEXT
QUICKLYANDACCURATELYANDWITHAPPROPRIATEEXPRESSION
FLUENCYISCRITICALTOREADINGCOMPREHENSIONBECAUSEOF
THEATTENTIONFACTOROURBRAINSCANATTENDTOALIMITED
NUMBEROFTHINGSATATIMEIFMOSTOFOURATTENTIONIS
FOCUSEDONDECODINGTHEWORDSTHEREISLITTLEATTENTION
LEFTFORTHECOMPREHENSIONPARTOFREADINGPUTTINGTHE
WORDSTOGETHERANDTHINKINGABOUTWHATTHEYMEAN

If you paused to figure out some of the words and if your phrasing and expression was not very smooth, you have experienced what it feels like when you cannot read something fluently. If your summary lacked some important information, you have experienced the detrimental effects of the lack of fluency on comprehension. If you are developing a headache, you have experienced what a painful task reading can be to readers who lack fluency.

Fluency is the ability to read most words in context quickly and accurately and with appropriate expression. It is critical to reading comprehension because of the attention factor. Our brains can attend to a limited number of things at a time. If most of our attention is focused on decoding the words, there is little attention left for the comprehension part of reading—putting the words together and thinking about what they mean.

The paragraph you just read is exactly the same as the one written in caps with no punctuation and no spaces between words. If, this time, you read it quickly and effortlessly and with good comprehension, you read it the way you normally read everything—fluently.

In order to become avid and enthusiastic readers who get pleasure and information from reading, children must develop fluency. Children who have to labor over everything they read, as you did with the opening paragraph, will only read when forced to read and will never understand how anyone can actually enjoy reading!

Fluency is not something you have or don't have. In fact, how fluent a reader you are is directly related to the complexity of the text you are reading. If you are reading a text on a familiar topic with lots of words you have read accurately many times before, you probably recognize those familiar words immediately and automatically. All your attention is then available to think about the meaning of what you are reading. If you are reading a text on an unfamiliar topic with lots of new words, you will have to stop and decode these words in some way—using your understanding of letter–sound patterns to turn the printed letters into sounds and words. In order to comprehend what you have read, you may have to reread the text once or even twice so that your attention is freed from decoding and available for comprehending.

The National Reading Panel (2000) explains this relationship between reading comprehension and fluency:

> If text is read in a laborious and inefficient manner, it will be difficult for the child to remember what has been read and to relate the ideas expressed in the text to his or her background knowledge. (p. 11)

Fluency is fast, expressive reading. Close your eyes and try to imagine the voices of your good and your struggling readers as they read aloud. The good readers probably sound "normal." They identify almost all the words quickly and accurately and their voices rise and fall and pause at appropriate points.

Some   of   your   struggling   readers   however   read   one word   at   a   time   hes—si—ta—ting   and   and   and re—peat—ing   words.

Every teacher has had the experience of working with students who can read many words but for whom reading is a tortured, labored, word-by-word sometimes syllable-by-syllable, process. Dysfluent reading is slow, labored, and lacking in expression and phrasing. Fluency is the ability to quickly and automatically identify the words. Fluent reading is not saying one word at a time. Fluent reading puts words together in phrases and has the expression you would use if you were speaking the words. All your students can become fluent readers. This chapter will describe activities you can use to make it happen.

Provide Easy Reading for Everyone

Most of the reading you do is not at your reading level. In fact, most of what you read is much too easy for you! If your reading in the past month has included the latest best-selling novel, a travel guide in preparation for your summer break, a journal article on effective teaching strategies, and your favorite section of your local newspaper, you were most likely reading primarily at your independent level. Because these are all things you chose to read and were interested in, you had huge amounts of background knowledge for these topics and you instantly recognized 98 to 99 percent of the words.

The best readers in your classroom—the ones whose instructional reading levels are above the grade level they are placed in—also spend most of their time reading text that is very easy for them. The science and social studies textbooks in their desks are written at the average reading level for your grade, but they are easy for your best readers, who read above grade level. So are the books you assign them for guided reading and take-home readers. The books and magazine articles they choose to read for independent reading time at home and school are also probably very easy for them. Your best readers became fluent readers by reading and rereading lots of easy books. Many of these children have favorite books at home in their own personal libraries and have read these books over and over. Many good readers get "hooked" on a series of books—the *Arthur* books or the *Babysitter Club* books, for example, and they devour these books.

Now think about the materials your struggling readers are reading. They probably have the same grade-level science and social studies books in their desks, and these books are much too hard for them to read. The books you assign them for guided reading and as take-home readers are, you hope, at their level—but that doesn't mean they are easy. The reading level of most children is determined to be the level at which they can read 92 to 95 percent of the words and can comprehend 75 percent of the ideas. Even in material that is determined to be at their instructional reading level, they will encounter a word they don't recognize every two or three sentences. When they encounter these unfamiliar words, they have to stop and use whatever decoding strategies they have to figure out these words, and this stopping to decode interrupts their fluency and interferes with comprehension.

Our best readers are fluent readers who spend a huge proportion of their reading time reading things that are easy for them. Our struggling readers spend a huge proportion of their reading time struggling through text that is much too hard and a little bit of time working to read material that is at their level. When reading both the too-hard text and the on-their-level text, they have to work hard to read and their reading is not fluent. The first commitment you have to make to help all your students become fluent readers is to make sure that they all are spending some of their time reading easy text—text in which they are interested (and thus for which they have background knowledge) and text in which they can recognize 98 to 99 percent of the words.

At this point, you may be thinking, "Easier said than done! I struggle to find appropriate materials at the instructional levels of my struggling readers. Where will I find easy books? And if I find easy books, won't my students be insulted if I offer them these 'baby' books?"

Finding easy materials for your struggling readers and getting them to read them is actually easier than you think. Recently, many publishers have published sets of small informational books. These books have very little text on the page, and the text is accompanied by engaging pictures—often photos. Because these books are informational and on high-interest topics—trucks, turtles, magnets, football, and much more—your students won't perceive them as "baby" books. If you include them in your read-aloud (they only take two minutes to read!), and you marvel at all the interesting facts in the book, your

Easy Informational Books

Once you start looking, you will be amazed at how many you can find. These are a few of my favorite sets. Hopefully, many more will be available by the time this book is printed.

- National Geographic publishes hundreds of small informational books as part of its Windows on Literacy series. Some of the titles in their Social Studies sets include: *The Park*, *What's on the Ships?*, *What Did They Drive?*, and *The Earth*. Science titles include: *When a Storm Comes*, *Spiders Spin Silk*, and *Fossils*. All of these books feature limited amounts of text brought to life through incredibly engaging photos.

- Scholastic publishes a Rookie Read-About Science series that also has small amounts of text and engaging photos. Titles include: *What Is Friction?*, *All about Light*, and *What Magnets Can Do*.

- HarperCollins has a Let's Read and Find Out about Science series. Captivating illustrations bring the text to life in titles including: *Energy Makes Things Happen*, *Switch On, Switch Off*, and *What's It Like to Be a Fish?*

students won't be embarrassed to be seen reading and enjoying the books you obviously enjoy.

Depending on the age of your children, a magazine subscription to *Zoobooks*, *Your Big Backyard* or another magazine easy enough for your struggling readers may provide the needed easy reading resources. It is not essential that your children be able to read every word or every article in these magazines. Just as adults do, children tend to pick and choose from magazine articles and read the ones they are most interested in. Those high-interest articles will be easier to read because they are usually on topics with which your struggling readers have a lot of background knowledge and vocabulary.

tech tips

Are you excited about providing all your students with easy reading materials but short on funds? Go to Donors Choose and enter your request there. Donors Choose is a clever but simple idea. Many people are concerned about schools that lack the resources to provide their students with the extras that PTOs in wealthier communities can often provide. Teachers can write short grant proposals explaining what they need and why and how much the items will cost. Donors can log on and use their credit cards to fund worthy projects. As of today, 74,784 projects have been funded. (Donors Choose is now available in all 50 states.)

Independent reading is a critical daily component of a balanced reading program in any classroom. A significant amount of time every day in every classroom should be devoted to children choosing for themselves something to read and then settling down to read it. Independent reading is often promoted in terms of the motivation and interest children develop when they have time to pursue their own personal interests through books. In addition, reading easy materials during independent reading promotes fluency.

Model Fluent, Expressive Reading

In addition to making sure everyone in your classroom has some easy reading in their reading diets, you can promote fluency by providing opportunities for all your students to hear and participate in fluent reading. Include teacher read-aloud, echo reading, and choral reading in your weekly plans, and your students will all know what fluent, expressive reading sounds like and feels like.

✳ Teacher Read-Aloud

Regardless of what grade level you teach, make time in your busy schedule to read aloud to your students each day. Reading to students is your best opportunity to demonstrate for them that reading is an activity you enjoy and that books and magazines are a reliable source of entertainment and information. Reading to students is the best way to motivate them to read. Most children report that their favorite books and magazines are those someone initially read aloud to them.

Your read-aloud time is also your opportunity to "ham it up!" Give different voices to the characters as you read their words. Read scary parts in a "frightened" voice. Read about lost pets and forgotten homework in a "worried" voice. Read interesting facts in a "that's amazing" voice. Most of your best readers will have experienced hundreds of hours of being read to by a caring adult before ever entering school. They know that when you read, your reading needs to sound like you are talking. When reading aloud or to themselves, they try to produce the phrasing and intonation of talking—to make it sound like speech! Seize the opportunity every day when you read aloud to your students to model for them what expressive, fluent reading sounds like.

✳ Echo Reading

One teacher had been doing echo reading for months when a child suddenly asked, "What's an echo?" The teacher invited class members to explain what an echo is and discovered that many children hadn't heard an echo. After some "field research," the teacher located a spot in the auditorium where sound would echo, and the class all got to hear their voices echoing back to them. Echo reading made a lot more sense to them after that and they tried to "be the echo." It is easy to

Multilevel Plays

Rigby publishes a set of *Tales and Plays* that are particularly useful because in the same book the story is told in a traditional tale format and then as a play. These tales and plays are written on many different reading levels and include favorites such as *Town Mouse and Country Mouse* and *Robin Hood and the Silver Trophy*. Another set of plays perfect for echo reading is the *Speak Out! Reader's Theatre* series published by Pacific Learning. In the Speak Out plays, different parts of the plays are written on different reading levels. Benchmark Education also publishes plays with multileveled scripts. Their plays include fables, legends, myths, and a wide variety of science and social studies topics. Using these scripts, you can group together children who read on a variety of reading levels and assign children parts that match their levels.

forget that our students don't know everything we know. If your children haven't heard an echo, you might try to find a place to take them where they can have firsthand experience with echoes.

Echo reading is the perfect venue for modeling expressive oral reading because in echo reading, your voice is the first voice and your students are trying to make their voice sound just like your voice. Echo reading is usually done one sentence at a time and is fun to do when the text has different voices. If you teach young children, consider using some of your children's favorite big books for echo reading. Children enjoy doing the different voices in *Brown Bear, Brown Bear, I Went Walking,* and *Hattie and the Fox.* Echo reading also works well for stories such as *There's an Alligator under My Bed,* in which one boy is telling the story. Stories told in the first-person format are called "I" stories. When you echo read "I" stories, try to sound the way the different voices would sound. Some favorite "I" stories include *One of Three* by Angela Johnson, *Enzo the Wonderfish* by Cathy Wilcox, and *My Friend* by Taro Gomi.

Elementary children of all ages enjoy plays, and echo reading is the perfect format for reading plays. There are many books of reproducible plays available, and several sets of leveled readers include plays.

In addition to plays you find, you can easily turn some of your children's favorite stories into plays using a Reader's Theatre format. The trick to turning a story into a play is to choose a story with lots of dialogue and to include a narrator who describes what you can't describe with dialogue. Imagine that your students have read *The Little Red Hen*—or you have read it aloud to them. Here is the beginning of a Reader's Theatre you could easily create:

Narrator: The Little Red Hen was walking in the barnyard. Her friends, the cat, the pig, and the duck, were playing. The Little Red Hen found a grain of wheat.

Hen: Who will help me plant this wheat?

Cat: Not I!

Dog: Not I!

Pig: Not I!

Narrator: So the Little Red Hen planted the wheat herself. The wheat grew and grew.

Hen: Who will help me cut this wheat?

Cat: Not I!

Dog: Not I!

Pig: Not I!

As you can see, you don't need any particular talents to turn a favorite story with lots of dialogue into a Reader's Theatre play. If you teach older students, you can have them take a story and turn it into a play. Let different groups create different plays. Make copies for everyone and use the echo reading format to model fluent, expressive reading of all the plays. Have students take the plays home and corral their family members into reading the plays at home. This is one take-home reading assignment the whole family will willingly participate in.

❋ Choral Reading

Another format you can use to model expressive oral reading is choral reading. When you do choral reading of plays, assign groups of students to the different roles. If you are doing a choral reading of *The Little Red Hen*, for example, divide your students into five groups and let different groups chorally read the parts of the narrator, hen, cat, duck, and pig. Reassign the parts and read it several times so that all your students get to read all the parts. Make sure that you assign your struggling readers to the easier parts first. For much of *The Little Red Hen*, the cat, duck, and pig roles only require the students to read, "Not I!" After a couple of readings, your struggling readers may be able to fluently read the hen's part. If your struggling readers are very dysfluent readers, you may not want to assign them the narrator's part, which always requires the most sophisticated reading skills.

In addition to choral reading of plays and Reader's Theatres, consider leading your students in reading some poetry you have arranged in a choral reading format. Nursery rhymes and other rhymes and finger-plays are naturals for choral reading. Begin by reading the rhyme to your children using the echo reading format. After the echo reading, assign different groups of voices to read different parts. Keep the choreography simple by having the children count off to read different parts or assigning girls and boys to read different parts. Here is an example for the beginning of *Five Little Monkeys*:

All: Five little monkeys jumping on the bed.

Voice 1:   One fell off and bumped his head.

> ***All:***   Momma called the doctor and the doctor said
>
> ***Voice 2:***   "No more monkeys jumping on the bed!"

For English Language Learners

Modeling fluent reading through echo and choral reading offers an excellent opportunity for your students learning English to practice their reading skills in a comfortable, supportive environment. Using poems and plays with repeated patterns will help them develop their understanding of English syntax and add some common phrases to their speaking vocabularies.

After reading the rhyme the first time, reassign the students so that those who were voice 1 now read the part of voice 2.

Many of these poems lend themselves to pantomiming. Divide your class into actors and readers. For actors, you will need five monkeys, the doctor, and the momma. Have all the readers read the first line chorally—"Five little monkeys jumping on the bed." Then stop the readers so the five monkeys can pantomime jumping on the bed. Continue leading your readers to read and stopping them so the actors can act. Read the poem several time so that all your students get to be actors as well as readers.

Rereading Develops Fluency

One of the major ways that people become fluent readers is by reading something over several times. At first, a lot of attention is on identifying the words. On the second reading, people are able to read in phrases as their brains put the phrases together into meaningful units. The third time, people read more rapidly with good expression and in a seemingly effortless way.

Rereading is important for fluency, and if you reread the previous sections of this chapter, you will find that getting your students to reread text plays a role in many of the activities. When you model expressive reading through echo and choral reading, you lead the students through several readings of the plays and poems. Having your students take copies of the plays and poems home and engage their families in echo and choral reading provides more opportunities for rereading.

There are various ways to include repeated readings as part of your classroom routines. This section will describe four ways many teachers have found to work well with children across the elementary grades: recorded reading, radio reading, timed repeated reading, and paired repeated reading.

❋ Recorded Reading

Children—and many adults—enjoy listening to recorded books. Many of these books are recorded by authors or professional readers, and they are marvelous models of fluent expressive reading. Have your readers who need to work on fluency select a book on their reading level and then let them listen to that book as many times as they need to until they can read the book fluently. When your students are able to read the book fluently without the aid of the recording, let them show off their fluency skills by reading the book to whomever you can find to listen. Send them to a class of younger-aged students and let them read the book to a small group in that class. Let them take the book home and challenge them to see how many signatures they can collect on an "I can read this book" card. Young children like to read to their pets and stuffed animals. Grandparents would love to hear their precious grandchild reading the book over the phone.

Consider recording some of the books and magazine articles as you are reading them aloud to your students. Have your students participate by clapping as a turn-page signal. Likewise, you may want to record some of the echo and choral reading you do with your students. If you record just a few pieces you are reading to your students, you will soon have a large recorded library customized to the interests of your students. Children often want to read the book the teacher has read to them. Recording some of what you read to your students makes this possible for more of your students.

❋ Radio Reading

Radio reading (Rasinski, 2010) is a way of doing repeated reading that many teachers use as an alternative to round-robin reading or as part of literature circles. To do radio reading, you need to form groups of four to six students who read at approximately the same level. The group reads the selection together for the first reading or has someone read the selection to them so that they get a general sense of what is happening. Next, you assign portions of the text to each child in the group. Assign longer, more complex portions to the best readers in the group and shorter, less complex portions to children whose reading skills are not as strong.

Children practice reading their portion aloud until they can read it perfectly and with expression. You may want to assign partners within each group to practice reading their portions and help each other. You may also want to have each child take their portion home and practice reading it to an adult or older sibling.

In addition to practicing reading the portion, each child makes up two questions. One question should be a literal "right there" question:

"Where did the three bears find Goldilocks?"

The second question should be an inferential "think and search" question:

"How did Goldilocks feel when she woke up and saw the three bears?"

On the next day, the group reassembles and each child reads his or her portion as if it were being read on the radio. Many teachers use a microphone or headset as a prop so that students feel like real radio announcers. After all students have read their portions aloud, they ask their literal and inferential questions. The answers to these questions—particularly to the inferential questions, which do not have one right answer—lead to a lively discussion of the text.

The first time you do radio reading with a group of children, you may need to let them listen to a radio announcer or model for them how radio announcers read. It is important for children to understand that reading accurately with good expression is a big part of radio announcers' jobs, and they have to practice what they read before going on air to make sure they can read it well. Radio reading gives repeated reading a "real-world" purpose and children a different and engaging way to read text. You may also find it a welcome addition to your classroom reading routines. If you have three or four reading groups, they can all engage in radio reading at the same time, reading text at their level and focusing on fluency and comprehension.

❋ Timed Repeated Reading

For timed repeated reading, you need a passage of interest to the student that is at the student's instructional level. The passage should be short, no more than 150 words. Give the student the passage and tell him or her to read it silently and to get ready to read it orally with few errors and at a comfortable rate. After silent reading, have the student read the passage to you, count the oral reading errors (the three most frequently occurring errors are words left out, words changed, and words added in), and time the reading. If the student makes more than five errors per 100 words, the passage is too difficult to use, and an easier one should be chosen. If no more than five errors per 100 words are made by the student, tell the reader the time it took and help her or him correct any errors. Then have the student practice reading the material again. Repeat this process until the student has read the passage three or four times. While some students are practicing, another can be reading to you, which makes it possible to use repeated readings with a small group of readers.

❋ Paired Repeated Reading

Paired repeated reading is just like repeated reading but without timing. In other words, the student reads and rereads a passage to make fewer errors, not to increase rate. Students of similar reading ability can be paired for repeated reading. They like listening to each other read to count errors. Teachers should make sure, however, that students do not interrupt each other during reading but wait until the selection is finished before helping the reader make corrections.

Summary

Fluency includes three components: accuracy, speed, and expression. Developing fluency needs to be one of the major goals of reading instruction. When children are first starting to read, their reading is not apt to be fluent. They must stop at almost all the words and take a second or two to recognize the word or figure it out. As their word identification skills develop and their reading vocabularies increase, their reading becomes more fluent.

Allington (2009) suggests three reasons some students struggle to become fluent readers. First, much of what struggling readers are given to read is much too difficult. Second, struggling readers read much less than more capable readers. Finally, teachers often ask struggling readers to read aloud and then immediately interrupt that reading to correct reading errors. These struggling readers come to rely on the teacher to correct their errors and don't develop self-monitoring strategies.

Fluency develops when children do lots of reading—including a great deal of easy text. In addition to making sure that all students are reading some text that is easy for them, teachers can model fluent, expressive reading in their teacher read-aloud and by including echo and choral reading lesson formats.

Repeated reading helps children develop fluency because with each reading, their word identification becomes quicker and more automatic, freeing attention for expression, phrasing, and comprehension. Letting children choose books they want to read and practice reading those books along with a recording help build both fluency and confidence. Other engaging formats for repeated reading include radio reading and paired repeated reading.

In English, people are exposed to words such as **of, said, the, have, they,** and many others daily. These words are called high-frequency words because they are seen and heard in everything we read and write. In order to read fluently, children need to instantly recognize these high-frequency words. Building this automatic and rapid recognition of high-frequency words is the topic of the next chapter.

chapter 7

High-Frequency Words

One hundred words account for almost half of all the words we read and write (Fry, Fountoukidis, & Polk, 1985). Ten words—**the**, **of**, **and**, **a**, **to**, **in**, **is**, **you**, **that**, and **it**—account for almost one-quarter of all the words we read and write. As soon as possible, children should learn to read and spell these high-frequency words.

When children at an early age learn to recognize and automatically spell the most frequently occurring words, all their attention is freed for decoding and spelling less frequent words and, more importantly, for processing meaning. Stopping to figure out a new word while reading, or stopping to say the word slowly and figure out how you might spell it while writing, requires time and mental energy. In fact, stopping to think about a new word takes attention away from meaning. Short-term memory is the place that holds words or other bits of information. The short-term memory span for most people is about seven words. When we read, we hold the words in short-term memory until we have enough words to make meaning from them. Meaning can then go into long-term memory. This frees up all our short-term memory space for more words, and the process continues. So it goes, until we need our short-term memory space for something else—like figuring out the pronunciation of a new word. Writing works the same way. We spell most words automatically, and when we have to stop to figure out the spelling of a word, our attention moves from what we are writing to how to spell a particular word.

Decoding or figuring out the spelling of a new word takes all our short-term memory space. In fact, when this decoding process begins, all words already read or written and stored in short-term memory are dumped out (into the garbage disposal, I think). This dumping explains why, once the new word is decoded or spelled, we must quickly reread any prior words in that sentence so that we can put them in short-term memory again. It also explains why children who have to decode many words often don't know what they have read after they read it! Their short-term memory space keeps getting preempted for decoding tasks, and they can't reread every sentence over and over. So they never get enough words in short-term memory from which to make meaning to put in long-term memory. All their attention is required for figuring out words, and there is no capacity for putting together meaning. In order to read and write fluently with comprehension and meaning, children must be able to automatically read and spell the most frequent words. As the store of words they can automatically read and spell increases, so will their speed and comprehension.

The second reason you want your students to automatically recognize and spell high-frequency words is that many of the most frequent words are not pronounced or spelled in logical ways: If **the** were pronounced like other words with the same spelling pattern, it would rhyme with **he**, **me**, and **be**; **to** would rhyme with **go**, **no**, and **so**; **said** would rhyme with **maid** and **paid**; and **have** would rhyme with **cave** and **wave**. If **they**, **was**, and **come** were spelled logically, they would be spelled the way many children spell them—**t-h-a-y**, **w-u-z**, and **c-u-m**.

The apparent lack of logic in how the most frequent words are spelled and pronounced has a logical—and historical—explanation. The way we pronounce words changes over time. The words used most often are, of course, the words whose pronunciation has changed the most. In most cases, pronunciation shifts to an easier pronunciation. It is quicker and easier to get your tongue in position to say "the" in the usual way than it is to make it rhyme with **he**, **me**, and **we**. "Said" takes longer to say if you make it rhyme with **paid** and **maid**. Children should learn to read and spell the most frequently occurring words because these are the words they will read and write over and over. Many of them cannot be decoded, and if you spell them logically, you will often be wrong.

The problem is that many struggling readers have a great deal of difficulty learning these words. They often know them today and forget them tomorrow. This chapter will focus on strategies that have been successful in teaching everyone—even the children who need multiple practices—to read and spell the most frequent words.

Building Meaning for High-Frequency Words

The first problem many children have with the high-frequency words is that most of these words have no meaning. Unlike **dinosaur**, **apples**, and **happy**, words like **are**, **is**, and **have** are functional, connecting, abstract words children cannot connect any meaning to. How do you explain, demonstrate, or otherwise make sense of words like **of**, **for**, and **from**? In addition, what meaning they do have changes from minute to minute. **There** is the opposite of **here**, but if you move across the room, there becomes here! **This** becomes **that** and **these** become **those**.

In addition to the problems these words create by having no concrete consistent meaning, many of the frequently occurring words share the same letters. Besides the often confused **of**, **for**, and **from** and the reversible words **on/no** and **was/saw**, beginners are always confusing the **th** and the **w** words:

the	there	their	this	that
they	them	then	these	those
what	want	went	when	who
why	were	where	will	with

To many children, remembering these words is like trying to remember the pronunciation of words in a foreign language when you don't know what they mean and they don't follow any standard spelling system. No wonder children know some words today and forget them tomorrow.

What kind of activities can you provide to ensure that all your students will learn to read and write these critical words? The most important factor to consider in teaching the highly frequent words seems to be the meaning—or, more specifically, the lack of meaning—factor.

In Chapter 4, we discussed learning letter names and how children who knew some concrete words that contained the letters remembered the letters better because they had associated the letters with the already known words. Associative learning is always more permanent than rote learning. Since these frequent words have no meaning in and of themselves, we must help the children associate them with something meaningful. To introduce the word **of**, for example, we might have pictures of a piece of pie, a can of Coke, and a box of cookies. These pictures would be labeled **a piece of pie**, **a bowl of soup**, and **a box of cookies** with the word **of** underlined. Next, the children would think of other things they like to eat and drink with the word **of**, such as a glass of milk, a piece of toast, and a stick of gum. The labeled pictures would then be displayed to help students associate meaning with this abstract word.

After an abstract word is associated with meaning, there must be practice with that word. This practice can take many forms, but it should not consist solely of looking at the word and saying it. Not all children are good visual learners. Many children need to do something in order to learn something. Chanting

figure 7.1 **Picture Posters to Build Meaning for the Word** *of*

a piece o̲f cake   a box o̲f cookies   a bowl o̲f soup

figure 7.2   **Picture Posters to Build Meaning for the Words** *of* **and** *for*

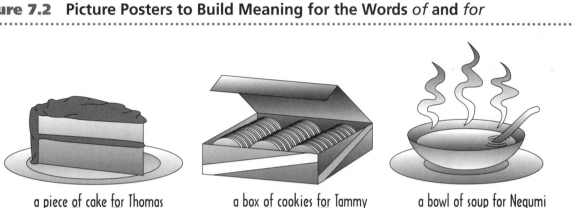

a piece <u>of</u> cake <u>for</u> Thomas   a box <u>of</u> cookies <u>for</u> Tammy   a bowl <u>of</u> soup <u>for</u> Negumi

the spelling of words and writing the words provide children with auditory and kinesthetic routes to learning and remembering abstract words.

Once the children can associate meaning with a word such as **of** and have practiced **of** enough times to be able to read it and spell it, it is time to introduce one of the words with which **of** is often confused, such as **for**. You might simply extend the picture posters already made for **of** by attaching another piece of paper to each and writing the word **for** and the name of one of the children in your class.

Have children name foods and tell who they are for; then provide chanting and writing practice with both the words **for** and **of**.

When **of** and **for** are firmly associated and can be read and written, then teach **from**. For each difficult word, think of some picture or sentence association your children would understand. Perhaps you have some children who came to your school from other states or countries. You could make some sentence posters with sentences such as:

Billy is **from** California.

José is **from** Mexico.

The children can then associate meaning with the word **from** because they know where these two classmates come from. Then provide practice with **of**, **for**, and **from**.

How much meaning you have to build for words and how much practice will be required to learn them varies with the different words and for different children. In general, the more abstract a word is and the more similar-looking abstract words there are, the more association and practice will be required to learn them. The following are the three principles for teaching abstract, function words:

1. Provide a way for students to associate meaning with the words.

2. Once meaning is associated, provide practice using a variety of learning modes.

3. If a common word has many easily confused words, teach one first. As soon as that one is learned, teach another and practice both. Then teach a third and practice all three.

Building Meaning Picture Card Kit

Really Good Stuff has a kit of pictures for 40 common abstract words. The pictures feature children of various ethnic groups, and each word is shown with a sentence and a picture that help students connect meanings to these abstract words.

Photos © 2011 Really Good Stuff®

For English Language Learners

Abstract, connecting words are the hardest words to learn in any new language. Imagine how much more quickly your English language learners absorb the concrete words—**table, big, run, milk, pizza**—that represent things they can see, do, touch, and eat. Unfortunately, the high-frequency words in any language are abstract, connecting words. Posters such as those described for **of, for,** and **from** are extremely important for your English language learners. Look at the high-utility list of words on page 94–95 and think about posters you could create for other abstract, confusing words.

Doing a Word Wall

Children need to associate meaning with the abstract connecting words, and they need to have them displayed in some readily accessible place so that they can find them when they need them while reading and writing. Many teachers display these words on the wall or on a bulletin board. They "have" a word wall. For struggling readers, having a word wall is not sufficient. You have to "do" the word wall.

Doing the word wall is not the same thing as having a word wall. Having a word wall might mean putting all these words up somewhere in the room and telling students to use them. Most struggling readers can't use them because they don't know them and don't know which is which! Doing a word wall means:

1. Being selective and limiting the words to those really common words that children need a lot in writing.

2. Adding words gradually—five or six a week.

3. Making words accessible by putting them where everyone can see them, writing them in big black letters, and using a variety of colors so that the constantly confused words (**for, from, that, them, they, this,** etc.) have different colors.

4. Practicing the words by chanting and writing them, because struggling readers are not usually good visual learners and can't just look at and remember words.

5. Doing a variety of review activities to provide enough practice so that the words are read and spelled instantly and automatically.

6. Making sure that word-wall words are spelled correctly in any writing students do.

Teachers who "do" word walls (rather than just have word walls) report that **all** their children can learn these critical words.

❋ Selecting Words for the Wall

The selection of the words varies from classroom to classroom, but the selection principle is the same. Include words students will need often in their reading and writing and that are often confused with other words.

High-Utility Wall Words

Teachers make their own decisions about which words to add to their word walls by observing which words children use frequently in their writing. This list is intended to be an example of the kinds of words that might be included if the word wall is to have the highest utility for the children. This list has high utility in multiple ways:

- It includes the most frequent words—those that make up half of all the words children read and write.

- There is an example word for each initial consonant: **b, c, d, f, g, h, j, k, l, m, n, p, r, s, t, v, w, y, z** (including both common sounds for **c** and **g**).

- There is an example for the most common blends: **bl, br, cl, cr, dr, fl, fr, gr, pl, pr, sk, sl, sm, sn, sp, st, str,** and **tr;** the common digraphs **ch, sh, th, wh;** and the two-letter combinations **ph, wr, kn, qu.**

- There is an example for the most common vowel spelling patterns:

at	make	rain	day	car	saw	caught
went	eat	see	her	new		
in	like	night	girl	thing		
not	those	coat	go	for	how	slow	out	boy	look	school
us	use	hurt				
my	very					

- There is an example for the highest-utility phonograms (Wylie & Durrell, 1970):

ack	ail	ain	ake	ale	ame	an	ank	ap	ash
at	ate	aw	ay	eat	ell	est	ice	ick	ide
ight	ill	in	ine	ing	ink	ip	it	ock	oke
op	ore	ot	uck	ug	ump	unk			

- It includes the most common contractions: **can't, didn't, don't, it's, won't,** and the most common homophones: **to, too, two; their, they're, there; right, write; no, know; one, won.**

- It includes words such as **favorite, teacher, school, family,** and **sister,** which young children use frequently in their writing.

Ideally, a classroom word wall would increase by five words per week and have about 100 to 120 words by the end of the year. This list contains 180 words, which is too many for any one word wall. In some schools, first-grade teachers pick the most frequent words for their walls. Second-grade teachers begin the year by gradually putting up some of the first-grade words that are particularly hard to spell—**they, were, because,** and so forth—and then add others.

about	don't	it	phone	they're
after	down	it's	play	thing
all	drink	joke	presents	this
am	each	jump	pretty	those
an	eat	junk	question	time
and	family	kick	rain	to
animal	father	know	ride	too
are	favorite	like	right	trip
as	first	line	run	truck
at	fly	little	said	two
be	for	long	sale	up
because	friend	look	saw	us
been	from	made	school	use
best	fun	mail	see	very
big	get	make	she	want
black	girl	many	sister	was
boy	give	me	slow	way
brother	go	more	skate	we
bug	good	mother	small	went
but	green	my	snap	were
by	gym	name	so	what
ball	had	new	some	when
can	has	nice	sports	where
can't	have	night	stop	which
car	he	no	street	who
caught	her	not	talk	why
children	here	now	teacher	will
city	him	of	tell	with
clock	his	off	than	won
coat	house	old	thank	won't
come	how	on	that	would
could	hurt	one	the	write
crash	I	or	their	you
day	if	other	them	your
did	in	out	then	zoo
didn't	into	over	there	
do	is	people	they	

First-grade teachers who are using a reading series usually select some highly frequent words taught in those books. Other teachers select their words from a high-frequency word list. In addition to high-frequency words, first-grade teachers often begin their word walls with the names of their children and add an example word for each letter in the alphabet—even if there is no high-frequency word for that letter.

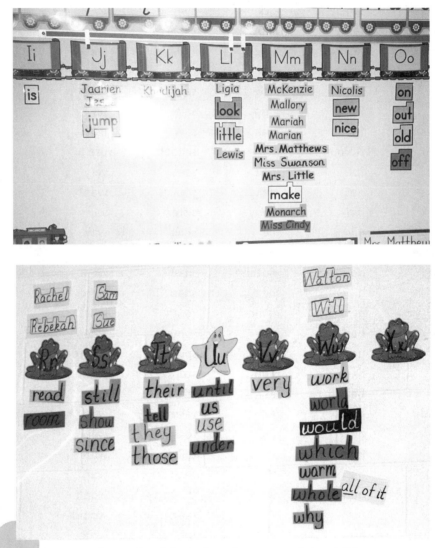

A primary grade word wall including the names of the children.

Beyond first grade, look for words commonly misspelled in your students' writing and add these words to the wall. Children frequently misspell homophones, and these can be added with a picture or phrase clue attached to all but one of the words. For example, we add a card with the number **2** next to **two** and attach the word **also** and the phrase **too late** next to **too**. Children learn to think about whether they are writing the number **two**, the "too late **too**," or "the

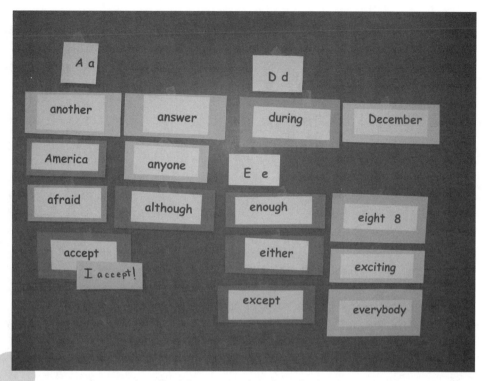

An upper grades word wall with commonly misspelled words including homophones and clues to their meaning.

other one." Once common, confusing, irregular words are on the wall, you may want to add words with a particular pattern—beginning letters, rhyming pattern, vowel pattern, ending—to provide an example for that pattern.

❋ Displaying the Words

Write the words with a thick, black-ink, permanent marker on pieces of different colored paper. Alternatively, use a large bold font to create the words and print them out. Use a variety of colors of paper to back the words. Place the words on the wall next to the letter they begin with. When easily confused words are added, make sure they are on a different color paper from the other words they are usually confused with. Cutting around the configuration is another helpful cue to those easily confused words. Children who are looking for **where** tend to distinguish it from **were** by its "**h** sticking up." Most teachers add five new words each week and do at least one daily activity in which the children find, chant, and write the words.

❋ Chanting and Writing the Words

To begin the word-wall practice, students number a sheet of paper from 1 to 5. Call out five words from the wall and give a quick sentence for each to ensure your students access meaning. Appoint a "pointer helper" whose job it is to point

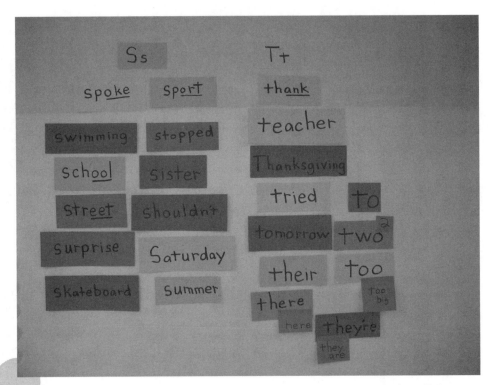

This teacher includes commonly misspelled words and an example for all the common beginning sounds. Common rhyming patterns are underlined.

to each word on the wall to focus everyone's attention on the right word. Lead your students to clap and chant the spelling of the word in a rhythmic "cheering" fashion three times.

"street s-t-r-e-e-t; s-t-r-e-e-t; s-t-r-e-e-t street

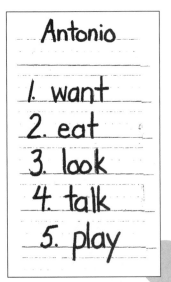

After chanting the word, have students write the word. Many teachers tie this daily writing of word-wall words into handwriting instruction and model for the children how to make each letter as the children write the words. When all five words have been cheered for and written, lead the students to check or fix their own papers. On the day new words are added, the new words are the words called out, cheered, and written. These new words are often reviewed on the second day. During the rest of the week, however, any five words from the wall can be called out. Words with which children need much practice are called out almost every day.

Word-Wall Words Written.

"On-the-Back" Activities

Most teachers allot 10 minutes each day for the daily word-wall practice. Early in the year, it takes the whole 10 minutes to call out, chant, write, and check five words. As the year goes on, children become much faster at chanting, writing, and checking the words and can do five words in five to six minutes. At this point, you can add an "on-the-back" activity (called this because you have the children turn over their word-wall paper and do this activity on the back). The on-the-back activity is designed to provide additional practice with word-wall words and to help children learn that some of the words on the wall can help them spell lots of other words. Several of the most popular and productive on-the-back activities are described next.

✳ Easy Rhyming Activity

Half the high-frequency words do not follow the logical patterns—but half do. Many teachers put a star or sticker on word-wall words that children can use to help them spell lots of rhyming words or underline the rhyming pattern. This activity helps children learn how to use the starred or underlined words to spell lots of other words. To begin this activity, you might tell the children:

> "All of the words we have on our word wall are important words because we see them over and over again in the books we read and they help us write. But some words are important in another way. Some of the words on our wall will help us spell lots of other words that rhyme with them. **It** is one of those helpful words. Today, we are going to practice using **it** to spell five other words we use a lot in our writing. Turn your paper over and number from 1 to 5. The first word **it** will help you spell is **bit**. You might be writing about how your brother **bitten** by a dog. Let's say **bit** slowly and listen for the first sound. Yes, **bit** begins with the letter **b**. Everyone write **b**. Now, words that rhyme usually have the same spelling pattern. The spelling pattern in a short word begins with the vowel and continues until the end of the word. Because **it** begins with a vowel, **i**, the whole word **it** is also the spelling pattern. Write **i-t** after **b** and you can spell **bit**."

The on-the-back lesson continues as the teacher gives the children possible scenarios in which they would need to use **it** to help them spell a rhyming word:

> "What if you were writing about the baseball game and wanted to say you got a **hit**? Say **hit** slowly. Write the first letter, **h**, and then finish the rhyming word with the spelling pattern **i-t**."

"You might be writing about how you taught your dog to **sit**. Everyone write **s-i-t**."

"You might write about going to the mall to buy a new winter jacket because last year's jacket wouldn't **fit**."

"The last rhyming word is one that begins with two letters. What if you're writing about your cat and want to tell that when she is really mad, she will **spit** at something? Say **spit** slowly with me, stretching it out and listening for two sounds at the beginning. Good, you hear an **s** and a **p**. Now finish your word with the **i-t** pattern."

For the on-the-back rhyming activity, have children write five words that rhyme with one of the word-wall words. Put it in a "What if you are writing and need to spell" context because knowing how rhyming words help you spell other words is useful only if you do it when you are writing and trying to spell a word. Use several examples, trying to choose words the children might actually need to write. Include some words with single beginning letters and others where you have to listen for two letters. Model how you "stretch out the word," listening for the beginning sounds, and then finish the word with the spelling pattern—the vowel and what follows.

If you have the word **eat** on your word wall, you might have students spell rhyming words by having them pretend they are writing sentences such as:

I hope Wake will **beat** Carolina this Saturday.

We had a storm, and the **heat** was off at my house.

We had company, and I had to get my room clean and **neat**.

I was good at school, so my Dad took me to the mall for a **treat**.

Some kids will try to **cheat** to win the game.

play
say
day
tray
clay
spray

On-the-Back Rhyming Words for *ay* Pattern.

When you do these rhyming activities, be sure to give the children the rhyming word rather than ask them to tell you rhyming words. Some rhymes have more than one pattern, and by controlling which words you have them spell, you can avoid using words such as **feet** and **Pete**, which have another pattern. They will eventually have to learn to use their visual checking system to determine the correct pattern, but the first step is to get them spelling by pattern rather than putting down one letter for each sound. Here are a few more examples for rhyming words your students can spell based on word-wall words.

At will help you spell **cat, bat, hat, brat,** and **flat**.

Look will help you spell **cook, book, hook, brook,** and **crook**.

Went will help you spell **bent, dent, tent, sent,** and **spent**.

Not will help you spell **hot, got, lot, spot,** and **trot**.

Ram will help you spell **ham, Sam, Pam, clam,** and **Spam**.

Land will help you spell **hand, sand, band, stand,** and **brand**.

Can will help you spell **Dan, man, ran, tan,** and **plan**.

Will will help you spell **Bill, fill, pill, still,** and **spill**.

Make will help you spell **bake, cake, rake, lake,** and **shake**.

❉ Harder Rhyming Activity

There is another rhyming "on-the-back" lesson format that is harder but closer to what your students actually have to do to use the word-wall words to spell a word they need while writing. To do this rhyming format, make sure that all the words you call out for them to write on the front of the paper have some words that rhyme and share the same spelling pattern. You might call out the words **make, thing, like, went,** and **will**. Help your students to notice that all these words are helpful words (starred or underlined words). Tell them that you are going to pretend to be writing and need to spell a word that rhymes with one of these five words. Say some sentences you might be writing, emphasizing the word you need to spell, and let them decide which of the five helpful words they wrote on the front will help you. Have them write each rhyming word once everyone has agreed on its spelling.

We like to cook chicken on the **grill**. (**will**)

I was so scared I started to **shake** all over. (**make**)

My brother **spent** his whole allowance on baseball cards. (**went**)

We are going to **sing** at my church on Sunday morning. (**thing**)

I want a new **bike** for my birthday. (**like**)

Once you have begun to use this new rhyming format, alternate it with the easier one in which your sentences use rhymes for only one of the words. The harder one helps children who are ready to learn how thinking of a rhyming word can help them spell lots of words. The easier format is still important for children who are still developing their sense of rhyme and how rhyme helps us spell.

❉ Easy Ending Activity

Another on-the-back activity helps children learn how to spell word-wall words that need an ending. Imagine that the five word-wall words you called out for them to locate, cheer for, and write were:

girl   boy   friend   brother   sister

Have them turn their papers over and write the words **boys**, **sisters**, **brothers**, **friends**, and **girls**.

On another day, call out five words that can have **ed** endings, such as **want**, **look**, **jump**, **kick**, and **play**. Then have them write these words with the **ed** ending on the back. On another day, do a similar activity with words to which **ing** can be added.

For the easy endings activities, limit the ending to just one, and don't include words that need spelling changes. Once students get good at adding **s**, **ed**, and **ing**, do some more complex on-the-back activities with endings.

✳ Harder Ending Activity

Make your on-the-back activity with endings more complex by including different words and endings. Imagine that your students have written these five words on the front of their paper:

> want   eat   look   talk   play

Have them turn their papers over. Then say something like:

> "Today we are going to work on how to spell these word-wall words when they need a different ending. I will say some sentences that some of you might write, and you listen for the word-wall word that has had an ending added:
>
> My friends and I love **eating** at McDonald's.
>
> We were **looking** for some new shoes.
>
> I was **talking** on the phone to my Grandma.
>
> My mom **wants** the new baby to be a girl.
>
> My friend spent the night and we **played** games until 11:00."

After each sentence, have your students identify the word-wall word and the ending, decide how to spell it, and write it on their papers.

Once your students can spell words by adding **s**, **ed**, and **ing**, include some endings with spelling changes—the **e** dropped, a **y** changed to **i**, or a letter doubled. Since you and your students decide ahead of time what to write, everyone should be spelling them correctly.

When students have learned to spell word-wall words with the most common endings, include some words in which **y**, **ly**, **er**, and **est** are added. Show them how they can spell **jumpy**, **rainy**, and **funny** by adding **y** to **jump**, **rain**, and **fun**, and how to spell **nicely** and **friendly** by adding **ly**. You can add **er** and **est** to **new**, **little**, and **pretty**. **Talk**, **jump**, **kick**, **ride**, **make**, **eat**, and **quit** can become the person who does them by adding **er**. Of course, you will help them decide what spelling changes they need as they write these words.

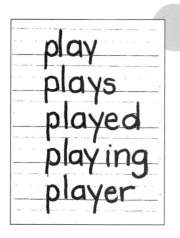

On-the-Back Activity with Endings Added to *play*.

❋ Combining Rhyme and Endings

Once your children are good at spelling words that rhyme with word-wall words and adding endings, it is time to combine these two formats. Begin with an easy rhyming format in which the words rhyme with just one word-wall word and have endings added. Here is an example using the word-wall word **down**. The sentences you say in which the children need to identify a word with an ending that rhymes with down might be:

My favorite thing at the circus was the **clowns**.

I saw the teacher **frowning** at me.

In the play, I was **crowned** the king.

My little brother fell in the pool and almost **drowned**.

I have lived in three different **towns**.

You could also do this with the harder format. When children are writing, they often need to spell a word that rhymes with one of the word-wall words and has an ending added. Make sure, however, that everyone spells the word aloud correctly before writing it, because this could be frustrating for some of your students. The children have written the words **tell**, **school**, **but**, **make**, and **rain** on the front.

My sister won the third-grade **spelling** bee.

I am going swimming as soon as the **pools** open.

My brother makes money **cutting** all the lawns in the neighborhood.

We almost had a wreck when the **brakes** didn't work on our truck.

I **trained** my dog to stay when I tell him to.

WORDO and Be a Mind Reader: Painless Practice with Word-Wall Words

WORDO is a variation of the ever-popular Bingo game. Children love it and don't know they are getting a lot of practice reading and writing common, confusing words. All you need to play WORDO are some WORDO sheets with

9 or 25 blocks and some small pieces of paper or objects for students to use to cover words as they fill in the blocks. Keep a supply of these grid sheets on hand and you are ready when the assembly program is canceled or the music teacher suddenly goes home sick.

Pick words from the wall your students need to practice. Write each word you pick on an index card and have students write it on their WORDO sheets in any block they choose. When all students have filled up their sheets with the 9 or 25 words called out, you are ready to play.

Shuffle your index cards and call the words one at a time. Have students chant the spelling of each word and then cover. The first student to have a complete row covered wins WORDO. Be sure to have the winner tell you the words covered and check to see that the words have been called and are spelled correctly. Students can then clear their sheets and play again. You might let the winner become the next caller and you can play the winner's sheet. Children love watching their teachers lose!

could	boy	was
friend	this	very
want	two	can't

there	night	they	their	won't
people	know	right	were	where
than	other	many	then	off
write	with	too	of	to
they're	some	for	two	from

In Be a Mind Reader, the teacher thinks of a word on the wall and then gives five clues to that word. Choose a word and write it on a scrap of paper, but do not let the students see what word you have written. Have students number their paper from 1 to 5, and tell them that you are going to see who can read your mind and figure out which of the words on the board you are thinking of and have written on your paper. Tell them you will give them five clues. By the fifth clue, everyone should guess your word, but if they read your mind they might get it before the fifth clue.

For your first clue, always give the same clue: "It's one of the words on the wall." Students should write next to number 1 the word they think it might be. Each succeeding clue should narrow down what it can be until by the fifth clue there is only one possible word. As you give clues, students write the word they believe it is next to each number. If succeeding clues confirm the word a student has written next to one number, the student writes that word again by the next number. Clues may include any features of the word you want students to notice. (It has more than two letters. It has less than four letters. It has an **e**. It does not have a **t**.) After the fifth clue, show students the word you wrote on your scratch paper and say, "I know you all have the word next to number 5, but who has it next to number 4? 3? 2? 1?" Some students will have read your mind and will be pleased as punch with themselves! Here are clues for the word **them**:

1. It's one of the words on the wall.
2. It has four letters.
3. It begins with **th**.
4. The vowel is an **e**.
5. It finishes the sentence **I gave my books to** _____.

Theme Boards

Word-wall space is reserved for really important words—words we want all students to learn to read and spell automatically, fluently, correctly, every time, everywhere! In every classroom there are other words students need—but the need changes as units, topics, and themes change. In addition to a word wall, most elementary classrooms have a theme board on which to display these words. The words on the board change as units, topics, and themes change.

Two theme boards from primary classrooms.

Summary

In English, approximately 100 words make up half of all the words we read and write. In order to read fluently, children must instantly and automatically recognize these high-frequency words. Unfortunately, many of these words are very hard for children to learn because they are abstract function words that don't have any tangible meaning and because many of them do not follow regular phonics patterns. Doing a word wall with these common, confusing words can help all your students to become automatic at reading and spelling these words. To do a word wall, you select words your students need most, add them gradually to the wall, and provide daily practice with the words. When you lead your students to "cheer" the words, they are using their auditory-rhythmic channel to learn these words. When they write the words, they are using their kinesthetic channel.

As you provide daily practice, the most important goal you have for your students is that they learn to read and spell the words you choose for your word wall.. You can, however, extend your daily word wall practice to teach your students how to read and spell many other words that have the same rhyming pattern as a word-wall word or that add endings to word-wall words. On-the-back activities give the daily word-wall practice more scope and allow your quick word learners to learn hundreds of other words.

chapter 8

Fluency Assessment and Interventions

Fluency assessment has become a regular part of literacy instruction since the National Reading Panel recommended that fluency be assessed and Response to Intervention (RTI) mandated assessment of reading skills, including fluency. In elementary classrooms throughout the country, children are given one-minute fluency checks and a Words Correct per Minute (WCPM) score is calculated. The most commonly used assessment is the Dynamic Indicators of Basic Early Literacy Skills (DIBELS) (Good & Kaminski, 2002). In this and similar tests, students are given a grade-level passage that they read orally. Their rate of reading is determined by considering the number of words correctly read in one minute. This assessment is quick to give and simple to score. You listen to the child read, mark the word he or she was on at the one-minute mark, and then subtract the number of errors from the total number of words. The use of these one-minute fluency checks has become so widespread in elementary schools that we seldom stop to consider what we are actually measuring.

In Chapter 5, Caldwell's (2009) definition and steps for assessment were described. Assessment is collecting and analyzing data to make decisions about how children are performing and growing. To conduct a valid assessment, you first identify what you want to assess. Second, you collect evidence. Next, you analyze that evidence. Finally, you make a decision and act on that decision. Many people, including Jay Samuels (2007), the recognized expert on automaticity and fluency in reading, do not consider these WCPM measures valid measures of fluency. Samuels notes:

> One criticism I have of the DIBELS tests is that, despite their labels, they are not valid tests of the construct of fluency as it is widely understood and defined. They only assess accuracy and speed. By attaching the term fluency to their tests, they create the false assumption that that is what the tests measure. (p. 564)

In addition to speed and accuracy, fluency always includes expression. We say a person is a fluent reader if his or her reading "sounds like speech." That expression is very important because it is an indicator of comprehension. Read the following list of words aloud:

a

and

care

children

cynics

entrust

harm

in

is

minds

modern

no

of

paid

paying

plumbers

see

skeptics

smaller

than

the

their

they

those

to

wage

whom

Now read aloud this quote, attributed to John F. Kennedy:

Modern cynics and skeptics see no harm in paying those to whom they entrust the minds of their children a smaller wage than is paid to those to whom they entrust the care of their plumbing.

You probably noticed that the words in the list and the words in the quote are the same words. When you read the quote, however, you read it in phrases. Your voice went up and down and you sounded like you were talking. You read the quote with appropriate speed, accuracy, and expression. If after reading the quote, the little voice in your head commented,

"That sure hasn't changed!"

That commentary demonstrates your comprehension!

Fluency Is More Than Speed!

So, the problem with using a quick, simple WCPM measure to assess fluency is that it doesn't measure fluency. WCPM assessments measure reading speed. Often, but not always, they measure accuracy. Imagine that Tracy, a fourth-grader, read the following passage, leaving out words she was probably unfamiliar with. Words with strikethroughs are words Tracy omitted.

> Frogs are found on every ~~continent~~ except ~~Antarctica~~. Frogs are cold-~~blooded~~ animals. Their bodies stay the same ~~temperature~~ as the air or water around them.
>
> Frogs begin their lives as tiny eggs. The eggs grow and turn into ~~tadpoles~~. ~~Tadpoles~~ have big heads and long tails. They have gills like fish so they can ~~breathe~~ under water. As ~~tadpoles~~ grow, they ~~develop~~ back legs and then front legs. Their tails ~~shrink~~ and ~~disappear~~. They ~~develop~~ lungs. Now they can ~~breathe~~ on land. The change from eggs to ~~tadpoles~~ to frogs is called ~~metamorphosis~~.
>
> Frogs are ~~carnivores~~, which means they eat meat. Small- and-medium sized frogs eat ~~insects~~ such as flies, ~~mosquitoes~~, and ~~dragonflies~~. Larger frogs eat larger insects and worms. Very large frogs eat small animals ~~including~~ baby snakes, mice, and turtles. Frogs do not eat dead ~~insects~~ or animals.

Before calculating Tracy's speed and accuracy, what would you say about Tracy's reading? What does she do when she comes to a word she is probably not familiar with? If you asked her to retell what she read, how good would you expect her comprehension to be? Most teachers would agree that Tracy is not very accurate in word identification and that her retelling will probably lack crucial information. The 100th word is **they**, and she made 12 errors in the first 100 words—an accuracy score of 88 percent, which is below the 95 percent accuracy rate generally considered instructional level for word identification. (She skipped the words **tadpole** and **develop** several times but words missed multiple times are only counted once.)

Now, calculate her speed. The passage has 142 words. At the one-minute mark, Tracy was reading the word **worms** in the third paragraph—the 122nd word. To calculate WCPM for Tracy, you subtract the numbers of errors—12—from 122 and determine that Tracy read 110 words correctly in one minute. This puts her in the acceptable range for a fourth-grader reading a fourth-grade passage at the beginning of the year, and according to the DIBELS norms, Tracy would be considered a fluent, low-risk reader. Most teachers would agree that she was not a fluent reader and would indeed be concerned about her reading progress.

Imagine how another fourth-grader, Scott, might read the same passage. Bold words are words he hesitated on but read correctly. Substitution errors are careted in. Words omitted are struck through.

> Frogs are found on every ∧ ^country^continent except **Antarctica**. Frogs are cold-blooded animals. Their bodies stay the same **temperature** as the air or water around them.
>
> Frogs begin their lives as tiny eggs. The eggs grow and turn into tadpoles. Tadpoles have big heads and long tails. They have gills like fish so they can breathe under water. As tadpoles grow, they **develop** back legs and then front legs. Their tales shrink and disappear. They develop lungs. Now they can breathe on land. The change from eggs to tadpoles to frogs is called ~~metamorphosis~~.
>
> Frogs are ~~carnivores~~, which means they eat meat. Small- and medium-sized frogs eat insects such as flies, **mosquitoes**, and **dragonflies**. Larger frogs eat larger insects and worms. Very large frogs eat small animals including baby snakes, mice, and turtles. Frogs do not eat dead insects or animals.

At the 100-word mark, Scott has three errors. He read **continent** as **country** and left out the words **metamorphosis** and **carnivores** after attempting to pronounce them. The bold words are words Scott hesitated on but correctly decoded. Scott's word identification accuracy is 97 percent (three errors in 100 words), a little above the 95 percent word-identification level needed to determine that his word-identification accuracy level is instructional level for this fourth-grade passage.

Now, let's compute Scott's WCPM score. At the one-minute point, Scott was reading the word **lungs**, the 78th word. Subtract the three errors from 78 and his score is 75, putting him at some risk for failure if he were reading this passage early in fourth grade.

Which child do you consider the better reader? By only considering WCPM, you would conclude that Tracy was progressing well and that Scott was in trouble. Most teachers would conclude the opposite. Tracy and Scott are extreme examples, not the typical profiles of fourth-grade readers, but readers like Tracy and Scott do exist.

According to Caldwell (2009), once you have identified what you want to assess and have collected data, you analyze the evidence and then decide what to do based on your analyses. Simply looking at speed does not give you much to analyze. In fact, Tracy may have learned how to "game the system." Perhaps she figured out that you could read more words correctly in one minute if you just skipped words you didn't immediately recognize rather than waste time trying to figure out these words. To validly assess fluency, you need to collect information on speed, accuracy, expression, and comprehension and analyze the results of your data. You can then truly make wise decisions about who needs additional instruction and what kind of instruction they will benefit from.

Extending One-Minute Measures to Truly Measure Fluency

I hope you are now convinced that it is impossible to make judgments about fluency and about which of your students are at risk for reading failure based only on the number of words read correctly in one minute. You can, however, modify the measures you are now using and collect data that will allow you to make valid decisions about the progress and needs of your students. This modification is based on the suggestions included in a must-have resource, *Fluency: Differentiated Interventions and Progress-Monitoring Assessments* (Johns & Berglund, 2010). In addition to graded passages you can use for fluency assessments, this book is chock-full of practical strategies you can use to improve fluency for all your students.

Because fluency is the ability to read with accuracy, appropriate speed, and expression, you will need to add a valid measure of accuracy and include a way to determine if students are reading with expression. Because you never want students to read without thinking about comprehension, you want to be sure they know before they read that you want them to be able to tell you what they read when they finish reading. After reading, have them retell what they read and rate their comprehension. You can also analyze their oral reading to see if students are quickly reading the high-frequency words commonly called sight words.

❋ Measuring Accuracy

To get an accuracy measure, rather than just putting a check on words read correctly, make a record of the errors students make. Using the simple system described for recording Tracy's and Scott's reading, you can strike through any omitted words and caret in any substitution or mispronunciation errors. You can put an *H* for any words they hesitate on and then correctly decode so that you will know which words they are successfully decoding. Sometimes, students make an error and then go back and correct that error. This is a very good sign because it means they are monitoring their reading and realizing when something they read does not make sense. You might want to note this with an *SC* for self-correction above the word. Any words that are self-corrected are not counted as errors. Recording what a student reads does not take any more time than making check marks, and keeping these records will give you data that you can analyze and that will help you make wise decisions about needed instruction.

❋ Measuring Expression

As each student reads and you record their reading, also listen for their phrasing and expression. Most teachers find that they can use a simple four-point scale to make a judgment about the expression aspect of fluency.

Oral Reading Expression Scale

Level 4	Reads in phrases with expression that sounds like speech
Level 3	Reads mostly in phrases and with some expression
Level 2	Reads mostly word by word with some phrases but little expression
Level 1	Reads like reading words in a list, word by word with little or no expression

❋ Measuring Comprehension

Before students read the passage, be sure to tell them that they should think about what they read because you will ask them to "retell" the major facts or events of what they read. When students finish reading, take the passage away and say:

"Now tell me everything you remember from your reading."

Listen while they tell you and ask questions if you are unsure of how much they comprehended. Rate their comprehension on a four-point scale.

Comprehension Scale

Level 4	Recalls most of the important events or facts and no misinformation
Level 3	Recalls a lot of events or facts and little misinformation
Level 2	Recalls some events or facts and may include some misinformation
Level 1	Recalls little except the topic

❋ Measuring Sight Word Recognition

Every passage you will use to assess fluency will contain some highly frequent words commonly called sight words. The first paragraph of the "Frogs" passage contains 8 high-frequency words.

are

around

as

on

or

the

them

their

Being able to instantly and automatically recognize the high-frequency words is critical for fluency. Mispronouncing or hesitating on any of these words will slow down reading, interfere with expression, and probably impede comprehension. When analyzing your students' oral reading, note any high-frequency words they mispronounce, omit, or hesitate on.

❋ Recording the Results of Your Enhanced Fluency Assessment

Here is a record sheet you might use to record the results of your fluency assessment.

Fluency Assessment Record Sheet		
Name_____ Date_____		Grade Level_____
Speed Words read in one minute minus errors	WCPM _____	_____ At risk _____ Some risk _____ Low risk
Accuracy First 100 words minus errors	% Accuracy _____	_____ Instructional level _____ Below instructional level
Expression Rating Scale Level 4 sounds like speech Level 1 word by word		_____ Level 4 _____ Level 3 _____ Level 2 _____ Level 1
Comprehension Rating Scale Level 4 recalls most important ideas/events Level 1 recalls almost none		_____ Level 4 _____ Level 3 _____ Level 2 _____ Level 1
Accuracy Analysis (not including high-frequency words)	List words student mispronounced or omitted	List words student hesitated on but pronounced correctly
Accuracy Analysis of High-Frequency Words	List common words (for, there, etc.) mispronounced or omitted	List common words student hesitated on but correctly pronounced

✳ Extending the Fluency Assessment

The assessment just described will give you an accurate assessment of reading fluency for most of your students. If, however, you have a student whose reading level is not even close to the level of the passage used for testing, the results of the assessment won't tell you very much. Imagine that you give this fluency assessment to Carl. His word-identification accuracy is below 90 percent and he shows little or no comprehension. For Carl, this passage is just too hard to use for an accurate fluency measure. To determine fluency, you need to have Carl read an easier passage. When you find a passage on which Carl shows more than 90 percent word-identification accuracy and comprehends some or most of the important events, you can look at his speed and expression on that passage to determine how fluently he reads when reading material at his reading level.

Another extension you may want to consider is to adapt the way you measure comprehension. Imagine that Paula reads the passage with acceptable accuracy, speed, and expression but shows little or no comprehension of what she read. Does Paula have a comprehension problem? Perhaps, but it is also possible that in spite of the fact that you told her to think about what she was reading, she was so concentrating on getting the words right and reading quickly with expression that she could not also think about what she was reading. There is a simple way to determine why Paula comprehended so little. Ask her to read the passage again silently and think about what she was reading so that she can tell you about the important ideas or events. After she reads it silently, listen to her retelling and ask questions as needed to determine how much she understood. If her comprehension is adequate after rereading it silently, you do not need to worry about Paula's comprehension since most of the reading she does will be done silently for meaning rather than orally for a fluency assessment.

Fluency Interventions

Once you have collected and analyzed data on the variables that comprise fluency, you are ready to implement or enhance the instruction you are providing students to increase their fluency. Think about fluency instruction in your classroom to decide what you may need to modify.

✳ Easy Reading for Everyone

A lot of what your students read across a school day will require some effort and concentration, but they also need to do some reading that is effortless—reading in which they can immediately recognize almost all the words and comprehend almost everything. Look back at the suggestions in Chapter 6 for making easy reading acceptable and a regular part of your classroom routines. Implementing these ideas will take you a long way toward your goal of having some of the reading your students do be effortless.

If you teach older children and many of them struggle with reading and never engage in reading that is easy, you may need to implement some additional routines to provide the effortless reading experience. Many older students consider easy books "baby books." Linda Fielding and Cathy Roller (1992) attack this "baby book attitude" head-on in a *Reading Teacher* article, "Making Difficult Books Accessible and Easy Books Acceptable." Among the many practical ideas they offer for making easy books acceptable, Fielding and Roller suggest:

- Model, by reading aloud, the use and enjoyment of easy books.
- Alter purposes for easy reading by having older children read these books to younger buddies.
- Allow children to make tape recordings of favorite books.
- Make the expanding world of easy nonfiction picture books readily available.

I have seen all four of these strategies successfully used; I have even seen them combined effectively. For instance, in one school, a fourth-grade teacher with many children still reading—not very fluently—at first- and second-grade levels decided that the children needed to do lots of easy reading. She partnered each child with a kindergartner and arranged for a weekly reading time. She then gathered up a lot of easy books, including many Dr. Seuss titles, Clifford books, and many nonfiction picture books (including alphabet books, some of which are listed in Chapter 4). Across the course of a week or two, she read these books to her students and let each student choose one book to prepare to read to the kindergarten buddy. When the children had chosen their books, they practiced reading the book several times—with a partner—to the tape recorder and finally to the teacher. By the time her children trotted down to the kindergarten—easy books proudly in hand—all the children were fluent readers of their book.

Following their return to their fourth-grade classroom, they talked about their experience reading to their kindergarten buddies and whether or not their book was a good choice. The teacher made a chart on which each child listed the book read aloud that week. The following day, the teacher and the children gathered and reviewed the chart showing who had read what. The teacher also reminded them of some other books no one had chosen the first week and led them to choose their second book. The partner reading, tape-recorder reading, and reading to the teacher continued as it had for the first week, except that if a child chose a book that another child had read the previous week, that child became the "expert" on that book and read the book to or listened to the new reader read the book at least once. The second trip to the kindergarten went more smoothly than the first, and the children returned, discussed the kindergartners' responses to the books, and listed the second book they had read on the chart.

By the fourth week, the easy-reading-for-fluency program was up and running with minimal help from the teacher. Many children chose books their friends had chosen previously, and they enjoyed reading together and often recorded the book together in preparation for performing their weekly "civic volunteer" duty!

❈ Models of Fluent, Expressive Reading

A lesson I learned my first year of teaching still applies today. If students are not doing something you want them to do, assume they don't know how to do it and show them. I wanted my students to read together in partners. The first time I partnered them up and told them to read, they did everything but read. When I expressed my dismay that "my class couldn't partner read" to a veteran teacher, she asked:

"Did you show them how to partner read?"

The next day we modeled and role-played partner reading, and lo and behold, my class could partner read. I also learned this lesson when I wanted them to "explore" some stuff in science, work with math manipulatives, and perform countless other tasks I just took for granted that everyone knew how to do.

Chapter 6 suggests that you provide models of expressive oral reading by reading aloud to your students in a "hammy" expressive way and make choral and echo reading of plays and poetry a regular part of your literacy routines. If you teach older students, you might have thought that these suggestions for providing these models of expressive oral reading were only needed for younger students. But what if your older students read in a word-by-word fashion with little phrasing? What if their reading does not sound like speech? Reading in phrases with expression is an indicator of comprehension, but it also promotes comprehension because a student has to understand what he or she is reading to recognize the phrases and turn the words into speech.

So if you have students who need to read with expression, be sure you include some hammy teacher read-alouds and some echo and choral reading of plays and poetry. Everyone enjoys watching their teacher ham it up, and big kids also like performing and being hammy.

If you decide to implement the reading buddy program described in the previous section, be sure to include some lessons of how your students should read expressively to their kindergarten buddies. Model this as you read aloud the easy-to-read books, and have your students listen to their recorded readings and assess their own expressiveness as they prepare to read the books to their buddies.

Among the many engaging activities to build fluency included in John and Berglund (2010) are several activities I especially like to use when teaching students to read with expression. In Say It Like the Character, students read stories that have lots of dialogue. They decide how the character is feeling and then practice reading it to show how the character is feeling. To get them started, you might help them brainstorm a list of different ways they feel by asking them questions such as:

How would you feel if your dog died?

If your dog got lost?

If you won a contest?

If you scored the winning basket in a game?

If you were going to go on a trip to Disney World?

If your birthday party was three days away?

Make a list of their responses and have them refer to this list as they think about how characters in what they are reading would feel and how they would sound. Have students decide how their character is feeling and practice reading the dialogue the way they would say it if they were feeling that way.

scared	excited	impatient	proud	confused
happy	surprised	nervous	worried	sad
angry	afraid	confused	bored	upset

Just Joking is another activity Johns and Berglund suggest for helping students learn to read with expression. Kids love jokes and will readily read joke books. Read some jokes to them aloud and help them to see that how the joke is read—and particularly how the punch line is delivered—is a big part of what makes the joke funny.

❋ Read It Again!

Rereading something several times until you can quickly and effortlessly identify all the words and read it with expression is one of the most powerful ways to build fluency. In addition to echo and choral reading, in which students often practice

tech tips

There are many Internet sites that have jokes for kids. On some, your students can submit their favorite jokes. Here are a few jokes to get you in the spirit. I have eliminated spaces between words in the answer so that you will have to think about them!

What do you do if you're getting chased by a blue tiger and a purple dog?
  Getoffthemerrygoround!

What do you get if you cross a teacher with a vampire?
  Lotsofbloodtests!

Why did the apple cross the road?
  ToseehisGrannySmith!

The teacher stood in front of the class "Stand up if you're an idiot." John stood up. "John, why do you think you're an idiot?"
  "Idon't.Ijusthatetoseeyoustandingtherebyyourself!"

reading their parts several times before the performance, Chapter 6 suggests four other repeated reading lesson formats: recorded reading, radio reading, timed repeated reading, and paired repeated reading

If fluency is an issue for the majority of your students you may want to consider two other lesson formats that have been shown to increase fluency for whole classrooms of children. In Fluency Development Lessons, students read a short passage several times in one day's lesson. In Fluency-Oriented Reading Instruction students read fairly long passages across a week's time.

Fluency Development Lessons (FDL)   In 1998, Tim Rasinski and Nancy Padak published a study that drew everyone's attention to how widespread fluency problems are for disabled readers. Rasinski and Padak had looked at a large number of remedial readers and evaluated their abilities in comprehension, decoding, and fluency. Almost all the children were well below grade level in all three areas, but fluency was by far the biggest area of concern. The children read the test passages in such a slow and laborious manner that the investigators were surprised that they had any comprehension at all. In response to their findings, Rasinski and Padak developed a lesson for teaching fluency, which they call a Fluency Development Lesson, or FDL Here is how the FDL strategy works. This is adapted from a more detailed and rich explanation in Tim Rasinski's (2010) wonderfully practical book, *The Fluent Reader*.

The teacher chooses a short passage—often a poem—that is apt to be appealing to the students and reads the passage aloud several times, modeling fluent reading. Meaning for the poem/passage and for any difficult vocabulary words is built through discussion.

Using individual copies of the poem, or a large-size version of it written on a chart, the teacher and the class do a choral reading. The poem is read chorally several times, often with different children reading different parts or verses.

The children are paired and take turns reading the passage to each other. Each person reads the passage three times. The children help each other and respond to each other's reading with praise, support, and encouragement.

When the class gathers together again, children can volunteer to read the passage aloud for everyone. If possible, children read the passage to other classes or to other school personnel.

Each child chooses two or three words from the passage to add to their personal word banks. They study these words and often use them in a variety of word sorts and games.

Children put one copy of the text in their poetry folders and are given a second copy to take home. They are encouraged to read the passage to whoever will listen. Children and parents alike report that this is one "homework" assignment they all look forward to.

The following day, the previous day's passage is read again and then the whole cycle begins with a new passage. Rasinski recommends a fast pace for this activity and suggests that once the class learn the routines, the whole FDL can be completed in 15 to 20 minutes.

FDLs are easy to do and enjoyed by both teachers and students. Rasinski reports that children engaged in these lessons made greater gains in reading than a similar group of children who read the same passages but did not use the FDL procedure. FDLs would be a welcome addition to any classroom routine but would be especially helpful in remedial and special education classes.

Fluency-Oriented Reading Instruction (FORI)   FORI also has students reading text multiple times but in FORI the text is a longer passage from a reading program. Like FDL, the lesson begins with the teacher reading the text aloud while students follow along silently in their books. Following the teacher read-aloud, the story is discussed and the teacher builds vocabulary, comprehension, and other strategies related to the story.

On the second day, the teacher and students do an echo reading of the story. The teacher reads several sentences aloud and then the students echo the reading, trying to use the phrasing and expression used by the teacher. After the echo reading, students do some kind of comprehension activity, usually writing a short response. That night, students take the story home to read it to a family member.

On the third day, students and teachers do a choral reading of the story. On the fourth day, students read the story with a partner, taking turns reading each page. If there is time, the partners read the story again, switching the pages read. On the final day of the week, students do some extension activities related to the story.

Research on FORI (Kuhn et al., 2006; Stahl & Heubach, 2005) demonstrated gains made by the FORI students when compared with students at another school using the same text in a more traditional way. Students whose reading instruction followed the FORI format made nearly two years of progress in one year of instruction. At the end of the year, only two of 105 students in the FORI classrooms were reading below grade level.

❋ High-Frequency Words

A little over 100 words **make up** half **the** words **in** everything **you** read! There are 14 words in the previous sentence. The eight bold words are some of the common functional and connecting words that are among the 100 most frequent words. Chapter 7 pointed out that these words are difficult for children to remember because they have no meaning and many of them are not decodable. The reason that the chapter on teaching these common words is included in the fluency section is that no one can read fluently if they hesitate on these words and spend time and attention trying to figure them out. The activities in Chapter 7 will help your students learn these high-frequency words, which are critical to fluency.

But what if only a few of your students have difficulty remembering these words? Teachers who have just a few students who still stumble over common words have found that making a personal portable word wall for these students can help them learn these words. You can easily construct this personal word wall by dividing the two inside flaps of a file folder into spaces for all the letters of the

A	B	C	D	E	F
are also about	before	can't could	don't	enough	first favorite
G getting	H have	I I'm into	J	K know knew	L let's
M myself	N new	O one our	P people	Q	R really
S said school	T then there threw to	U until	V very	W want was wear whether	X	YZ your you're

A personal word wall made from a file folder.

alphabet. Since many of the common confusing words begin with the letters **t** and **w**, leave extra space next to these letters.

Observe the reading and writing of your students who need personal word walls. If they stumble on a common word in their reading or confuse one of these words with another word (**was** for **saw**; **for** for **from**; **with** for **will**) or if they misspell a common word in their writing (thay, sed, becuz) add these words to their folder. Use different colors of permanent marker to help students distinguish the words.

Take a few minutes each day to read these words with your students. Give them a clue sentence or phrase to anchor the word (piece **of** pizza; I **was** hungry; I **don't** like carrots!) and make sure they know how it is used in speech. Help them to cheer the spelling of the word in a rhythmic fashion so that they can use their auditory channel to retrieve the word. When they are writing or reading, have them open their word wall and use it to help them remember the words that confuse them.

Summary

To be valid, assessment must measure what it is intended to measure. Common one-minute assessments, which measure the number of words students can read correctly in one minute, only measure speed of reading. Reading fluency, however, includes not only speed but accuracy, expression, and comprehension. Popular one-minute measures can easily be extended to include accuracy, expression, and comprehension. Looking at these four variables will give you a complete picture of how fluently a child reads.

In addition to the activities suggested in Chapters 6 and 7, there are specific interventions you can implement if fluency is a major concern for some of your students. Older students who won't read what they consider to be "baby books" can be enticed to read these if you set up a big buddy reading program with a kindergarten or first-grade classroom.

Older students who are not fluent in reading will benefit from your modeling expressive reading for them, and they will also enjoy participating in echo and choral reading. Activities such as Say It Like the Character and Just Joking are engaging ways to help older students learn to read with phrasing and expression.

Rereading in various formats including recorded reading, radio reading, timed repeated reading and paired repeated reading promote fluent reading. Two classroom lesson formats, Fluency Development Lessons (FDL) and Fluency-Oriented Reading Instruction (FORI), can help all students increase fluency and become better readers.

Some children are not fluent because they stumble over, misread, or simply skip common, abstract words. Creating a personal word wall for these students can help them learn to automatically and quickly recognize these high-frequency words and thus remove this stumbling block to fluency.

part three

Using Phonics and Spelling Patterns

Most of the words people read and write are one- and two-syllable *regular* words, which, because they are consistent with the rules of spelling and pronunciation, people can decode and spell even if they have not seen them before. Developing the ability to independently read and write most regular words is a complex process and takes time and practice with a variety of activities.

In English, the vowels are variant and unpredictable. The letter **a** commonly represents the sound in **and, made, agree, art, talk,** and **care.** Names have been given to some of these sounds. **And** has a short a; **made** has a long a; **agree** is a schwa; the **a** in **art** is **r** controlled. There are no names for the sound **a** represents in **talk** and **care.** Further complicating things are

the many words in which **a** doesn't do any of these six common things—**eat**, **coat**, **legal**—and the fact that even the consistent sounds can be spelled in many different ways. The long **a** sound is commonly spelled by the patterns in **made**, **maid**, and **may**. The sound **a** has in **talk** is spelled by an **aw** in **saw** and an **au** in **Paul**.

When one stops to think about all the possible sounds and spelling patterns for the vowels, it is a miracle that anyone becomes an accurate and fast decoder of English words. And yet that is exactly what happens! All good readers can quickly and accurately pronounce the made-up words **gand**, **hade**, **afuse**, **sart**, **malk**, **lare**, **jeat**, **foat**, **pregal**, **maw**, and **naul**.

In schools, teachers have traditionally taught students many rules and jargon: the **e** on the end makes the vowel long; vowels in unaccented syllables have a schwa sound; when a vowel is followed by **r**, it is **r** controlled. Children have been taught so many rules and jargon because it takes over 200 rules to account for the common spelling patterns in English. Although these rules do describe the English alphabetic system, it is doubtful that readers and writers use these rules to decode and spell words. So how do they do it?

As readers develop some fluency, they decode words by using spelling patterns from the words they know. **Made**, **fade**, **blade**, and **shade** all have the same spelling pattern, and the **a** is pronounced the same in all four. When you see the made-up word **hade**, your mind accesses that known spelling pattern and you give the made-up word the same pronunciation you have for other words with that spelling pattern. Spelling patterns are letters that are commonly seen together in a certain position in words. The **al** at the end of **legal**, **royal**, and the made-up word **pregal** is a spelling pattern. Sometimes a spelling pattern can be a single letter, as the **a** is in **agree**, **about**, **adopt**, and the made-up word **afuse**. Using words you know to decode unknown words is called *decoding by analogy*.

Spelling patterns are quite reliable indicators of pronunciation—with two exceptions. The first exception was explained in Chapter 7. The most frequently used words are often not pronounced or spelled like other words with that spelling pattern. **To** and **do** should rhyme with **go**, **so**, and **no**. **What** should rhyme with **at**, **cat**, and **bat**. **They** should be spelled like **way** and **stay**. **Said** should be spelled like **red** and **bed**. It is precisely because the most frequent words have the least predictable pronunciations and spellings that you need to provide daily practice with word-wall words so that all children learn to read and spell them.

The second exception in spelling patterns is that some spelling patterns have two common sounds. The **ow** at the end of words occurs in **show**, **grow**, and **slow**, but also in **how**, **now**, and **cow**. The **ood** at the end of **good**, **hood**, and **stood** is also found at the end of **food**, **mood**, and **brood**.

Children who are constantly cross-checking meaning with the pronunciations will not be bothered by these differences, as long as the word they are reading is in their listening-meaning vocabulary.

Whereas spelling patterns work wonderfully well for pronouncing unfamiliar words, they don't work as well for spelling! There are often two or more spelling patterns with the same pronunciation. When trying to read the made-up word **nade**, you would simply compare its pronunciation to other words with that spelling pattern—**made**, **grade**, and **blade**. If, however, I didn't show you **nade**, but rather pronounced it and asked you to spell it, you might compare it to **maid**, **paid**, and **braid** and spell it **n-a-i-d**. Most words can be correctly pronounced by comparing them to known spelling patterns. To spell a word correctly, however, you must often choose between two or more possible spelling patterns.

Part Three contains activities that will help children use patterns to decode words. In Chapter 9, you will learn how Making Words can help all levels of children move forward in their decoding and spelling abilities. Chapter 10 focuses on rhyming patterns with a variety of activities you can use to teach children to decode and spell using patterns. Once children are decoding and spelling based on patterns, teachers help them develop their visual checking system and decide which pattern is the correct spelling. Chapter 11 presents you with strategies for teaching your students how to decode and spell big words. Chapter 12 has an explanation and examples of how you can use the Making Words lesson format with older students. Chapter 13 includes a variety of assessments to help you measure your students' progress in mastering our complex English phonics/spelling system. Chapter 13 also includes coaching suggestions and some interventions you can use with older struggling readers.

chapter 9

Making Words

Making Words (Cunningham & Cunningham, 1992) is a popular activity with both teachers and children. Children love manipulating letters to make words and figuring out the secret word that can be made with all the letters. While children are having fun making words, they are also learning important information about phonics and spelling. As children manipulate the letters to make the words, they learn how small changes, such as changing just one letter or moving the letters around, result in completely new words. Children learn to stretch out words and listen for the sounds they hear and the order of those sounds. When you change the first letter, you also change the sound you hear at the beginning of the word. Likewise, when you change the last letter, you change the sound you hear at the end of the word. These ideas seem commonplace and obvious to those of us who have been reading and writing for almost as long as we can remember. But they are a revelation to many beginners—a revelation that gives them tremendous independence in and power over the challenge of decoding and spelling words.

Making Words lessons are an example of a type of instruction called Guided Discovery. In order to truly learn and retain strategies, children must discover them. But some children do not seem to make discoveries about words very easily on their own. In a Making Words lesson, teachers guide children toward those discoveries by carefully sequencing the words they are to make and giving them explicit guidance about how much change is needed.

Making Words lessons have three parts. In the first part, the children make words. Begin with short, easy words, and move to longer, more complex words. The last word is always the secret word—a word that can be made with all the letters. As children arrange the letters, a child who has successfully made a word goes up to the pocket chart or chalk ledge and makes the word with big letters. Children who don't have the word made correctly quickly fix their word so that they're ready for the next word. The small changes between most words encourage even those children who have not made a word perfectly to fix it because they soon realize that having the current word correctly spelled increases their chances of spelling the next word correctly. Each lesson includes 9 to 15 words, including the secret word that can be made with all the letters. When it is time to make the secret word, children have one minute to try to come up with the word. After one minute, if no one has discovered the secret word, give them clues that allow them to figure it out.

In Part Two of a Making Words lesson, children sort the words into patterns. Many children discover patterns just through making the words in the carefully sequenced order, but some children need more explicit guidance. This guidance happens when all the words have been made and the teacher guides the children to sort them into patterns. Depending on the sophistication of the children and the words available in the lesson, words might be sorted according to their beginning letters—all the letters up to the vowel. Alternatively, to focus on just one sound–letter combination, the teacher might ask children to sort out all the words that start with **qu**, **br**, or **sh**. Once the words with these letters are sorted, the teacher and children pronounce the words and discover that most words that have the same letters also have the same sounds—an important discovery for all emerging readers and writers.

Another pattern children need to discover is that many words have the same root word. If they can pronounce and spell the root word and if they recognize root words with endings, prefixes, or suffixes added, they are able to decode and spell many additional words. To some children, every new word they meet is a new experience! They fail to recognize how new words are related to already known words and, thus, are in the difficult—if not impossible—position of starting from "scratch" and just trying to learn and remember every new word. To be fluent, fast, automatic decoders and spellers, children must learn that **play**, **playing**, **played**, **plays**, **player**, and **replay** have **play** as their root and use their knowledge of how to decode and spell **play** to quickly transfer to these related words. Whenever possible from the letters available, Making Words lessons include related words. We tell the children that people are related by blood and words are related by meaning. We ask the children to find any related words and sort them out, and then we create sentences to show how these words are related.

Each lesson contains several sets of rhyming words. Children need to recognize that words that have the same spelling pattern from the vowel to the end of the word usually rhyme. When they sort the words into rhyming words and notice that the words that rhyme have the same spelling pattern, children learn rhyming patterns and how to use words they know to decode and spell lots of other words.

The final part of a Making Words lesson is the Transfer step. All the working and playing with words you do while making words are worth nothing if children do not use what they know when they need to use it. Many children know letter sounds and patterns and do not apply these to decode an unknown word encountered during reading or to spell a word they need while writing. All teachers know that it is much easier to teach children phonics than it is to actually get them to use it. This is the reason that every Making Words lesson ends with a Transfer step. Once the words are sorted according to rhyme, you then help the children transfer their letter–sound knowledge to writing. To do this, you ask the children to pretend they are writing and need to spell a word:

> "Pretend you're writing and you need to spell the word **stray**. You stretch out **stray** and hear the beginning letters **str**. If you can think of the words we made today that rhyme with **stray**, you will have the correct spelling of the word."

figure 9.1 Steps in Teaching a Making Words Lesson

1. Place the large letter cards needed in a pocket chart or on the smart board.

2. Have children pass out letters or pick up the letters needed.

3. Point to the letters on the large letter cards, and have the children hold up their matching small letter cards.

4. Write the number 2 (or 3 if no two-letter words are in this lesson) on the board. Tell them to take two letters and make the first word. Have them say the word after you stretch out the word to hear all the sounds.

5. Have a child who makes the first word correctly make the same word with the large letter cards in the pocket chart or on the smart board. Do not wait for everyone to make the word before sending a child to make it with the big letters. Encourage anyone who did not make the word correctly at first to fix the word when he or she sees it made correctly.

6. Continue to make words, giving students clues, such as "Change the first letter only" or "Move the same letters around and you can make a different word" or "Take all your letters out and make another word." Send a child who has made the word correctly to make the word with the large letter cards. Cue students when they are to use more letters by erasing and changing the number on the board to indicate the number of letters needed.

7. Before telling students the last word, ask, "Has anyone figured out the secret word—the word we can make with all our letters?" If someone has, congratulate them and let them make it. If not, give them clues until someone figures out the secret word.

8. Once all the words have been made, display the words made, one at a time (in the same order that the children made them) on the smart board or in the pocket chart. Have the children say and spell the words with you as you do this. Have the children sort these words for patterns—including beginning letters, rhymes, and related words.

9. To encourage transfer to reading and writing, show students how rhyming words can help them decode and spell other words. Say some words that rhyme and have students spell these new words by deciding which words they rhyme with.

The children decide that **stray** rhymes with the **ay** words they made and that **stray** is spelled s-t-r-a-y. Finish the lesson by having them spell several more words by deciding which of the words they made it rhymes with.

A Sample Making Words Lesson

As the teacher who is teaching the lesson, you are the only person who can decide exactly what to say to your students and how to cue them about the different words. Your children will relate better to example sentences you come up with that relate to their communities and their lives. With the caveat that you can do this much better for your children can than I—who have never seen your children— here is a sample that you can use to construct your own lesson cues. This sample lesson is taken from *Making Words First Grade* (Cunningham & Hall, 2008).

✳ Beginning the Lesson

The children all have the letters: **a e g m n s t.**

These same letters—big enough for all to see—are displayed in a pocket chart or on a smart board. The letter cards have lowercase letters on one side and capital letters on the other side. The vowels are in a different color.

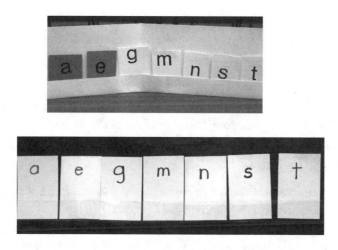

The words the children are going to make are written on index cards or on cards for the smart board. These words will be used for the Sort and Transfer steps of the lesson.

The teacher begins the lesson by having the children hold up and name each letter as the teacher points to the big letters.

"Hold up and name your letter as I point to each letter. Let's start with your vowels. Show me your **a** and your **e.** Now show me your **g, m, n,**

s, and **t**. Today you have seven letters. In a few minutes, we will see if anyone can figure out the secret word that uses all seven letters."

❋ Part One: Making Words

"Use three letters to spell the word **eat**. We **eat** at 11:25."

(Find someone with **eat** spelled correctly and send that child to spell **eat** with the big letters.)

"Use three letters to spell **net**. In tennis, you try to hit the ball over the **net**."

"Change the first letter in **net** to spell **met**. I **met** my cousin at the mall."

"Change the first letter again to spell **set**. It is my job to **set** the table."

"Add a letter you can't hear to **set** to spell **seat**. Please stay in your **seat**."

(Quickly send someone with the correct spelling to make the word with the big letters. Keep the pace brisk. Do not wait until everyone has **seat** spelled with their little letters. It is fine if some children are making **seat** as **seat** is being spelled with the big letters.)

"Change the first letter in **seat** to spell **neat**. On Fridays, we leave our classroom clean and **neat**."

"Change the first letter again to spell **meat**. Vegetarians don't eat **meat**."

"Use the same letters in **meat** but move them around so they spell **team**. Do you have a favorite football **team**?"

"Use four letters to spell **east**. The sun rises in the **east**."

"Clear your holders and start over to spell another four-letter word: **stem**. Most plants have a root, leaves, and a **stem**."

"Use a letter you can't hear to turn **stem** into **steam**. When you heat water, it turns into **steam**."

"I have just one word left. It is the secret word you can make with all your letters. See if you can figure it out."

(Give the children one minute to figure out the secret word. Then give clues if needed.) Let someone who figures it out go to the big letters and spell the secret word: **magnets**.

❋ Part Two: Sorting the Words into Patterns

Place the word cards in the pocket chart or display them on the smart board as the children pronounce and chorally spell each. Give them a quick reminder of how they made these words:

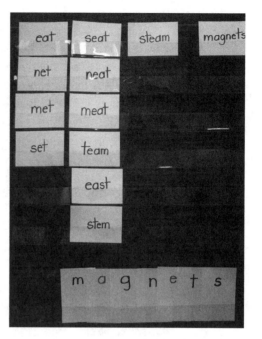

"First we spelled a three-letter word, **eat, e-a-t.**"

"We spelled another three-letter word, **net, n-e-t.**"

"We changed the first letter to spell **met, m-e-t.**"

"We changed the first letter again to spell **set, s-e-t.**"

"We added the **a** you don't hear to change set to **seat, s-e-a-t.**"

"We changed the first letter to spell **neat, n-e-a-t.**"

"We changed the first letter again to spell **meat, m-e-a-t.**"

"We used four letters to spell **east, e-a-s-t.**"

"We spelled one more four-letter word, **stem, s-t-e-m.**"

"We added the silent **a** to change stem to **steam, s-t-e-a-m.**"

"Finally, we spelled the secret word using all our letters, **magnets, m-a-g-n-e-t-s.**"

Next have the children sort the rhyming words. Take one of each set of rhyming words and place them in the pocket chart or in three columns on the smart board.

net   seat   team

Ask three children to find the other words that rhyme and place them under the ones you placed there.

eat	team	net
seat	steam	met
neat		set
meat		

Have the children chorally pronounce the sets of rhyming words.

✳ Part Three: Transfer

Tell the children to pretend it is writing time and they need to spell some words that rhyme with some of the words they made today. Have the children use whiteboards or half-sheets of paper to write the words. Say sentences that children might want to write that include a rhyming word. Work together to decide which words the target word rhymes with and to decide how to spell it.

> "Boys and girls, let's pretend it is writing time. Terry is writing about going fishing and he is trying to spell the word **stream**. Let's all say **stream** and stretch out the beginning letters. What three letters do you hear at the beginning of **stream**?"

Have the children stretch out **stream** and listen for the beginning letters. When they tell you that **stream** begins with **str**, write **str** on a card and have the children write **str** on their papers or whiteboards.

Take the card with **str** on it to the pocket chart or smart board and move it under each column of words as you lead the children to chorally pronounce the words and decide if **stream** rhymes with them:

> "Net, met, set, stream." Children should show you "thumbs down."
>
> "Seat, neat, meat, eat, stream." Children should again show you "thumbs down."
>
> "Team, steam, stream." Children should show you "thumbs up."

Finish writing **stream** on your card by adding **eam** to **str** and place **stream** under **team** and **steam**. Have the children write **eam** next to **str**.

> "Now let's pretend Carla is writing and telling you that she and her family went out for pizza last night as a special **treat**. Carla is trying to spell **treat**. Let's stretch out **treat** and listen for the two letters we hear at the beginning of **treat**."

Write **tr** on the card and have the students write **tr**.

Hold the card under each column of words as you lead the children to chorally pronounce the words and decide if **treat** rhymes with them:

> "Net, met, set, treat." Children should show you "thumbs down."
>
> "Seat, neat, meat, eat, treat." Children should show you "thumbs up."

Finish writing **treat** on your card by adding **eat** to **tr** and place **treat** under **seat**, **neat**, **meat**, and **eat**. Have the children write **eat** next to **tr** to complete their word.

Follow the same procedure to lead the children to use the rhyming word to spell **wet**.

We hope this sample lesson has helped you see how a Making Words lesson works and how Making Words lessons help children develop phonemic awareness, phonics, and spelling skills. Most important, we hope you see that in every lesson children will practice applying the patterns they are learning to reading and spelling new words.

Making Words Homework

Because students like to manipulate the letters and come up with their own words, a Making Words Take-Home Sheet is a popular activity. The sheet has the letters across the top and blocks for writing words. Students write capital letters on the back and then cut the letters apart. They manipulate the letters to make words and then write them in the blocks. When writing the letters at the top, write them in alphabetical order—vowels and then consonants—so as not to give away the secret word. Before children take the sheet home, have them turn it over and write the capital letters on the back. Children love being the "smart" ones who "know the secret word" and watching parents and other relatives try to figure it out.

Additional Making Words Lessons

Here are some lessons to get you started. More lessons can be found in the Making Words books referenced at the end of this book.

❋ One-Vowel Lessons

One-vowel lessons are a great way to start the year. Be sure to have your children stretch out the words and listen for all the letters before making them.

> ### tech tip
>
> Would you like to know our secret to planning a good Making Words lesson? Go to wordplays.com and click on Words in a Word. Enter the word you have chosen for the secret word, and like magic, all the words that can be made from the letters of the secret word appear. Choose the words that will give you lots of sorting possibilities. Don't tell your students about this site. It's our secret!

blast	1. Make: **al as at sat bat tab stab/bats last blast** (Words separated by / can be made with the same letters.) 2. Sort beginning letters Sort rhymes: **at, sat, bat; tab, stab; last, blast** 3. Transfer: **past, fat; cab, fast**
string	1. Make: **is in it sit rig ring/grin sing sting string** 2. Sort beginning letters Sort rhymes: **it, sit; in, grin; sing, sting, string** 3. Transfer: **swing, fit; spin, win**
trunks	1. Make: **us sun run rut nut nuts/stun rust trunk trunks** 2. Sort beginning letters Sort rhymes: **sun, run, stun; rut, nut** 3. Transfer: **stun, hut; cut, spun**
spent	1. Make: **pen ten/net pet pest/pets nets/nest/sent spent** 2. Sort beginning letters Sort rhymes: **pen, ten; net, pet; pest, nest; pets, nets; sent, spent** 3. Transfer: **test, tent; jets, west**
ponds	1. Make: **so no/on Don/nod pod pods nods pond ponds** 2. Sort beginning letters Sort rhymes: **so, no; on, Don; nod, pod; pods, nods** 3. Transfer: **rod, rods; Ron, Bo**

✱ Theme/Holiday Lessons

valentines	1. Make: **an van vet vent vest nest sent vine base valentines** 2. Sort v words: **van, vet, vent, vest, vine, valentines** Sort rhymes: **an, van; sent, vent; nest, vest** 3. Transfer: **bent, chest; spent, west**
elephants	1. Make: **pet pest past last east least sheep sleep asleep please elephants** 2. Sort related words: **sleep, asleep** Sort rhymes: **past, last; sleep, sheep, asleep; east, least** 3. Transfer: **beast, blast; steep, feast**
football	1. Make: **to too all fall ball tall tool fool foot football** 2. Sort related words: **foot, ball, football** Sort rhymes: **all, fall, ball, tall; tool, fool** 3. Transfer: **school, stall; mall, stool**
dancers	1. Make: **an can car cars/scar care dare dance scare scared dancers** 2. Sort related words: **scare, scared; dance, dancers** Sort rhymes: **an, can; car, scar, dare, care, scare** 3. Transfer: **plan, stare; scan, par**
teacher	1. Make: **at cat eat ear hear heat each reach teach/cheat there teacher/cheater** 2. Sort related words: **teach, teacher; cheat, cheater** Sort rhymes: **at, cat; eat, heat, cheat; reach, each, teach; ear, hear** 3. Transfer: **spear, peach; beach, treat**

figure 9.2 Steps in Planning a Making Words Lesson

1. Choose your secret word, a word that can be made with all the letters. In choosing this word, consider child interest, the curriculum tie-ins you can make, and the letter–sound patterns to which you can draw children's attention through the sorting at the end.

2. Make a list of other words that can be made from these letters. (wordplays. com will allow you to do this quickly!)

3. From all the words you could make, pick 12 to 15 words using these criteria:
   - Words that you can sort for the pattern you want to emphasize
   - Little words and big words to create a multilevel lesson. (Making little words helps your struggling students; making big words challenges your highest-achieving students.)
   - Words that can be made with the same letters in different places (barn/bran) so children are reminded that ordering letters is crucial when spelling words
   - A proper name or two to remind the children that we use capital letters
   - Words that most students have in their listening vocabularies

4. Write all the words on index cards or create cards for your smart board and order them from shortest to longest.

5. Once you have the two-letter words together, the three-letter words together, and so on, order them so you can emphasize letter patterns and how changing the position of the letters or changing/adding just one letter results in a different word.

6. Choose some letters or patterns to sort for.

7. Choose some transfer words—uncommon words you can read or spell based on the rhyming words.

8. Store the cards in an envelope. Write the words in order on the envelope, the patterns you will sort for, and the transfer words.

❋ Lessons with Children's Names

Alexander	1. Make: **Ed Ned Rex and land Alan Alex lead/deal real relax leader/dealer relaxed Alexander** 2. Sort related words: **lead, leader; deal, dealer; relax, relaxed** Sort rhymes: **and, land; deal, real** 3. Transfer: **squeal, stand; steal, grand**
Barney	1. Make: **ear Ray bay ban ran bran/barn yarn year near earn yearn Barney** 2. Sort beginning letters Sort rhymes: **Ray, bay; ban, ran, bran; barn, yarn; ear, year, near; earn, yearn** 3. Transfer: **learn, clear; stray; clan**
Clifford	1. Make: **of off for old oil coil foil Lori cold fold Ford cord Cliff Clifford** 2. Sort beginning letters Sort rhymes: **old, cold, fold; Ford, cord; oil, coil, foil** 3. Transfer: **told, boil; broil, scold**
Dorothy	1. Make: **hot rot Rod Roy try dry toy hood hoot root Troy door/odor Dorothy** 2. Sort beginning letters Sort rhymes: **hot, rot; Roy, Troy; hoot, root; try, dry** 3. Transfer: **boot, sky; shoot, shot**
Frederick	1. Make: **kid rid Eric Fred Rick Dick fire fired/fried cried/cider rider Derrick Frederick** 2. Sort related words: **fire, fired** Sort rhymes: **kid, rid; fried, cried; rider, cider** 3. Transfer: **tried, spider; slid, spied**
Brianna	1. Make: **in an Ian ran ban Nan Anna rain barn/bran brain/Brian Brianna** 2. Sort br words: **bran, brain, Brian, Brianna** Sort rhymes: **an, ran, ban, bran, Nan; rain, brain** 3. Transfer: **Spain, span; clan, chain**

For English Language Learners

When planning Making Words lessons, try not to include words your students do not have in their listening vocabularies. If you have English language learners in your classroom, you may not want to include some of the less common words in these lessons. Before the children make each word, have them pronounce the word. This is important for all children because they need to hear their voice making the sounds that form the word. This "pronouncing the word" step is crucial for your English language learners who might not be as quick to access the word from their oral vocabularies. As students are making each word, give them a sentence containing that word. If you have English language learners, you may want to give them a richer sentence that contains more information about the word being made.

Summary

Making Words is a favorite activity of many children. You can choose the secret word to go with a unit you are studying, a story you have read, a phonics skill you want to emphasize, or an interesting-to-your-children name. Each lesson includes 10 to 15 words that will make a multilevel lesson with short, easy words at the beginning and more complex words at the end. Be sure to include some rhyming words for the Sort and Transfer steps. If there are several words that begin with particular letter combinations you want to emphasize, include them so that you can sort them and notice the beginning letters and sounds. When related words occur, include them and sort for these to help children begin to realize how you decode and spell longer words by recognizing the root word and endings.

chapter 10

Rhyme-Based Decoding and Spelling Activities

Making Words lessons do focus on rhyme during the Sort and Transfer steps. They also focus children's attention on single letters as they process the letters sequentially to spell the words. In addition to Making Words, there are many other activities that help children focus on and learn rhyming patterns that help them decode and spell thousands of words. In this chapter, you will learn how to do Rounding Up the Rhymes, Using Words You Know, Reading/Writing Rhymes, and What Looks Right? activities to help your students use rhyming patterns to decode and spell words.

For English Language Learners

If your English language learners come from Spanish-speaking homes, you will need to be alert to some confusion these children may have, given the different sounds some letters represent in Spanish versus English. Spanish-speaking children often experience great difficulty with vowels because the vowel system in Spanish is much simpler than that in English. Spanish does not have the vowel sounds represented by the **a** in **man**, the **e** in **pen**, the **i** in **is**, the **u** in **up**, the **er** in **her**, the **ou** in **could**, the **a** in **along**, or the **au** in **caught**. Furthermore, some sounds that both English and Spanish share are spelled differently in Spanish. The **a** sound in **cake**, for example, is spelled with an **e** in Spanish. The **e** sound in **bee** is spelled with an **i**. The **i** sound in **like** is spelled with an **ai**. The **o** sound in **on** is spelled with an **a**. When teaching phonics to children whose first language is Spanish, it is probably best to start with the letters that have the same sounds. The consonant letters **p**, **b**, **t**, **k**, **m**, **n**, **f**, **s**, **w**, and **y** have almost the same sounds in both languages and provide a good place to begin. As children develop some confidence in their decoding ability, the sounds that do not exist in Spanish and the letters that have different sounds in Spanish and English can be introduced.

Learning the Most Common Rhyming Patterns

As children are learning the beginning sounds and how they can use these sounds to figure out words, they should also be learning some of the most common rhyming patterns. These rhyming patterns are sometimes called *rimes*, *spelling patterns*, *word families*, or *phonograms*. Thirty-seven spelling patterns allow children to read and spell over 500 words commonly used by young children (Wylie & Durrell, 1970). Because these 37 spelling patterns help students decode and spell so many words, you may want to display these someplace in your room. Put a key word and picture with these common rimes and encourage your students to use these rimes to decode and spell many other words.

Rounding Up the Rhymes

Rounding Up the Rhymes is an activity to follow up the reading of a book, story, or poem that contains lots of rhyming words. Here is an example using that timeless book, *I Wish That I Had Duck Feet* (Seuss, 1972). The first reading of anything should be for meaning and enjoyment. In Dr. Seuss's *I Wish That I Had Duck Feet*, a boy wishes he had duck feet so that he could splash and wouldn't have to wear shoes—until he realizes his mother wouldn't want him in the house like that. The boy goes on to wish for deer horns, a whale spout, a long tail, and a long nose—until he thinks of the complications each would cause and finally decides to "be just me." As with so many other Seuss books, this one has enormous appeal for children.

figure 10.1 Most Common Rhyming Patterns

Here are the 37 high-frequency spelling patterns (with possible key words):

ack (black)	ap (cap)	est (nest)	ing (king)	ot (hot)
ail (pail)	ash (trash)	ice (rice)	ink (pink)	uck (truck)
ain (train)	at (cat)	ide (bride)	ip (ship)	ug (bug)
ake (cake)	ate (skate)	ick (brick)	it (hit)	ump (jump)
ale (whale)	aw (claw)	ight (night)	ock (sock)	unk (skunk)
ame (game)	ay (tray)	ill (hill)	oke (Coke)	
an (pan)	eat (meat)	in (pin)	op (mop)	
ank (bank)	ell (shell)	ine (nine)	ore (store)	

After enjoying the book, point out to the children that in addition to a silly story and great illustrations, Dr. Seuss books are fun to read because of all the rhyming words. Tell the children that you are going to read several pages of *I Wish That I Had Duck Feet* again and they can help you "round up the rhymes." Read the first page and have students help you decide that the rhyming words are **why** and **dry**. Write these words on two index cards and place them one under the other in a pocket chart. Read the next page and have the children identify the rhyming words **me** and **see**. Continue to read until you have six or seven sets of rhyming words.

why	me	brown	play	floor	don't	instead
dry	see	town	way	door	won't	head

Now, reread these pages again. As you get to the rhyming words, point to them in the pocket chart and have the children say them.

Next, have the children help you identify the spelling pattern. Explain that the spelling pattern in a short word includes all the letters beginning with the first vowel and going to the end of the word. After naming the vowels—**a**, **e**, **i**, **o**, **u**, and sometimes **y**—pick up the first set of rhyming words **why** and **dry**, have the children tell you the spelling pattern in each, and underline the spelling pattern. In **why** and **dry**, the spelling pattern is only the **y**. Put **why** and **dry** back in the pocket chart and pick up the next set of rhymes—**me** and **see**. Have the children say them and hear once more that they do rhyme. Then underline the spelling patterns: **e** and **ee**. They do rhyme, but they have a different spelling pattern. Explain that you want to keep only the rhymes with the same spelling pattern, then toss **me** and **see** in the trash can.

Continue with the remaining pairs, deciding first that they rhyme and then underlining the spelling pattern to see if it is the same. There are now six pairs of rhyming words with the same spelling pattern in the pocket chart:

wh<u>y</u>	br<u>own</u>	pl<u>ay</u>	fl<u>oor</u>	d<u>on't</u>	inst<u>ead</u>
dr<u>y</u>	t<u>own</u>	w<u>ay</u>	d<u>oor</u>	w<u>on't</u>	h<u>ead</u>

The final part of this activity is the transfer step—how to use rhyming words to read and spell other words. Begin the transfer part of this activity by telling children something like:

"You know that when you are reading books and writing stories, there are words you have never seen before. You have to figure them out. One way people figure out how to read and spell new words is to see if they already know any rhyming words or words that have the same spelling pattern. I am going to write some words and you can see which words with the same spelling pattern will help you read them. Then we are going to spell some words by deciding which words they rhyme with."

Write two or three words that rhyme and have the same spelling pattern as the words in the pocket chart. Let the children underline the spelling pattern and put each word in the pocket chart under the other words with the same spelling pattern. Help the children use the rhyme to decode the words.

Finally, say two or three words that rhyme. The children decide what words they rhyme with and use the spelling pattern to spell them. Here are the *I Wish That I Had Duck Feet* words along with the new words read and spelled based on their rhymes and spelling patterns.

why	brown	play	floor	don't	instead
dry	town	way	door	won't	head
sky	clown	tray	poor		bread

Steps in Teaching a Rounding Up the Rhymes Lesson

1. Read a book with lots of rhyming words.

2. Choose several pages of the book to reread.

3. After reading each page, have students tell you which words rhyme. Write these words on cards and display them in your pocket chart or on your smart board.

4. Have children read the rhyming words with you and underline the spelling pattern.

5. Discard any rhymes that have different spelling patterns.

6. Show students some new words that rhyme and have the same pattern as the words displayed. Have students put these new words with the rhyming words from the book and use the rhyming words to decode the new words.

7. Say a few words that rhyme and have the same spelling pattern. Have students decide which words they rhyme with and use that rhyming pattern to spell the new words.

Using Words You Know

Another activity that helps children learn patterns and how patterns help you read and write is called Using Words You Know. To plan a Using Words You Know lesson, choose three or four words that your children can read and spell and that have many rhyming words spelled the same way. Although about half the word-wall words are irregular words such as **they**, **was**, and **have**, other words follow the expected pattern. Many teachers put a star on those word-wall words such as **big, play, not, make, ride,** and **thing** that help students spell lots of other words and use these in a Using Words You Know activity. You can also use words from your Key Word/Picture Rhyming Board.

Using Words I Know Lessons

Really Good Stuff publishes a book that contains 45 Using Words I Know lessons. You can also plan your own lessons using a good rhyming dictionary, many of which can be found at various online sites.

For the first lessons, choose three or four words that have very different vowel and ending sounds. When your students begin to understand how they can use rhyming words to decode and spell other words, teach lessons in which the words sound alike at the end but have different rhymes.

Here is an outline of how this first lesson might go.

1. Head three columns with three words all your students can read and spell. Have students divide a piece of paper into three columns and head them with the same three words.

   ride   day   hot

2. Tell students that you are going to show them some words and that they should write them under the key word with the same spelling pattern. Show them words that you have written on index cards. Let different students go to the board and write the words there as the rest of the students are writing them on their paper. Do not let the students pronounce the words until they are written on the board. Help the students pronounce the words by making them rhyme. Here are some words to use.

side	stay	gray	slide	shot
cot	stray	spot	wide	tray

3. Once all the words are written, have students verbalize the strategy they used to read the words:

   "If d-a-y is day, then s-t-r-a-y must be stray. If r-i-d-e is ride, s-l-i-d-e is slide."

4. Explain to students that thinking of rhyming words can also help them spell. This time you will not show your students the words. Rather, you will say words and your students will have to decide which key word they rhyme with and then spell them using the spelling pattern of the key word. First, say some words (but do not show them to your students). Next, have the children write these words under the appropriate key word. Finally, have a student write each word on the chart or board. Here are some words you might pronounce and have your students spell:

bride	rot	clay	hide	spray
trot	glide	slot	pay	tide

   Again, help them verbalize their strategy by leading them to explain,

   "If ride is spelled r-i-d-e, glide is probably spelled g-l-i-d-e. If hot is spelled h-o-t, slot is probably spelled s-l-o-t."

5. End this part of the lesson by helping students verbalize that in English, words that rhyme often have the same spelling pattern and that good readers and spellers don't sound out every letter but rather they try to think of a rhyming word and read or spell the word using the pattern in the rhyming word.

6. Explain to the students that using the rhyme to help read and spell words works with longer words too. Show students some longer words written on index cards and have them write them under the appropriate word. Once the word is written on the board or chart, have them pronounce the word, making the last syllable rhyme with the key word

teapot	birthday	delay
riptide	landslide	jackpot

7. Now say some longer words, but this time do not show them to your students. For each of these longer words, have students decide which key word the last syllable rhymes with and then have them spell the longer word using the spelling pattern of the key word. Give help with the spelling of the first part if needed.

inside	robot	relay
mascot	beside	subway

8. Again, end the lesson by helping students notice how helpful it is to think of a rhyming word they are sure how to spell when trying to read or spell a strange word.

In most classrooms, this lesson would take two days. One-syllable words would be read and spelled on the first day and two-syllable words on the second day.

After doing several more lessons in which the key words are very different (and, best, night; ten, make, sit; will, hop, thing), choose words that end with the same sound but have a different rhyme. It is the vowel part of the word that most students find difficult to decode and spell, and they need to make distinctions between words that sound alike at the end and words that rhyme. Here is a lesson in which the words have the same ending sound.

Key words:	**eat, kite, vote, date**
One-syllable words to read:	**quote, white, note, plate, wrote, skate, write**
One-syllable words to spell:	**treat, gate, bite, beat, cheat, state, seat**
Longer words to read:	**backseat, debate, excite, classmate, repeat, termite**
Longer words to spell:	**promote, defeat, remote, inflate, rebate, retreat, invite**

Some teachers worry that if they do lessons such as this one in which rhyming words can be spelled two different ways, students will choose rhymes with the wrong patterns. That is precisely why we never ask children to give us the rhyming words. We give them the rhyming words and only choose rhymes that are spelled alike. On another day, we could work with the other rhyming pattern. Here are words you could use in that lesson.

Key words: **street, night, coat, at**

One-syllable words to read: **goat, flight, tweet, throat, sight, flat, might**

One-syllable words to spell: **feet, splat, fight, boat, light, chat, tight**

Longer words to read: **lifeboat, parakeet, flashlight, acrobat, hardhat, steamboat**

Longer words to spell: **delight, tonight, inflate, stoplight, combat, raincoat**

It is very important for Using Words You Know lessons (and the transfer steps of Rounding Up the Rhymes and Making Words lessons) that you choose the rhyming words for the students to read and spell rather than ask them for rhyming words. In English, there are often two spelling patterns for the same rhyme. If you ask the children what rhymes with **cream** or **cool**, they may come up with words with the **e-e-m** pattern such as **seem** and words with the **u-l-e** pattern such as **rule**. The fact that there are two common patterns for many rhymes should not hinder the children while reading. When new readers see the word **drool**, their brains think of other **o-o-l** words such as **cool** and **school**. They make this new word **drool** rhyme with **cool** and **school** and then check out this pronunciation with the meaning of whatever they are reading. If they were going to write the word **drool** for the first time, they wouldn't know for sure which spelling pattern to use, and they might think of the rhyming word **rule** and use that pattern. Spelling requires both a sense of word patterns and a visual checking sense. When a person writes a word and then thinks, "That doesn't look right!"

Steps in Teaching a Using Words You Know Lesson

1. Display and talk about the words children know.

2. Make as many columns as needed on the board and on student papers. Head these with the known word and underline the spelling pattern.

3. Show one-syllable words written on index cards. Have the children write them under the word with the same pattern and use the rhyme to pronounce the words.

4. Say one-syllable words and have the students decide how to spell them by deciding which word they rhyme with.

5. Repeat the preceding procedure with longer words.

6. Help students explain how words they know help them read and spell lots of other words, including longer words.

and then writes it using a different pattern, he or she is demonstrating a developed visual checking sense. Once children become good at spelling by pattern—rather than putting down one letter for each sound—teachers can help them develop their visual checking sense through two activities: Reading/Writing Rhymes and What Looks Right? During Using Words You Know lessons, the teacher is trying to get the students to spell based on pattern, and "finesses" the problem of two patterns by choosing the words the teacher presents to them.

Reading/Writing Rhymes

Reading/Writing Rhymes is another activity that helps students learn to use patterns to decode and spell hundreds of words. In addition, all beginning letters (onsets) are reviewed every time you do a Reading/Writing Rhymes lesson. Once all the rhyming words are generated on a chart, students write rhymes using these words and then read each other's rhymes. Because writing and reading are connected to every lesson, students learn how to use these patterns as they actually read and write. Here is how to do Reading/Writing Rhymes lessons.

❋ The Onset Deck

You will need an onset deck containing cards for all the beginning sounds. The cards, 3 × 5 index cards, are laminated and have the single-letter consonants written in blue, the blends in red, and the digraphs and other two-letter combinations in green. On one side of each card, the first letter of the onset is a capital letter. The onset deck contains 50 beginning letter cards including:

Single consonants: **b c d f g h j k l m n p r s t v w y z**

Digraphs (two letters, one sound): **sh ch wh th**

Other two-letter, one-sound combinations: **kn qu**

Blends (beginning letters blended together, sometimes called clusters): **bl br cl cr dr fl fr gl gr pl pr sc scr sk sl sm sn sp spl spr st str sw tr tw**

To begin the lesson, distribute all the onset cards to your students. Depending on how many students you have, each student will have two or three cards.

❋ Making the Chart of Rhyming Words

Once all the onset cards are distributed, write the spelling pattern you are working with 10 to 12 times on a piece of chart paper or a smart board. As you write it each time, have the children help spell it and pronounce it ("a-d, ad").

```
                           ad

        ___ ad                    ___ ad

        ___ ad                    ___ ad

        ___ ad                    ___ ad

        ___ ad                    ___ ad

        ___ ad                    ___ ad

        ___ ad                    ___ ad
```

Next, invite all the children who think they have a card that makes a real word to line up next to the chart or overhead board. As each child shows his or her card, blend the onset and the rhyming pattern together to decide if the word is a real word. If the word is indeed a real word, use the word in a sentence and write that word on the chart. If the word is not a real word, explain why you cannot write it on the chart. (If a word is a real word and does rhyme but has a different spelling pattern, such as **plaid** to rhyme with **ad**, explain that it rhymes but has a different pattern and include it on the bottom of the chart with an asterisk next to it.) Write names with capital letters and, if a word can be a name and not a name, such as **tad** and **Tad**, write it both ways. When all the children who think they can spell words with their beginning letters and the spelling pattern have come up, call children up to make the words not yet there by saying something like,

> "I think the person with the **f** card could come up here and add **f** to **ad** to make a word we know."

Try to include all the words that any of the children would have in their listening vocabulary, but avoid obscure words. If the pattern you wrote to begin your chart gets made into complete words, add as many more as needed. Finally, if you can think of some good longer words that rhyme and have that spelling pattern, add them to the list. (Spell and write the whole word here since children do not have the extra letters needed to spell it.)

```
                           ad

        ___ b ad                  ___ Ch ad

        ___ s ad                  ___ Br ad

        ___ m ad                  ___ d ad

        ___ p ad                  ___ t ad

        ___ gl ad                 ___ T ad

        ___ h ad                  ___ f ad

        granddad                  undergrad

        *plaid   add
```

❋ Writing Sentences with the Rhyming Words

After the chart of rhyming words is written, have children come up with oral sentences that have at least two of the rhyming words.

"Dad was mad at Brad."

"Chad went to see his granddad."

"Tad felt sad."

"Brad had a bad day."

Next, give the students eight minutes to write rhymes using as many words as they can. Be sure they understand that the rhymes can be silly. Writing these silly rhymes is more fun if done with a friend, so give your students the choice of writing by themselves or partnering with a friend. When the eight minutes are up, let children volunteer to read their silly rhymes to the class.

You can use the Reading/Writing Rhymes format to teach any of the common vowel patterns. If you are using a basal reader or curriculum guide that specifies an order in which the vowel sounds will be taught and tested, let that guide determine the order in which you make charts for Reading/Writing Rhymes. Just as for Using Words You Know, a rhyming dictionary is a good source for the rhyming words. Select the patterns that have the most rhyming examples. (Some patterns will generate some "bad" words. You can either not distribute the beginning letters that would make the "bad" words or tell the children that there are some words that could be made that "we never use in school" so we won't include them. And you don't need anyone to tell you what they are!)

❋ Reading/Writing Rhymes with Two or More Spelling Patterns

Some rhymes have two common spelling patterns. If you are reading and come to the new word **blight**, you can easily use the **ight** pattern to decode it. If you come to the word **cite**, you can use the **ite** pattern to decode it. But if you need to spell a word that rhymes with **tight** and **bite**, which spelling pattern should you use? You can use Reading/Writing Rhymes lessons to sensitize children to the different spelling patterns some rhymes share.

❋ A Two-Pattern Lesson

When spelling a word, there is no way to know which one is the correct spelling unless you recognize it as a word you know after writing it. (This is why people often write a word and think, "That doesn't look right," and then try writing it with the other pattern to see if that looks right.) When you are working rhymes that have two common spelling patterns, write both patterns on the same chart.

Students come to the front of the room and say the word their beginning letters will make, and you write it with the correct pattern. In many cases, there are two homophones, words that are spelled differently and have different meanings but the same pronunciation. Write both of these and talk about what each one means. (Artistic teachers sometimes draw a little picture next to one of these so that students can tell them apart.)

ail/ale	
_____ j ail	_____ wh ale
_____ n ail	_____ sc ale
_____ m ail	_____ m ale
_____ s ail	_____ s ale
_____ f ail	_____ t ale
_____ sn ail	_____ p ale
_____ t ail	_____ Y ale
_____ p ail	_____ s ale
_____ s ail	_____ st ale
_____ G ail	_____ g ale
_____ tr ail	_____
blackmail fingernail monorail	

Just as in the single-pattern lessons, have children come up with a couple of oral sentences using at least two of the words.

"I saw a snail trail."

"Tell me a tale about a whale with a tail."

"You can sail to see a whale."

"Gail got blown away by a gale."

"Gail paints her fingernails green."

"Gail found a snail on the trail."

After warming up with a few oral sentences, give your students eight minutes to write as many silly sentences using the words as they can. Each sentence must use at least two of the rhyming words. At the end of eight minutes, circle your students and let volunteers read some of their silly sentences.

❋ Vowel Patterns for Reading/Writing Rhymes Lessons

All the common vowel patterns can be taught through Reading/Writing Rhymes. Here are the vowel patterns that are common enough to merit teaching and that make good Reading/Writing Rhymes lessons:

Rhymes with only one common spelling pattern

ack	ad	am	an	ap	ash	at	ake	ar	ark	art
ay	aw	ank	ang							
ell	en	et								
ick	ip	ill	it	in	ice	ine	ing	ink		
op	ot	ock	ob	orn	ook	oom	oy	oil	out	
ug	ut	ump	unch							

Rhymes with two or more common patterns

ail/ale	ain/ane	ait/ate	ace/ase	and/anned
ants/ance	aste/aced	ax/acks	ays/aze	
ed/ead	est/essed	ead/eed	eak/eek	eal/eel
eap/eep	eat/eet			
ide/ied	ite/ight	ix/icks		
oak/oke	oat/ote	old/olled	oot/ute	
e/ea/ee	o/oe/ow	ade/aid/ayed	oan/one/own	
oal/ole/oll	ool/ule/uel	un/on/one		
are/air/ear	ear/eer/ere	ert/irt/urt	urn/ern/earn	ore/oar/oor/our
all/awl/aul	ew/ue/oo	y/igh/ie	ary/airy/erry/arry	ees/eas/ease/eeze

What Looks Right?

What Looks Right? is an activity by which children learn that good spelling requires visual memory and how to use their visual memory for words along with a dictionary to determine the correct spelling of a word. In English, words that have the same spelling pattern usually rhyme. If you are reading and you come to the unknown words **plight** and **trite**, you can easily figure out their pronunciation by accessing the pronunciation associated with other **ight** or **ite** words you can read and spell. The fact that there are two common spelling patterns with the same pronunciation is not a problem when you are trying to read a word, but it is a problem when you are trying to spell it. If you were writing and trying to spell **trite** or **plight**, you could just as easily spell them **t-r-i-g-h-t** and **p-l-i-t-e**. The only way to know which is the correct spelling is to write it one way and see if it "looks right" or check your probable spelling in a dictionary. What Looks Right? is an activity to help children learn how to use these two important self-monitoring spelling strategies.

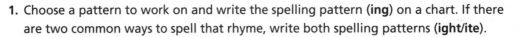

Steps in Teaching a Reading/Writing Rhymes Lesson

1. Choose a pattern to work on and write the spelling pattern (**ing**) on a chart. If there are two common ways to spell that rhyme, write both spelling patterns (**ight/ite**).

2. Distribute all 50 cards in the onset deck to your students.

3. Have students who think they have a beginning letter card that will make a real word with the rhyming pattern line up next to the chart.

4. Have each child put his or her beginning letter card next to the pattern and have the class blend the letters to form the word. Put the word quickly into a sentence to make sure students know you only want to include real words. If you are working with two rhyming spelling patterns, have students hold their word between the two patterns written on the chart.

5. If the word is a real word, add the letters to the spelling pattern to spell the word. If you are working with two patterns, write it next to the one that spells the word. If there are two homophones (**sail**; **sale**) that can be spelled, write both and explain which word has which meaning. If the word is a name, write it with a capital letter.

6. Write any words that are not spelled with the pattern with an * on the bottom of the chart (***plaid**).

7. Add any two-syllable words that you think your students would have meanings for.

8. Have all your students read the rhyming words. Let a few students volunteer oral sentences using at least two of the rhymes.

9. Give students eight minutes to write as many sentences as they can. Each sentence must use at least two of the rhyming words. Let children work together to create these silly sentences if they choose to.

10. When the eight-minute time limit is up, gather your students and let volunteers share some of their sentences.

Here is a sample lesson for the **oat–ote** pattern. Using your "old-fashioned" board or your smart board, create two columns and head each with an **oat–ote** word most of your students can both read and spell. Have the children set up two columns on their paper to match your model:

coat   vote

Have your students pronounce and spell the words and lead them to realize that the words rhyme but have a different spelling pattern. Tell them that there are many words that rhyme with **coat** and **vote** and that they can't tell just by saying the words which spelling patterns some words will have. Next say a word that rhymes with **coat** and **vote**, such as **goat**, and write it both ways, saying, "If the word is spelled like **coat**, it will be **g-o-a-t**. If it is spelled like **vote**, it will be **g-o-t-e**." Write these two possible spellings under the appropriate word.

Tell the children to decide which one "looks right" to them and to write only the one they think is correct. As soon as they decide which one looks right and write it in the correct column, have them use the dictionary to see if that spelling can be found. If they cannot find the one that looked right, then have them look up the other possible spelling. Cross out the spelling you wrote that is not correct and continue with some more examples. For each word, again model both possible spellings: "If it is spelled like **coat**, it will be **g-o-a-t**, but if it is spelled like **vote**, it will be **g-o-t-e**." Write the word both ways, and have your students write it the way it looks right and then look in the dictionary to see if the word is spelled the way they thought.

Here is what your columns of words would look like after several examples:

coat	vote
goat	~~gote~~
boat	~~bote~~
float	~~flote~~
~~noat~~	note
~~quoat~~	quote
throat	~~throte~~
bloat	~~blote~~

To make your lesson more challenging, include some longer words in which the last syllable rhymes with **coat** and **vote**. Proceed just as before to write the word both ways, have students choose the one that looks right, write that word, and look for it in the dictionary. For the **coat–vote** lesson, here are three longer words you might use:

~~promoat~~	promote
~~devoat~~	devote
~~remoat~~	remote

Here is a lesson for the **ait–ate** pattern. Notice that several of these pairs are both real words. Children should find both **gate/gait** and **plate/plait**. This is an excellent time to talk about homophones and how the dictionary can help in deciding which word to use. Also notice the words that follow the double asterisks. When encountering common words such as **great**, **eight**, **weight**, and **straight** that don't follow the pattern, point these out to your students, explaining that most—but not all—words that rhyme with **date** and **wait** are spelled **a-t-e** or **a-i-t**.

What Looks Right? is a versatile strategy and can be used to help children become better spellers of longer words. Here are two lessons for the **tion/sion** and **le/el/al** patterns.

Working with all these rhyming words also offers a wonderful opportunity to have your children write some poetry. Select a poem or two your children will like and read it to them several times. Then have them decide which words rhyme and whether the rhyming words have the same spelling patterns. Using these poems as models and the rhyming words you have collected as part of your spelling pattern lessons, students can write some interesting rhyming poetry.

<u>date</u>	<u>wait</u>
~~bate~~	bait
fate	~~fait~~
hate	~~hait~~
skate	~~skait~~
gate	gait
plate	plait
state	~~stait~~
rebate	~~rebait~~
debate	~~debait~~
donate	~~donait~~
hibernate	~~hibernait~~

**straight   eight   weight   great

<u>motion</u>	<u>pension</u>
action	~~acsion~~
station	~~stasion~~
~~mantion~~	mansion
mention	~~mension~~
lotion	~~losion~~
nation	~~nasion~~
~~tention~~	tension
attention	~~attension~~
~~extention~~	extension
~~divition~~	division
multiplication	~~multiplicasion~~

~~television~~   television

vacation   ~~vacasion~~

~~collition~~   collision

people	model	animal
~~travle~~	travel	~~traval~~
little	~~littel~~	~~littal~~
~~channle~~	channel	~~channal~~
~~locle~~	~~locel~~	local
~~equle~~	~~equel~~	equal
~~loyle~~	~~loyel~~	loyal
settle	~~settel~~	~~settal~~
poodle	~~poodel~~	~~poodal~~
bubble	~~bubbel~~	~~bubbal~~
~~tunnle~~	tunnel	~~tunnal~~
~~normle~~	~~normel~~	normal
~~generle~~	~~generel~~	general
possible	~~possibel~~	~~possibal~~
invisible	~~invisibel~~	~~invisibal~~
principle	~~principel~~	~~principal~~

Steps in Teaching a What Looks Right? Lesson

1. Choose a rhyme that has at least two common patterns. Head two columns on a chart with two words you think your students can spell and that show the two patterns (**eat/street**). Have your students head two columns on their papers with the same words.

2. Remind students that some rhyming words have two common spelling patterns. Tell them that if they write the word the way they think it is spelled and it doesn't look right, they should try the other pattern. If they want to be sure they have it spelled correctly, they can find the word in the dictionary.

3. Write a word that can only be spelled one way both ways in each column. For the first words, choose words you think most of your students can spell (**cheat**, **sweet**, **seat**).

4. Have students decide which spelling they think is correct and write only that spelling on their papers.

5. When they have made their choice, have students look in the dictionary to check their choices.

6. Cross out the misspellings on your chart and have students change their spelling if it was not correct.

7. Continue to write pairs of words. Include some homophones if there are any (**beat/beet**, **meat/meet**, **feat/feet**).

8. For each pair of spellings, have students choose the one they think looks right, write that spelling on their paper, and use dictionaries to confirm the spelling. For homophones, have students read the dictionary definition to decide which word has which meaning.

For English Language Learners

All four lesson formats in this chapter can be enhanced for English language learners by making sure they connect meaning to the words. In Rounding Up the Rhymes, the rhyming words come from a book and you use the pictures in that book to develop meaning for any words your English language learners might not have in their oral vocabularies. For transfer words, choose words you are sure they know or give them a rich sentence explanation for the transfer word before asking them to read it or spell it. Use pictures along with your key words in Using Words You Know lessons and be sure to put words they are reading and spelling in a rich context before they attempt to read or spell them. In Reading/Writing Rhymes, you and your students decide that a word is a real word by putting it in a sentence that connects meaning. Use more elaborated sentences to help your English language learners make connections for each word. Our English spelling system is complex and is particularly hard for children whose first language is not English. Doing What Looks Right? lessons will help your English language learners develop a visual checking sense and teach them how to use a dictionary to help spell words.

Summary

All the activities in this chapter help focus children's attention on rhyming patterns and how these rhyming patterns help them decode and spell words. As children engage in the activities, they are constantly reviewing all the beginning letters as they combine these with the rimes to figure out words. All four lesson formats have a lot of scope. There are many different skills children can learn from each lesson. All the activities emphasize transfer. Most teachers know that it is much easier to teach children phonics than it is to actually have them use phonics when they need to figure out how to decode a new word while reading or spell a new word while writing.

While rounding up the rhymes, some children are still developing their phonemic awareness as they decide which words rhyme and learn that rhyming words usually—but not always—have the same spelling pattern. As they use the words rounded up to read and spell new words, children who need it are getting practice with beginning letter substitution. Children who already have well-developed phonemic awareness and beginning letter knowledge are practicing the important strategy of using known words to decode and spell unknown rhyming words. Rounding Up the Rhymes facilitates transfer because the rhymes are from books and children are thus more apt to recall this strategy when reading other books. At the end of the Rounding Up the Rhymes lesson, students decode and spell some new words using the rhyming words they rounded up from the book.

Using Words You Know lessons provide children who still need it with lots of practice with rhyming words and with the idea that spelling pattern and rhyme are connected. Depending on what they already know, some children realize how words they know can help them decode, whereas other children realize how these words help them spell. If you want to make the lesson a bit more multilevel at the upper end, include a few longer words that rhyme and help students see how their known words can help them spell the rhyming part of longer words. Using Words You Know lessons promote transfer to reading and writing because they show children explicitly how all the words they know can help them decode and spell other, less familiar words.

Reading/Writing Rhymes and What Looks Right? lessons both teach a wide range of phonics skills. All beginning letters, including the common single consonants, digraphs, and blends, are reviewed each time the teacher distributes the onset cards for Reading/Writing Rhymes. Phonemic awareness is developed as children say all the rhyming words and blend the vowel pattern with the beginning letters. Children whose word awareness is more sophisticated learn that there are often two spellings for the long vowel patterns and develop their visual checking sense as they see the rhyming words with the different patterns. They also learn the correct spelling for many of the common homophones. The addition of some longer rhyming words helps them learn how to decode and spell longer words. In What Looks Right? lessons, children learn to use the dictionary to check a possible spelling. They also learn how the dictionary can help in deciding which way to spell a word when there are two words that sound the same but have different spellings and meanings.

Transfer to reading and writing is a part of every Reading/Writing Rhymes and What Looks Right? lesson. In Reading/Writing Rhymes, children blend onsets and rimes together to decode words. They then immediately transfer those rhyming words into their writing by composing some silly sentences. When children decide which of two possible spellings "looks right" and confirm their choice by consulting the dictionary, they are learning how to decide if a word they write looks right and how to use a dictionary if they need to confirm spelling or to choose the correct homophone. All four lesson formats described in this chapter teach your students phonics they can actually put immediately into use as they go about all the reading and writing they do during the school day.

chapter 11

Decoding and Spelling Big Words

Pick up any newspaper or magazine and read the first few sentences of any article and notice the big words—words that have eight or more letters:

> The SAT—*Scholastic Aptitude* Test—*denounced* as biased and *ineffective* by many *consumers*—is still the *gatekeeper* in most *American* schools. College *admissions officers* often *downplay* the *significance* of the exam in the *application* process but then brag about their school's scores in *recruitment brochures*.
>
> *Historically*, as a strike *deadline approaches*, the labor *negotiators go underground* and stop talking to the media. Fear of having the talks *derailed* by leaks causes both sides to stop talking and keep *bargaining*.

The first thing that strikes you in looking at these big words is that they are the "meaning-carrying" words. Without them, you wouldn't know very much. The second thing you should notice is that these words are relatively low-frequency words. You could read many articles and pages in books before once again encountering **recruitment**, **historically**, and **derailed**.

Starting at about the fourth-grade level, most of what we read contains a high percentage of big, relatively unfamiliar, low-frequency words. Because these big words contain most of the meaning, we cannot comprehend what we read unless we can pronounce and access meaning for these words. All good readers are able to quickly pronounce and associate meaning with words they have rarely ever read before. How does this happen? How did you pronounce and make meaning for words such as **admissions**, **derailed**, and **underground** the first time you encountered them in your reading?

Linguists, who study how language works, tell us that in English, morphemes are the keys to unlocking the pronunciation, spelling, and meaning for big words. *Morphemes* are roots, prefixes, and suffixes that combine in a variety of ways to make up big words. The word **admission** is simply the word **admit**—with the spelling changes that always occur when **sion** is added to words ending in **t**. The first time you saw **admissions**, your brain probably accessed similar words such as **permission**, **omission**, and **emission**. Using these other similar words, you quickly pronounced **admission**. Since you were probably aware that when you **permit** something, you give your **permission**, when you **omit** something, you have an **omission**, and the fumes that your car **emits** are called **emissions**, you probably also recognized the relationship between the word you had read many times—**admit**—and this new word **admissions**. Similarly, pronouncing and making meaning for **derailed** was not difficult if your brain thought of similar words such as **deported** and **declassified**. **Underground** is a compound word—its pronunciation and meaning are obvious by thinking of the pronunciation and meaning of the two root words, **under** and **ground**.

Morphemes—roots, prefixes, and suffixes—are the keys to unlocking the pronunciation, spelling, and meaning for big words. When you see a big new word you have never encountered before in your reading, your brain thinks of similar big words and uses these big words and the understanding it has about how these big words work to quickly pronounce and access meaning for the new big word. But what if your brain doesn't have very many big words stored there? What if you have some big words but you have never realized how they were related to your smaller words? Children who lack big words that they can quickly access, and associate meaning for, are helpless from fourth grade up when they encounter big words.

Good readers decode and spell new words by comparing them to words they can already read and spell. Decoding and spelling big words—multisyllabic words with anywhere from 7 to 20 letters—is also dependent on patterns from similar words. Morphemes are meaningful parts of words. The word **internationalize** has four morphemes:

> **inter**—a prefix meaning "between"
>
> **nation**—a root word
>
> **al**—a suffix that commonly turns a noun into an adjective
>
> **ize**—a suffix that commonly turns nouns and adjectives into verbs

Children need to realize that many of the big words they encounter while reading are just words they already know with parts added to the beginning (prefixes) and parts added to the end (suffixes). It is important to note here that it is not the terminology—the jargon—that children need to learn. When you first saw the word **modernize**, your brain didn't say,

> "I see the root word **modern** with the prefix **ize**."

Rather, your brain recognized the familiar parts, put the parts together, and pronounced the word. You may also have used other **ize** known words such as **legalize** and **unionize** to build meaning for **modernize**. Activities in this chapter will help your students learn how roots, prefixes, and suffixes help them decode, spell, and build meaning for thousands of big words. The focus of this chapter, as of all the other chapters in *Phonics They Use*, is on how to help students use these morphemic parts, not just recognize them.

Modeling: How to Figure Out a Big Word

When you model, you show someone how to do something. In real life, people use modeling constantly to teach skills. For example, you would not think of explaining how to ride a bike. Rather, you demonstrate and talk about what you are doing as the learner watches what you do and listens to your explanation. Vocabulary introduction is a good place to model for students how you figure out the pronunciation of a word. The word should be shown in a sentence context so that students are reminded that words must have the right letters in the right places and make sense. Following is an example of how you might model for students one way to decode **entertainment**:

> "I am going to write a sentence on the board that has a big word in it. I will 'think aloud' how I might figure out this one. After I show you how I decode this one, I will let several of you model how you would decode other words."

Write on the board: **Different people like different kinds of entertainment**.

> "Now I am going to read up to the big word and tell you how I might figure it out. If you figure out the word before I do, please don't say it and ruin my performance!"

Read the sentence and stop when you get to **entertainment**.

> "This is a long word, but I can probably figure it out if I think of some other words I know."

Cover all but **enter**.

> "The first chunk is a word I know—**enter**. The second chunk is like **container** and **maintain**."

Write **container** and **maintain** on the board, underlining the **tain**.

> "Finally, I know the last chunk is like **argument** and **moment**."

Write **argument** and **moment** on the board, underlining the **ment**.

> "Now I will put the chunks together: **enter-tain-ment**. Yes, that's a word I know, and it makes sense in the sentence because my brother and I certainly are different, and we don't like the same TV shows or movies or anything."

Since English is not a language in which letters or chunks have only one sound, you might also write the word **mountain** on the board, underlining the **tain** and pointing out to students that the letters **t-a-i-n** also commonly have the sound you hear at the end of **mountain**. Have students try pronouncing **entertainment** with the different sounds for the **tain** chunk. Point out that it sounds right and makes a word you know when you use the sound of **tain** you know from **maintain** and **container**. Remind students that if they use the probable sound of letters together with the sense of what they are reading, they can figure out many more words than if they just pay attention to the letter sounds, ignoring what makes sense, or if they just guess something that makes sense, ignoring the letter sounds.

For **entertainment**, the chunks helped only with the pronunciation of the word. Sometimes the word has morphemes—prefixes, suffixes, or root words—that also help with the meaning of the word. The next example shows what a teacher might do and say to introduce the word **international**.

Write on the board: **The thinning of the ozone layer is an international problem**.

"Today, we are going to look at a big word that is really just a little word with a prefix added to the beginning and a suffix added to the end."

Underline **nation**.

"Who can tell me this word? Yes, that's the word **nation**, and we know **nation** is another word for **country**. Now let's look at the prefix that comes before **nation**."

Underline **inter**.

"This prefix is **inter**. You probably know **inter** from words like **interrupt** and **internal**. Now let's look at what follows **inter** and **nation**."

Underline **al**.

"You know **al** from many words, such as **unusual** and **critical**."

Write **unusual** and **critical** and underline the **al**.

"Listen as I pronounce this part of the word."

Underline and pronounce **national**.

"Notice how the pronunciation of **nation** changes when we put **a-l** on it. Now let's put all the parts together and pronounce the word **inter-nation-al**. Let's read the sentence and make sure **international** makes sense."

Have one of your students read the sentence; then confirm that ozone thinning is indeed a problem for many nations to solve.

"You can figure out the pronunciation of many big words if you look for common prefixes, such as **inter**, common root words, such as **nation**, and common suffixes, such as **al**.

"In addition to helping you figure out the pronunciation of a word, prefixes and suffixes sometimes help you know what the word means or where in a sentence you can use the word. The word **nation** names a thing. When we describe a nation, we add the suffix **al** and have **national**. The prefix **inter** often means 'between or among.' Something that is **international** is between many nations. The Olympics are the best example of an **international** sports event."

This sample lesson for introducing the word **international** demonstrates how you can help your students see and use morphemes to decode polysyllabic words. As in the sample lesson for **entertainment**, you point out words students might know that have the same chunks—in this case, morphemes.

If you teach elementary students, you probably introduce numerous new words as you teach the different subject areas. Modeling how to decode a big word can happen when you are teaching reading as well as when you are teaching the content areas of math, science, and social studies.

Word Detectives

There are two questions I would like to put into the mouths of every teacher from fourth grade through high school. These two questions are:

"Do I know any other words that look and sound like this word?"

"Are any of these look-alike/sound-alike words related to each other?"

The answer to the first question should help students with pronouncing and spelling the word. The answer to the second question should help students discover what, if any, meaning relationships exist between this new word and others in their meaning vocabulary stores. This guideline and these two simple questions could be used by any teacher of any subject area. Imagine that students in a mathematics class encounter the following new word:

equation

The teacher demonstrates and gives examples of equations and helps build meaning for the concept. Finally, the teacher asks the students to pronounce

equation to determine if they know any other words that look and sound like **equation**. Students think of:

addition   multiplication   nation   vacation

equal   equator

The teacher lists the words, underlining the parts that look the same. Students pronounce the words, emphasizing the part that is pronounced the same. The teacher then points out to the students that thinking of a word that looks and sounds the same as a new word will help them quickly remember how to pronounce the new word and will also help them spell the new word.

Next, the teacher explains that words, like people, sometimes look and sound alike but are not related. If this is the first time this analogy is used, the teacher will want to spend some time talking with the students about people with red hair, green eyes, and so on who have some parts that look alike but who are not related and about others who are.

"Not all people who look alike are related, but some are. This is how words work too. Words are related if there is something about their meaning that is the same. After we find look-alike, sound-alike words that will help us spell and pronounce new words, we try to think of any ways these words might be in the same meaning family."

With help from the teacher, the students discover that **equal**, **equator**, and **equation** are related because the meaning of **equal** is in all three. An equation has to have equal quantities on both sides of the equal signs. The equator is an imaginary line that divides the earth into two equal halves.

Imagine that the students who were introduced to equations on Monday during math and were asked to think of look-alike, sound-alike words and consider if any of these words might be "kinfolks" had a science lesson on Tuesday in which they did some experiments using **thermometers** and **barometers**. At the close of the lesson, the teacher pointed to these words and helped the students notice that the **meters** chunk was pronounced and spelled the same; the teacher next asked the students if they thought these words were just look-alikes or were related to one another. The students concluded that both were used to measure things and that the **meters** chunk must be related to measuring, like in **kilometers**. When asked to think of look-alike, sound-alike words for the first chunk, students thought of **baron** for **barometers** but decided these two words were probably not related. For **thermometer**, they thought of **thermal** and **thermostat** and decided that all these words had to do with heat or temperature and were related.

Now imagine that this lucky class of students had a social studies lesson on Wednesday during which the teacher pointed out the new word **international** and asked the two critical questions, a music lesson on Thursday in which they were preparing for a trip to the **symphony** and the teacher asked the two critical questions, and a tennis lesson on Friday in which they practiced their **forehand** and **backhand** strokes and the teacher asked the two critical questions—this time about these crucial tennis words.

Throughout their school day, your students encounter many new words. Because English is such a morphologically related language, most new words can be connected to other words by their spelling and pronunciation, and many new words have meaning-related words already known to the student. Some clever, word-sensitive children become word detectives on their own. They notice the patterns and use these to learn and retrieve words. Others, however, try to learn to pronounce, spell, and associate meaning with each of these words as separate, distinct entities. This is a difficult task that becomes almost impossible as students move through the grades and the number of new words increases each year. Readers do not need to be taught every possible pattern because the brain is programmed to look for patterns. Some students, however, do not know what the important patterns in words are and that these patterns can help them with pronouncing, spelling, and meanings for words. Asking the two critical questions for key vocabulary introduced in any content area would add only a few minutes to the introduction of key content vocabulary and would turn many students into word detectives.

Teaching Common Prefixes and Suffixes

Four prefixes, **un**, **re**, **in** (and **im**, **ir**, **il** meaning "not"), and **dis**, account for 58 percent of all prefixed words. Add 16 more prefixes—**en/em**, **non**, **in/im** (meaning "in"), **over**, **mis**, **sub**, **pre**, **inter**, **fore**, **de**, **trans**, **super**, **semi**, **anti**, **mid**, and **under**—and you can account for 97 percent of all prefixed words (White, Sowell, & Yanagihara, 1989). Children who can read, spell, and attach meaning to these 20 prefixes have a jump-start on decoding, spelling, and understanding a huge number of multisyllabic words.

For suffixes, **s/es**, **ed**, and **ing** account for 67 percent of the suffixed words. Add **ly**, **er/or**, **ion/tion**, **ible/able**, **al**, **y**, **ness**, **ity**, and **ment** and you account for 87 percent of the words. The remaining suffixes with some utility are **er/est** (comparative), **ic**, **ous**, **en**, **ive**, **ful**, and **less** (White, Sowell, & Yanagihara, 1989). Again, learning to read, spell, and understand how meaning is affected for a relatively small number of suffixes gives readers a huge advantage with multisyllabic words.

✽ A Prefix Lesson Framework

The modeling during vocabulary introduction and the Word Detectives activities described earlier take advantage of whatever words occur in the course of content-area instruction. Most students can also profit from some explicit instruction with the most common prefixes. Teach all the prefixes using the same

For English Language Learners

Prefixes, suffixes, and roots are the building blocks of big words. When students are decoding or spelling a big word, they need to recognize that most big words are smaller words with meaningful parts added to the beginning and end. Because prefixes and suffixes add meaning to words, it is especially important that English language learners become very quick and fluent at seeing and using these word part patterns. As children progress through the upper grades of school, reading is the major way they add new words to their meaning vocabularies. For polysyllabic words, readers figure out word meanings by combining the information they get from context with the morphemic information they get from their knowledge of prefixes, suffixes, and roots. Learning how prefixes, suffixes, and roots combine to create new words gives your English language learners the necessary tools so they can increase their English vocabularies as they read.

lesson format. Begin with words containing the prefixes students already can read and spell and have meaning for. Use these known words to establish the pattern, and then move to less familiar words. Include examples of words in which the prefix has a discernible meaning and others in which the prefix helps with pronunciation and spelling but not with meaning. Here is an example lesson that could be used to teach the prefix **re**.

Write nine words that begin with **re** on index cards. Include three words in which **re** means "back," three words in which **re** means "again," and three words in which **re** is just the first syllable and has no apparent meaning. Use words for which your students are apt to have meanings. Place these words randomly along the chalk ledge, invite students to pronounce them, and then ask what "chunk" the words all have in common. When students notice that they all begin with r-e, arrange the words in three columns on the board and tell the students to think about why you have put together **rebound**, **return**, and **replace** in one column; **redo**, **replay**, and **rework** in the second column; and **record**, **refuse**, and **reveal** in the third column. If students need help, tell them that for one column of **re** words, you can put the word **again** in place of the **re** and still have the meaning of the word. Explain that for another column, you can put the word **back** in place of **re**. Once students have figured out in which column the **re** means "back" and in which the **re** means "again," label these columns **back** and **again**. Help students see that when you refuse something, you don't fuse it back or fuse it again. Do the same with **record** and **reveal**.

Back	Again	
rebound	redo	record
return	replay	refuse
replace	rework	reveal

Have students set up their own papers in three columns, the first two headed by **back** and **again** and the last not headed, and have them write the words written on the board. Then say some other **re** words and have students write them in the column they think they belong in. As each word is written, ask someone where he or she wrote it and how he or she spelled it. Write it in the appropriate column on the board. Conclude the activity by having all the **re** words read and replacing the **re** with **back** or **again** when appropriate. Help students summarize that sometimes **re** means "back," sometimes **re** means "again," and sometimes **re** is just the first chunk of the word. Some additional words you might use are:

reusable	retire	retreat	rewind
recall	respond	remote	responsible
recoil	rewrite	refund	relief

When this activity is completed, leave the chart with these **re** words displayed and ask students to hunt for **re** words in their reading for the next several days. When they find a word that begins with **re**, they should decide which category it fits and add it to the chart. At the end of several days, review the chart and help students summarize what they learned about **re** as a pronunciation, spelling, and sometimes meaning chunk in words.

As you do other lessons with prefixes, your message to students should be the same. Prefixes are chunks at the front of words that have predictable pronunciations and spellings. Look for them and depend on them to help you spell and pronounce new words. Sometimes, they also give you meaning clues. If you are unsure about the meaning of a word, see if a common meaning for the prefix can help. Check the meaning you figure out to make sure it makes sense in the context in which you are reading. The Common Prefixes chart lists the most common prefixes, their common meanings, and examples of words in which the prefix helps with meaning, along with examples of words in which the prefix is only a help for spelling and pronouncing the word.

❋ The "Unpeelable" Prefixes

In addition to the prefixes, which can be understood by taking them off the root word and then combining the meanings, there are other common prefixes that do not leave recognizable words when they are "peeled off." The prefixes **con/com, ex, em,** and **per** do add meanings to words, but one would have to have a rather advanced understanding of Latin and Greek roots to see the meaning relationships. It is probably best just to help students see how these are predictable spelling and pronunciation chunks rather than try to show students how to analyze these words for meaning clues.

figure 11.1 Common Prefixes, Meanings, and Examples

Prefix	Meaning	Meaning Chunk	Spelling/ Pronunciation Chunk
re	back	replacement	refrigerator
re	again	rearrange	reward
un	opposite	unfriendly	uncle
in (im, ir, il)	opposite	independent	incident
		impossible	imagine
		irresponsible	irritate
		illegal	illustrate
in (im)	in	invasion	instant
		impression	immense
dis	opposite	dishonest	distress
non	opposite	nonliving	—
en	in	encourage	entire
mis	bad, wrong	misunderstand	miscellaneous
pre	before	prehistoric	present
inter	between	international	interesting
de	opposite/take away	deodorize	delight
sub	under	submarine	subsist
fore	before/in front of	forehead	—
trans	across	transportation	—
super	really big	supermarkets	superintendent
semi	half	semifinal	seminar
mid	middle	midnight	midget
over	too much	overpower	—
under	below	underweight	understand
anti	against	antifreeze	—

figure 11.2 "Unpeelable" Prefixes and Examples

Unpeelable Prefix	Examples
com/con	communities, competition, communism
	composer, computer, compassion
	continuous, construction, conclusion
	conversation, constitution, concrete
em	employee, embassy, embryo
ex	expensive, excitement, explain
per	performance, permanent, personality

✳ A Suffix Lesson Framework

Suffixes, like prefixes, are predictable indicators of pronunciation and sometimes signal a meaning relationship. The meaning signaled by suffixes, however, is not usually a meaning change, but rather a change in how and in what position the word can be used in the sentence. **Compose** is what you do. The **composer** is the person doing it. A **composition** is what you have once you have composed. Students need to become aware of how words change when they are signaling different relationships. They also need to realize that there are pronunciation changes in root words when suffixes are added.

The first suffixes you teach should be the most familiar to students and have the highest utility. The suffixes **er** and **ion** make particularly useful first lessons.

To teach **er**, write words on index cards that demonstrate the someone or something who does something, some comparative meanings, and some words that just end in **er**. Place the words randomly along the chalk ledge and have students notice that the words all end in **er**. Next, arrange the words in four columns, and help students see that column 1 words are all people who do something, column 2 words are things that do something, column 3 words mean "more," and column 4 words are those in which **er** is just the last chunk:

People Who Do	Things That Do	More	
reporter	computer	fatter	cover
photographer	pointer	skinnier	never
teacher	heater	greater	master

Label the first three columns "People Who Do," "Things That Do," and "More." Do not label the last column. Have pupils set up papers in four columns, labeling and listing the words just as you have done on the board. Call out some **er** words and have students write them in the column they think the words belong in. Then have students spell each word and tell you which column to put the word in. Remind students of spelling rules—changing **y** to **i**, doubling letters—as needed. Some **er** words you might use are:

after	richer	fighter	winner
winter	under	heavier	air conditioner
murderer	manager	copier	dishwasher
runner	diaper	writer	typewriter

A common suffix that is always pronounced the same way and that sometimes signals a change from a verb to a noun is **ion**. Students make this shift easily in their speech and need to recognize that the same shift occurs in reading and writing. Write **ion** words on index cards, some of which have a related "doing" word and some of which don't. After students notice that the words all end in **tion** and that the **tion** chunk is pronounced the same, divide the words to form two columns on the board. For example:

collection	nation
election	fraction
attraction	condition

Help students see that when they collect coins, they have a coin **collection**; adults elect leaders during an **election**; and a person has an **attraction** for someone he or she is attracted to. In **nation**, **fraction**, and **condition**, the **tion** is pronounced the same but the meaning of the word is not obvious by looking at the root word. Have students set up their papers in the usual way, then call out words for students to decide which group they fit with. Be sure to have students spell words as you write them on the board and talk about the meaning relationships where appropriate. Here are some starters:

traction	subtraction	construction	rejection
auction	expedition	tradition	interruption
mention	action	pollution	correction

Here are some **sion** words you could use in a similar activity:

confusion	invasion	vision	provision
extension	suspension	passion	expression
collision	mission	tension	explosion

Just as with prefixes, keep the chart displayed for several days and ask students to add words they find in their reading to the appropriate columns. The common suffixes chart shows the most common endings and suffixes, along with example words familiar to most children.

figure 11.3 Suffix/Endings and Examples

Suffix/Ending	Examples
s/es	heroes, musicians, signatures
(y-i)	communities, discoveries, countries
ed/ing	unfinished, performed, misunderstanding
(drop e)	nonliving, replaced, continuing
(double consonant)	swimming, forgetting
er/est	richest, craziest, bigger
en	forgotten, hidden, chosen
less	hopeless, careless, penniless
ful	beautiful, successful, pitiful
able	valuable, portable, incurable
ible	irresponsible, reversible, horrible
tion	transportation, imagination, solution
sion	invasion, impression, permission
ly	unfriendly, hopelessly, happily
er	composer, reporter, robber
or	governor, dictator, juror
ee	employee, referee, trainee
ian	musician, magician, beautician
ance	performance, attendance, ignorance
ence	independence, conference, persistence
ment	encouragement, punishment, involvement
ness	happiness, goodness, business
y	discovery, jealousy, pregnancy
ity	electricity, popularity, possibility
ant	unpleasant, tolerant, dominant
ent	different, confident, excellent
al	international, political, racial
ive	expensive, inconclusive, competitive

ous	continuous, humorous, ambitious
ic	prehistoric, scenic, specific
ify	classify, beautify, identify
ize	deodorize, modernize, standardize
ture	signature, creature, fracture

Teaching Common Root Words

So far, we have talked about working from prefixes and suffixes back to the root word. You can also teach your students how many different words they can read and understand from just one root word. Students need to learn that the pronunciation of a root word often changes as prefixes and suffixes are added. They also need to learn that the root sometimes helps them to come up with meanings. Some sample root-word activities are described next.

❋ Lessons with Simple Roots

For the first lessons, use some words that students know well to make the point that words they know are often the keys to unlocking the pronunciation, spelling, and meaning for hundreds of other words. **Play** makes a great first lesson.

Write the word **play** on the board. Tell students that a little word like **play** can become a big word when parts are added to the beginning and ending of the word. Write words that have **play** in them. Have the words pronounced and talk about how the meaning of the word changes. Have students suggest other words with **play**. Here are some starters:

plays	played	playing	player	players
playful	playfully	playable	replay	playfulness
misplay	ballplayer	outplay	overplay	playground
playhouse	playoff	playpen	playwright	screenplay

Other roots that have many words include **work**, **agree**, and **create**:

workable	homework	network	rework
working	legwork	housework	outwork
workers	unworkable	nonworker	woodwork
teamwork	overworked	paperwork	schoolwork
workshop	workout	groundwork	hardworking

agree	agreeable	agreeably	disagreement
agreed	agreement	nonagreement	agreeableness
agreeing	disagreeable	disagreeably	disagreeableness
creatures	creates	created	recreation
creator	creative	creating	creatively
creativity	uncreative	creation	recreational

❊ Lessons with More Complex Roots

Sometimes there are root words whose meanings must be taught so that students can see how words in that family are related in meaning. The most useful of these is the root word **port.**

Write the words **reporter**, **portable**, and **export** on the board. Pronounce the words as you underline **port** in each. Tell students that many words in English have the word **port** in them. Tell them to listen as you tell them some meaning for the three words on the board to see if they can hear a meaning all the words share.

A **reporter** carries a story back to tell others.
Something you can carry with you is **portable**.
When you **export** something, you take or carry it out of the country.

Help students understand that **port** often means "carry or take." Next write this list of words on the board one at a time and help students to see how the meanings change but are still related to **port**:

port	import
export	importer
exportable	transport
nonexportable	transportation

Label this list of words "Carry/Take."

Begin another list with the words **portion** and **portrait**. Underline **port**. Help students to see that not all words that have **port** in them have a meaning clearly related to "carry or take." Tell students that when they see a word containing **port** whose meaning they do not know, they should try to figure out a meaning related to "take or carry" and see if that meaning makes sense in the sentence. Have students set up their paper in two columns like your board. Then call out some words, some of which have the meaning of "carry or take" and some of which don't. Here are some possibilities:

importer	exporter	airport	deport
unimportant	porter	portray	passport
misreport	support	nonsupport	opportunity
seaport	important	portfolio	Portugal

You could do a similar activity with the root **press**. Write the words **depression**, **impress**, and **repress** on the board. Pronounce the words as you underline **press** in each. Tell students that many words in English have the word **press** in them. Tell them to listen as you tell them some meanings for the words on the board to see if they can hear a meaning all the words share.

"You make a **depression** when you push something down. You feel **depressed** when you feel pushed down. When you **repress** a feeling, you push it out of your mind. You **impress** people when you push your good image into their minds."

Help students understand that **press** often means "push." Next write these words on the board and help students to see how the meanings change but are still related to **press**:

press	oppress
express	oppressive
expressible	oppressiveness
inexpressible	

Tell students that when they see a word containing **press** whose meaning they do not know, they should try to figure out a meaning related to "push" and see if that meaning makes sense in the sentence they are reading.

Begin another column with the word **cypress**. Have students notice that **cypress** ends in **press** but there does not appear to be any "push" meaning in **cypress**. Here are some words, only one of which does not have any "push" meaning relationship.

expression	expressway	inexpressible	antidepressant
compression	pressure	pressurize	suppress
impressive	unimpressed	repressive	empress

Common Root Words

Some common root words that are easy for students to understand and that have many related words are:

port: report, export, transport, import, important, seaport, airport, passport, portfolio

press: impress, express, compress, pressure, depress, repress, impression

act: action, react, activity, active, inactive, activate

sign: signature, design, resign, designate, signal, insignia, significant

form: reform, inform, information, deform, uniform, formula, transform

meter: barometer, thermometer, kilometer, centimeter, millimeter, diameter

The Nifty Thrifty Fifty

All the activities described in this chapter so far will help children develop a store of big words they can read and spell and teach them how to analyze big words for familiar patterns. Because a limited number of prefixes, suffixes, and spelling changes can be found in thousands of multisyllabic words, all children should have example words for those that are thoroughly familiar to them. What words could older children learn to read, spell, and analyze so that the teacher could be sure they had examples for these common patterns?

I created such a list by deciding which prefixes, suffixes, and spelling changes were most prevalent in the multisyllabic words students might encounter. I included all the prefixes and suffixes determined to be most common in the White, Sowell, and Yanagihara (1989) study. Because I wanted to create a list that would provide the maximum help with all three big-word tasks, I added prefixes and suffixes such as **con/com**, **per**, **ex**, **ture**, **ian** not included in that study because they were not considered helpful from a meaning standpoint. These prefixes are, however, useful spelling and pronunciation chunks.

Having created the list of "transferable chunks," I then wanted to find the "most-apt-to-be-known" word containing each chunk. I consulted *The Living Word Vocabulary* (Dale & O'Rourke, 1981), which indicates for 44,000 words the grade level at which more than two-thirds of the students tested knew the meaning of the word. Because the test that determined whether students knew the meaning also required students to read the word, it can also be inferred that at least two-thirds of the students could decode and pronounce the word. The goal was to find words that two-thirds of fourth-graders could read and knew at least one meaning for. After much finagling, a list of 50 words was created that contains all the most useful prefixes, suffixes, and spelling changes. All but eight of these words were known by more than two-thirds of fourth-graders. Seven words—**antifreeze, classify, deodorize, impression, irresponsible, prehistoric**, and **semifinal**—were not known by two-thirds of fourth-graders but were known by two-thirds of sixth-graders. **International**, the most known word containing the prefix **inter**, was known by two-thirds of eighth-graders. Because this list of 50 words is apt to be known by so many intermediate-age and older students, and because it so economically represents all the important big-word parts, I named this list the Nifty Thrifty Fifty.

There are endless possibilities for how the list might be used. First, however, students must learn to spell the words. Teachers might want to start a word wall (see Chapter 7) of big words and add five words each week to the wall. They might take a few minutes each day to chant the spelling of the words and talk about the parts of the word that could be applied to other words. This talking should be as "nonjargony" as possible. Rather than talking about the root word **freeze** and the prefix **anti**, the discussions should be about how antifreeze keeps your car's engine from freezing up and, thus, it is protection against freezing. Students should be asked to think of other words that look

figure 11.4 The Nifty Thrifty Fifty

The Nifty Thrifty Fifty		
Key Word	Prefix	Suffix/Ending/ Spelling Change
antifreeze	anti (against)	
beautiful		ful (y-i) (full of)
classify		ify
communities	com (with or together)	es (y-i)
community	com (with or together)	
composer	com (with or together)	er (person or thing)
continuous	con	ous
conversation	con	tion
deodorize	de (take away)	ize
different		ent
discovery	dis (not or reverse)	y
dishonest	dis (not or reverse)	
electricity		ity
employee	em	ee (person)
encouragement	en (make or give)	ment
expensive	ex	ive
governor		or (person)
happiness		ness (y-i)
hopeless		less (without)
illegal	il (not or opposite)	
impossible	im (not or opposite)	
impression	im (in)	ion
independence	in (not or opposite)	ence
international	inter (between)	al
invasion	in (in)	ion
irresponsible	ir (not or opposite)	ible
midnight	mid (middle)	
misunderstood	mis (wrong or bad)	

(continued)

figure 11.4   Continued

The Nifty Thrifty Fifty		
Key Word	**Prefix**	**Suffix/Ending/ Spelling Change**
musician		ian (person)
nonviolent	non (not)	
overpower	over (more than or too much)	
patiently		ly
performance	per	ance
prehistoric	pre (before)	ic
prettier		er (y-i) (more)
promotion	pro (for or in favor of)	tion
rearrange	re (back or again)	
replacement	re (back or again)	ment
richest		est (most)
semifinal	semi (half or partly)	
signature		ture
submarine	sub (under or below)	
supermarkets	super (really big)	
swimming		ing (double m)
transportation	trans (across or through)	tion
underweight	under	
unfinished	un (not or opposite)	ed
unpleasant	un (not or opposite)	ant
valuable		able (drop e)
written		en (double t)

and sound like **antifreeze** and then decide if the **anti** parts of those words could have anything to do with the notion of "against."

"What is an **antibiotic** against?"

"What is an **antiaircraft** weapon?"

For suffixes, the discussion should center around how the suffix changes how the word can be used in a sentence.

> "A **musician** makes music. What does a **beautician**, **electrician**, **physician**, or **magician** do?"

> "When you need to replace something, you get a **replacement**. What do you get when someone **encourages** you?"

> "What do you call it when you **accomplish** something?"

Spelling changes should be noticed and applied to similar words.

> "**Communities** is the plural of **community**. How would you spell **parties**? **Candies**? **Personalities**?"

> "When we swim, we say we are **swimming**. How would you spell **swimmer**? **Drummed**?"

If this list is to become truly useful to students, they need to learn to spell the words gradually over time, and they need to be shown how the patterns found in these words can be useful in decoding, spelling, and figuring out meaning for lots of other words. Here is an example of how the first words might be taught:

1. Explain that in English, many big words are just smaller words with prefixes and suffixes. The Nifty Thrifty Fifty words include all the important prefixes and suffixes and spelling changes needed to read, spell, and figure out meanings for thousands of other words.

2. Add five or six words to your display each week. Use different colors and make the words big and bold so that they are easily seen.

3. Have students chant each word cheerleader-style with you. After cheering for each word, help students analyze the word, talking about meaning and determining the root, prefix, and suffix, and noting any spelling changes.

   > **composer**: A composer is a person who composes something. Many other words such as **writer**, **reporter**, and **teacher** are made up of a root word and the suffix **er**, meaning a person or thing that does something.

   > **expensive**: The word **expense** with the suffix **ive** added and the **e** in **expense** dropped. Another related word that students might not know is **expend**. You might be able to make the **expend-expense-expensive** relationship clear to them by using the sports terms **defend**, **defense**, and **defensive**.

encouragement: When you encourage someone, you give them encouragement. Many other words such as **argue, argument**; **replace, replacement** follow this same pattern. The root word for **encourage** is **courage**. So **encouragement** is made up of the prefix **en**, the root word **courage**, and the suffix **ment**.

impossible: The root **possible** with the suffix **im**. In many words, including **impatient** and **immature**, the suffix **im** changes the word to an opposite.

musician: A musician is a person who makes music. A beautician helps make you beautiful and a magician makes magic. **Musician** has the root word **music** with the suffix **ian**, which sometimes indicates the person who does something. There are no spelling changes, but the pronunciation changes. Have students say the words **music** and **musician**, **magic**, and **magician** and notice how the pronunciation changes.

4. Once you have noticed the composition for each word, helped students see other words that work in a similar way, and cheered for each word, have students write each word. Students enjoy writing the words more and focus better on the word if you give clues to the word such as:

   Number 1 is the opposite of discouragement.

   For number 2, write the word that tells what you are if you play the guitar.

   For number 3, write what you are if you play the guitar but you also make up the songs you play.

   Write the word that is the opposite of possible for number 4.

   The last word means costing a lot of money.

5. After students write all the words, have them check their own papers by once more chanting the letters aloud, underlining each as they say it.

When you have a few minutes of "sponge" time, practice the words by chanting or writing. As you are cheering or writing each word, ask students to identify the root, prefix, and suffix and talk about how these affect the meaning of the root word. Point out any spelling changes.

The following week, add another five or six words and follow the foregoing procedures. When you have enough words, begin to show students how parts from the Nifty Thrifty Fifty words can be combined to spell lots of other words. From just the 11 words **composer**, **discovery**, **encouragement**, **expensive**, **hopeless**, **impossible**, **impression**, **musician**, **richest**, **transportation**, and **unfinished**, students should be able to decode, spell, and discuss meanings for:

compose	pose	discover	encourage	courage
import	importation	possible	compress	compression
finished	transpose	dispose	discourage	discouragement
enrich	enrichment	uncover	richly	hopelessly
impress	inexpensive	transport	port	expose
express	expression	export	exportation	

As more and more words are added, students become quite impressed with the number of transfer words they can read, spell, and build meanings for.

figure 11.5 Nifty Thrifty Fifty Transfer Words

Here are just some of the words buildable from just the parts of the 50 words. The number grows astronomically when the prefixes and suffixes are attached to other root words students know.

300-Plus Words Your Students Can Spell Based on Nifty Thrifty Fifty Words			
antidepressant	arrange	arrangement	arranging
beautician	beautify	beauty	class
classifiable	classification	classified	classifying
commotion	communication	compose	composed
composing	compress	compression	conform
conformity	consignment	continual	continually
continue	continuing	converse	conversing
courage	courageous	courageously	cover
covered	declassify	decompose	deform
deformity	demotion	deodorant	depend
depended	dependence	depending	deploy
deport	deportation	deportee	depress
depressing	depression	design	designation
devalue	differ	difference	discontinue
discourage	discouraged	discouragement	discouraging
discover	discovered	discovering	dishonestly
dishonesty	displace	displacement	displease
disposal	dispose	electric	electrical
electrician	electrification	electrify	employ

(continued)

figure 11.5   Continued

300-Plus Words Your Students Can Spell Based on Nifty Thrifty Fifty Words			
employable	employer	employment	empower
empowerment	encourage	encouraged	encouraging
enrich	enrichment	expense	export
exportation	exported	expose	exposed
express	expressed	expression	expressionless
expressive	final	finalization	finalize
finalizing	finally	finish	finished
finishing	form	formal	formally
formation	freezable	freeze	freezer
freezing	govern	governable	governed
government	happier	happily	happy
historic	historical	historically	history
honest	honestly	honesty	hope
hoped	hopeful	hopefully	hopelessly
hoping	illegally	impatience	impatient
impatiently	import	importance	important
importation	imported	impossibility	impossibly
impress	impressed	impressionable	impressive
inexpensive	inform	informal	informant
information	informer	insignificant	interdependence
internationalize	internationally	invade	invaluable
invasive	invasiveness	irreplaceable	irresponsibly
legal	legally	marine	market
misinform	misplace	misplacing	motion
motionless	music	musical	musically
nation	national	nationalities	nationality
nationalize	night	noninvasive	nonviolence
nonviolently	odor	overexpose	overnight
overture	overweight	patience	patient

perform	performer	place	placing
pleasant	pleasantly	please	port
portable	pose	posed	possibility
possible	possibly	power	powerful
powerfully	powerfulness	powerless	powerlessly
prearrange	predispose	predisposition	press
pressed	prettiest	pretty	proposal
propose	rearrangement	rearranging	reclassify
recover	rediscover	refinish	reform
replace	replacing	report	reporter
repress	repressive	resign	resignation
response	responsibility	responsible	responsibly
responsive	responsiveness	reunification	revalue
rewrite	rewritten	rich	richer
richly	sign	signal	significance
significant	stood	subfreezing	super
superpower	swim	swimmer	transform
transformation	transformer	transport	transportable
transported	transporting	transpose	transposed
unclassifiable	unclassified	uncover	uncovered
underclass	undercover	underexpose	understood
undervalue	unemployable	unemployed	unemployment
ungovernable	unhappier	unhappiest	unhappily
unhappiness	unhappy	unification	unify
uninformed	unity	unpleasantly	unpleasantness
unresponsive	unwritten	value	valued
valuing	violence	violent	violently
weight	weightier	weightiest	weightless
weighty	write	writer	writing

Summary

Facility with big words is essential for students as they read, write, and learn in all areas of school and life. Many big words occur infrequently, but when they do occur, they carry a lot of the meaning and content of what is being read. English is a language in which many words are related through their morphology. Linguists estimate that every big word your students can read, spell, and analyze enables them to acquire six or seven other morphemically related words. Students who learn to look for patterns in the big new words they meet will be better spellers and decoders. If they learn to look further and consider possible meaning relationships, they will increase the size of their meaning vocabulary stores.

Big words—words of seven or more letters—are the words that carry the meaning of whatever we are reading. There are thousands of them and we don't see any of them very frequently. In order to be a good reader from third grade on, children must have strategies for decoding and spelling big words. Big words are decoded and spelled based on similar patterns from other big words. Many older students, however, do not have a store of big words they can fluently read and spell. This chapter has suggested ways of adding big words to the word stores of all your students. In addition, suggestions were made for teaching your students how to use big words to decode and spell other big words.

Many big words have recognizable roots, prefixes, and suffixes. These morphemic "chunks" are particularly useful because not only do they give clues to pronunciation and spelling, but they also help us determine the meaning of unfamiliar big words. This chapter described many activities that help children use roots, prefixes, and suffixes to decode, spell, and build meaning for polysyllabic words.

chapter 12

Making Words in Upper Grades

In Chapter 4 and Chapter 9, Making Words was described as a Guided Discovery lesson in which young children could learn the beginning letter and rhyming patterns that enable them to decode thousands of English words. In Chapter 11, you learned that the patterns in big words are not rhyming patterns but rather morphemic patterns. Most big words in English are combinations of word parts—prefixes, suffixes, and roots. Learning how these word parts combine to form words not only gives students tools for decoding and spelling thousands of polysyllabic words, but the morpheme patterns also give clues to meaning. Rhyming and beginning letter patterns do not contain these meaning clues. The **a-t-c-h** pattern in **catch**, **match**, **batch**, and **thatch** helps you read and spell these words, but these words share no meaning connection. Similarly, the **b-r** pattern in **branch**, **brace**, **bracket**, and **breakfast** cues you to pronunciation and spelling, but there is no meaning connection. The **u-n** morphemic pattern in **unhappy**, **unpleasant**, **untried**, and **unmatched**, however, cues you to pronunciation, spelling, and meaning. Similarly, the **a-b-l-e** morphemic pattern in **comfortable**, **unstoppable**, **reliable**, and **notable** provides meaning clues along with spelling and pronunciation clues. Some suffixes don't add to the meaning of a word but do indicate how that word can be used in a sentence. **Perform** indicates the action and **performance** is the thing performed. **Kind** describes the act of **kindness**. The word **national** describes things related to a nation. When you nationalize something, you make it national. Suffixes such as **ance**, **ness**, **al**, and **ize** are grammatical suffixes. When these grammatical suffixes are added to words, they change how these words can be used in a sentence.

When suffixes are added to words, the root word spelling is often changed. The **p** in **stop** is doubled when writing **unstoppable**. The **y** in **rely** changes to an **i** to spell **reliable**. The final **e** in **note** is dropped when **able** is added to create the word **notable**. These spelling changes are also a kind of pattern because they happen each time a certain suffix is added to a root word with a particular spelling. Sometimes the pronunciation of a root word changes when suffixes are added. The long vowel sound of **a** in **nation** becomes a short **a** sound in **national** and **nationalize**. The silent **g** in **sign** is pronounced in related words such as **signature** and **signal**. These spelling changes and pronunciation changes, although quite predictable, make using word parts to decode and spell big words more complicated. There is evidence that many older students— including high school students—do not recognize the relationship between words in which the spelling or pronunciation changes. These students are thus unable to use these morphemic clues as aids to pronunciation, spelling, and meaning.

Making Words lessons in upper grades always contain some related words—words that share the same root. During the Sort part, these related words are grouped together and teachers help students see how the words share meaning and notice any spelling changes that occur. Once the related words are sorted, students use them to read and spell some other words that share the same word parts, during the Transfer step of the Making Words lessons.

In this chapter, I will share with you three Making Words sample lessons in which students are guided to discover how morphemic patterns work as clues to the decoding, spelling, and meaning of big words. This first lesson comes from *Making Words Third Grade: 70 Hands-On Lessons for Teaching Prefixes, Suffixes, and Homophones* (Cunningham & Hall, 2009). In third grade, students need to learn the most common prefixes and suffixes and the spelling changes required when adding some of the suffixes. Third-grade students also need to learn the spelling of the common homophones and need continued practice with the more complex rhyming patterns. Lessons in *Making Words Third Grade* include opportunities for students to make and sort words with rhyming and morphemic patterns and homophones. (This lesson is #30 in *Making Words Third Grade*.)

A Third-Grade Making Words Lesson

The children all have a letter strip with these letters: **e o u f l p r w**.

These same letters are displayed in a pocket chart, smart board, or on plastic tiles on the overhead. Children turn over the strip and write the capital letters on the back and then tear the letters apart.

The words the children are going to make are written on index cards. These words will be placed in the pocket chart as the words are made and will be used for the Sort and Transfer parts of the lesson.

❋ Part One: Making Words

The teacher begins the lesson by telling students what word to make and how many letters each word takes.

> "Use three letters to spell the word **low**. We haven't had much rain and the water level in the lake is very **low**."

(Find someone with **low** spelled correctly and send that child to spell **low** with the pocket chart, smart board, or transparency letters.)

> "Use the same three letters to spell **owl**. We saw a white **owl** at the zoo."
>
> "Start over and use three letters to spell **few**. We have a **few** new students in our room this month."
>
> "Change the last two letters to spell **for**. I brought apples **for** snack time."
>
> "Add one letter to **for** to spell the number **four**. I have **four** pets."
>
> "Use four letters again to spell **flew**. I **flew** to Florida when I went to Disney World."

(Quickly send someone with the correct spelling to make the words with the big letters. Keep the pace brisk. Do not wait until everyone has spelled **flew** with their little letters. It is fine if some children are making **flew** as **flew** is being spelled with the big letters. Choose your struggling readers to go to the pocket chart when easy words are being spelled and your advanced readers when harder words are being made.)

> "Change one letter in **flew** to spell **flow**. We watched the water **flow** into the stream."
>
> "Use the same letters in **flow** to spell **wolf**. We were camping and heard a **wolf** howl."
>
> "Use four letters to spell **plow**. In the spring, farmers **plow** the fields."
>
> "Use five letters to spell **prowl**. Many wild animals **prowl** at night while we sleep."
>
> "Use five letters to spell **power**. **Power** is another word for strength."
>
> "Use five letters to spell **flour**. We use **flour** to bake bread and cookies."

Lesson 30: powerful

Letter strip: e o u f l p r w

Make:
low	four	prowl	flower	powerful
owl	flew	power		
few	flow	flour		
for	wolf			
	plow			

Sort: low   few   owl   power
       flow flew prowl flower

"Use six letters to spell the **flower** that grows in your garden. My favorite **flower** is a daisy."

"I have just one word left. It is the secret word you can make with all your letters. See if you can figure it out."

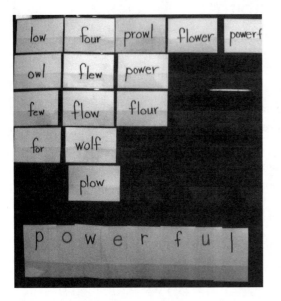

(Give the children one minute to figure out the secret word. Then give clues if needed. "Our secret word today is related to the word **power**.")

Let someone who figures it out go to the big letters and spell the secret word: **powerful**.

❋ Part Two: Sort Words into Patterns

Using the index cards with words you made, place them in the pocket chart as the children pronounce and chorally spell each. Give them a quick reminder of how they made these words:

"First we spelled a three-letter word **low, l-o-w**."

"We used the same letters to spell **owl, o-w-l**."

"We used three letters to spell **few, f-e-w**."

"We used three letters to spell **for, f-o-r**."

"We added the **u** to spell the number **four, f-o-u-r**."

"We used four letters to spell **flew, f-l-e-w**."

"We changed the vowel to spell **flow, f-l-o-w**."

"We moved the letters in **flow** to spell **wolf, w-o-l-f**."

"We used four letters to spell **plow, p-l-o-w**."

"We used five letters to spell **prowl, p-r-o-w-l**."

"We used five letters to spell **power, p-o-w-e-r**."

"We used five letters to spell the **flour** you bake with, **f-l-o-u-r**."

"We used six letters to spell the **flower** that grows in the garden, **f-l-o-w-e-r**."

"Finally, we spelled the secret word with all our letters, **powerful**, **p-o-w-e-r-f-u-l**."

Sort Homophones   Take one of each set of homophones and line them up in the pocket chart.

for

flower

Have two children come and find the homophones and place them next to the ones you pulled out.

for   **four**
flower   **flour**

Put the words in sentences to show the different meaning, pointing to the correct one as you say each.

"I got a new bike **for** my birthday."

"Two plus two equals **four**."

"The first **flower** just bloomed in my garden."

"**Flour** is used to make pizza dough."

Allow a few children to come and point to a homophone and use it in a sentence.

Sort Related Words   Remind the students that related words are words that share a root word and meaning. Place **power** and **powerful** next to each other in the pocket chart.

power   **powerful**

Use these related words in a sentence to show the meaning.

"When something has a lot of **power** or strength, we say it is **powerful**. Our town was struck by a **powerful** tornado."

Let volunteers share sentence using the word **powerful**.

Sort Rhyming Words   Take one of each set of rhymes and place them to form columns in the pocket chart.

low   **few**   **owl**   **power**

Have four children come and find the rhymes and place them under the words you pulled out.

low	few	owl	power
flow	flew	prowl	flower

Have the students read the rhyming words and confirm that they rhyme and have the same spelling pattern.

✳ Part Three: Transfer

During the transfer step, we help students use the related and rhyming words to spell other words.

Transfer Related Words   Have students use **power**, **powerful** to spell other words that end in **ful**. Give them help to spell the root word if needed.

cheerful   thankful   painful

Let volunteers share sentence that shows the meaning relationship between **cheer**, **cheerful**; **thank**, **thankful**; and **pain**, **painful**.

Transfer Rhyming Words   Have the students spell these words using the rhyming words to determine the spelling pattern.

howl   growl   tower   shower

Kevin C.

1. cheerful
2. thankful
3. painful
4. howl
5. growl
6. tower
7. shower

A Fourth-Grade Making Words Lesson

In fourth grade, we continue to sort rhyming words and include more words with morphemic patterns. Spelling changes are pointed out as needed during the Sort and Transfer parts of the lesson. This sample lesson is #29 in *Making Words Fourth Grade: 50 Hands-On Lessons for Teaching Prefixes, Suffixes, and Roots* (Cunningham & Hall, 2009).

The students all have a letter strip with these letters: **a   a   e   i   d   p   p   r   s**.

These same letters are displayed in a pocket chart, smart board, or on plastic tiles on the overhead. Students tear the letters apart and line them up on their desks.

The words the students are going to make are written on index cards. These words will be used for the Sort and Transfer steps of the lesson.

❋ Part One: Making Words

The teacher begins the lesson by telling students what word to make and how many letters each word takes.

> "Use three letters to spell the word **sip**. I took a little **sip** of my hot chocolate to make sure it wasn't too hot."

(Find someone with **sip** spelled correctly and send that student to spell **sip** with the pocket chart, smart board, or transparency letters.)

> "Change just the first letter to spell **dip**. It was a sweltering hot day and we took a quick **dip** into the pool to cool off."

> "Start over and use three letters to spell **air**. We need to put **air** in our bikes' tires before we can ride."

> "Add one letter to **air** to spell **pair**. I brought a new **pair** of boots."

> "Change one letter in **pair** to spell **paid**. I **paid** all my bills."

> "Change one letter in **paid** to spell **raid**. The hostages were freed during an early morning **raid** on the base."

> "Use four letters to spell **drip**. The plumber fixed the faucet so it doesn't **drip**."

> "Use four letters again to spell **side**. Which **side** of the field are you sitting on?"

(Quickly send someone with the correct spelling to make the words with the pocket chart, smart board, or overhead letters. Keep the pace brisk. Do not wait until everyone has **side** spelled with their little letters. It is fine if some students are making **side** as **side** is being spelled with the big letters. Choose your struggling readers to go to the pocket chart when easy words are being spelled and your advanced readers when harder words are being made.)

"Change one letter in **side** to spell **ride**. Did you ever **ride** a horse?"

"Add one letter to **ride** to spell **pride**. We work hard on our writing and take **pride** in the books we publish."

"Use five letters to spell **raise**. In the morning we **raise** the flag."

"Add one letter to **raise** to spell **praise**. After the concert, the whole school was full of **praise** for the band and chorus."

"Use six letters to spell **dipper**. Mom used a **dipper** to serve the punch."

"Use six letters to spell **appear**. I looked up and saw a rainbow **appear** in the sky."

"Use six letters to spell **repaid**. My friend got a job and **repaid** me the money I had loaned him."

"Add one letter to **repaid** to spell **prepaid**. When I went to pay for the tickets, I discovered my mom had **prepaid** them as a birthday gift."

"I have just one word left. It is the secret word you can make with all your letters. See if you can figure it out."

(Give the children one minute to figure out the secret word. Then give clues if needed. "Our secret word today is related to the word **appear**.")

Let someone who figures it out go to the big letters and spell the secret word: **disappear**.

❋ Part Two: Sort Words into Patterns

Using the index cards with words you made, place them in the pocket chart as the students pronounce and chorally spell each. Give them a quick reminder of how they made these words:

"First we spelled a three-letter word **sip, s-i-p**."

"We changed the first letter to spell **dip, d-i-p**."

"We used three letters to spell **air, a-i-r**."

"We added a letter to spell **pair, p-a-i-r**."

"We changed the last letter to spell **paid, p-a-i-d**."

"We changed the first letter to spell **raid, r-a-i-d**."

"We used four letters to spell **drip, d-r-i-p**."

"We used four letters to spell **side, s-i-d-e**."

"We changed the first letter to spell **ride, r-i-d-e**."

"We added one letter to spell **pride, p-r-i-d-e**."

"We used five letters to spell **raise, r-a-i-s-e**."

"We added one letter to spell **praise, p-r-a-i-s-e**."

"We used six letters to spell **dipper, d-i-p-p-e-r**."

"We used six letters to spell **appear, a-p-p-e-a-r**."

"We used six letters to spell **repaid, r-e-p-a-i-d**."

"We added one letter to spell **prepaid, p-r-e-p-a-i-d**."

"Finally, we spelled the secret word with all our letters, **disappear, d-i-s-a-p-p-e-a-r**."

Sort Related Words Draw the students' attention to the words on the index cards and remind them that related words are words that share a root word and meaning. Choose a set of related words and model for the students how to use those words in sentences to show how they are related. (Choose the most complex set of words to model.)

paid   repaid   prepaid

"I forgot my wallet, so my friend **paid** for my lunch. I **repaid** him the money I owed the next day. When I went to visit my mom for a month, I **prepaid** all my bills so they wouldn't be overdue when I got back."

"**Re** is a prefix that sometimes means back. If the money was repaid, it was paid back. **Pre** is a prefix that sometimes means before. If the bills were prepaid, they were paid before they were due."

Let volunteers choose other sets of related words and help them construct sentences and explain how the prefixes and suffixes change the root words.

dip   dipper

"A **dipper** is a thing you can use to **dip** things out. **Er** is a suffix that sometimes means the thing that does something."

appear   disappear

"On a cloudy day the sun will suddenly **appear** and then **disappear**."

"**Dis** is a prefix that sometimes makes a word mean the opposite."

Sorting the related words, using sentences that show how they are related, and explaining how prefixes and suffixes affect meaning or change how words can be used in a sentence is a crucial part of each Making Words lesson in fourth grade. Students often need help in explaining how the prefixes and suffixes work.

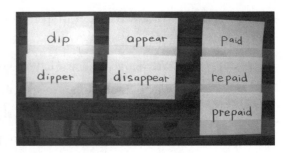

Sort Rhyming Words   Take one of each set of rhymes and place them to form columns in the pocket chart.

sip	air	raid	praise	ride

Have five students find the rhymes and place them under the words you pulled out.

sip	air	raid	praise	ride
dip	pair	paid	raise	side
drip		pride		price

Have the students read the rhyming words and confirm that they rhyme and have the same spelling pattern.

✳ Part Three: Transfer

The transfer step is the most important step of the lesson because it is when we teach students how rhymes, prefixes, suffixes, and roots help them read and spell lots of other words. Once we have sorted all the words into related words and rhymes, we say several new words and have students decide which word parts these words share with our related words and how they will help the students spell them. Finally, we say several words that rhyme with the rhyming words we made and use the rhyming patterns to spell these. It is very important to make this a learning experience rather than a test. Make sure everyone agrees how to spell the new words before letting anyone write the transferwords.

Ask the students to number a sheet of paper from 1 to 6. Pronounce a word that follows the pattern of some of the related words.

Transfer Related Words   Have students use **repaid** and **prepaid** to spell **review** and **preview**. Give them help to spell the root word if needed.

Let volunteers tell a sentence that shows the meaning relationship between **view**, **review**, and **preview**.

Have students use **appear** and **disappear** to spell two other words that begin with **dis**: **disagree** and **dislike**. Give them help to spell the root words if needed.

Let volunteers tell a sentence that shows the meaning relationship between **agree** and **disagree** and between **like** and **dislike**.

Transfer Rhyming Words   Have the students spell these words using the rhyming words to determine the spelling pattern.

> **glide**   **braid**   **clip**

> Zachary B.
> 1. review
> 2. preview
> 3. reappear
> 4. disagree
> 5. braid
> 6. bride
> 7. flip

A *Fifth-Grade Making Words Lesson*

By fifth grade, almost all students have learned the rhyming patterns that help us spell and decode short words. In fifth grade, we don't sort for rhyming words but focus exclusively on morphemic patterns. This sample lesson is #8 in *Making Words Fifth Grade: 50 Hands-On Lessons for Teaching Prefixes, Suffixes, and Roots* (Cunningham & Hall, 2009).

The students all have a letter strip with these letters:

a a e i u l m n p r t.

One student is assigned the job of "letter manipulator" for today's lesson. As students make each word at their desks, the teacher calls on a student who has the word made correctly to spell aloud the letters in that word. The letter manipulator moves the letters on the overhead or smart board so that all students have a visual image against which to check their spelling. (You can make clear letter tiles by cutting a sheet of transparency film into small squares and then writing the letters for the lesson on the squares, or you can copy the letter strips at the back of this book on a transparency and have the letter manipulator cut the letters on the plastic strip apart.)

Students tear or cut the letters apart and arrange them in alphabetical order—vowels first and consonants next. The words the students are going to make are written on index cards. These words will be placed in the pocket chart or along the chalk ledge and will be used for the Sort and Transfer parts of the lesson.

❋ Part One: Making Words

The teacher begins the lesson by telling students what word to make and how many letters each word requires. She or he gives a sentence for each word to clarify meaning.

> "Use four letters to spell the word **real**. The creatures in the movie were animated but they looked very **real**."

(Find someone with **real** spelled correctly and have that student spell **real** aloud so that the letter manipulator can spell **real** with the smart board or transparency letters.)

> "Use four letters to spell **ripe**. We pick strawberries when they are **ripe**."
>
> "Spell another four-letter word, **mine**. Would you like to work deep down under the earth in a coal **mine**?"
>
> "Let's spell one more four-letter word, **time**. What **time** do we go to lunch?"
>
> "Add one letter to **time** to spell **timer**. I put the cookies in the oven and set the **timer** for 15 minutes."
>
> "Use five letters again to spell **miner**. I am claustrophobic so I would not be a good coal **miner**."

(Quickly call on someone with the correct spelling to spell the word aloud for the letter manipulator. Keep the pace brisk. Choose your struggling readers to spell words aloud when easy words are being spelled and your advanced readers when harder words are being made.)

> "Use five letters to spell **ripen**. The strawberries are just beginning to **ripen**."
>
> "Use five letters to spell **paint**. We all love to **paint** in art class."
>
> "Use five letters to spell **plant**. In the spring we will **plant** flowers in our garden."
>
> "Add one letter to **plant** to spell **planet**. Mars is called the red **planet**."
>
> "Use six letters in to spell **unreal**. Everyone said that watching the tornado touch down felt very **unreal**."
>
> "Use six letters to spell **unripe**. Strawberries do not taste good when they are **unripe**."
>
> "Use seven letters to spell **planter**. I plant spring flowers in a hanging **planter**."
>
> "Use the same letters in **planter** to spell **replant**. Every year I **replant** the shrubs that die during the winter."

"Change the first two letters in **replant** to spell **implant**. If your heart does not have a steady beat, doctors can **implant** a pacemaker into your body to regulate your heartbeat."

"Use seven letters to spell **painter**. The **painter** is coming next week to paint the house."

"Use the same seven letters in **painter** to spell **repaint**. After the storm, the roof leaked and we had to **repaint** the kitchen."

"I have just one word left. It is the secret word you can make with all your letters. Move your letters around and see if you can figure out the word that can be spelled using all the letters. You have one minute to try to figure out the secret word, and then I will give you clues."

(Give the students one minute to figure out the secret word. Then give clues if needed. "Our secret word today is related to the word **planet**. Start with the word **planet** and add your other letters to it.")

Let someone who figures it out go to the smart board or overhead and spell the secret word: **planetarium.**

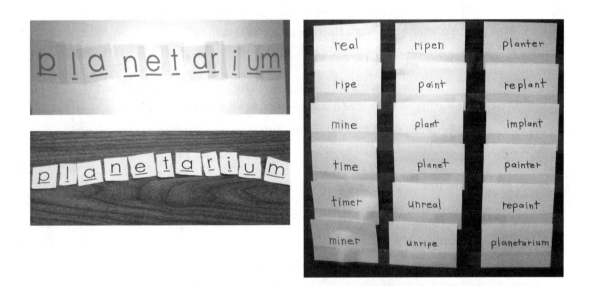

❋ Part Two: Sort Words into Patterns

Draw students' attention to the words on the index cards and have the words pronounced. Remind students that related words are words that share a root word and meaning.

Choose a set of related words and model for students how to use related words in sentences to show how they are related. (Choose the most complex set of words to model.)

plant   **planter**   **replant**   **implant**

"A **planter** is a container you plant things in. When you **replant** something, you **plant** it again. When you **implant** something, you plant it in something or somebody."

"The **er** suffix can be a person or a thing. **Re** is a prefix that sometimes means again. **Im** is a prefix that sometimes means in."

Let volunteers choose other sets of related words, and help them construct sentences and explain how the prefixes and suffixes change the root words.

paint   **painter**   **repaint**

"A **painter** is a person who **paints**. When you **repaint** something, you **paint** it again."

"**Er** is a suffix that sometimes means the person who does something. **Re** is a prefix that sometimes means again."

ripe   **ripen**   **unripe**

"The strawberries are starting to **ripen** and will soon be **ripe** enough to eat. **Unripe** strawberries taste terrible!"

"The suffix **en** changes how a word can be used in a sentence. The prefix **un** often turns a word into the opposite meaning."

real   **unreal**

"When you see something that is actually happening it is **real**, but sometimes things are so strange they seem **unreal**."

"The prefix **un** changes real into the opposite meaning."

time   **timer**

"To **time** the cookies baking, we set the **timer**."

"The suffix **er** sometimes means a thing."

mine   **miner**

"A **miner** is a person who works in a **mine**."

"The suffix **er** sometimes means a person."

planet   **planetarium**

"You can see all the different **planets** and how they move at a **planetarium**."

"Other words that end in **ium** and mean places are **aquarium**, **terrarium**, **auditorium**, **gymnasium**, and **stadium**."

Sorting the related words, using sentences that show how they are related, and explaining how prefixes and suffixes affect meaning or change how words can be used in a sentence is a crucial part of each Making Words lesson in fifth grade. Students often need help in explaining how the prefixes and suffixes work. For less common prefixes and suffixes, such as **ium**, it is helpful to point out other words students may know that begin or end with that word part.

✳ Part Three: Transfer

The transfer step is the most important step of the lesson because it is when we teach students how the prefixes, suffixes, and roots they are learning help them read and spell lots of other words. Once we have sorted all the words into related word sets, we say five or six new words and have students decide which word parts these words share with our related words and how they will help the students spell them. It is

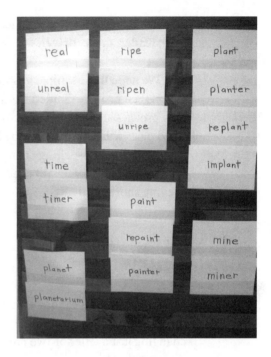

very important to make this a learning experience rather than a test. Make sure everyone knows how to spell the new part of the transfer word and which related words will help before letting anyone write the word.

Ask the students to number a sheet of paper from 1 to 6. Pronounce a word that follows the pattern of some of the related words.

Have the students use **unripe** and **unreal** to spell other words that begin with **un**. Give them help to spell the root word if needed.

unfair   **unpainted**

Let volunteers tell a sentence that shows the meaning relationship between **fair, unfair; painted, unpainted**.

Have the students use **repaint** and **replant** to spell other words that begin with **re**. Give them help to spell the root word if needed.

rebuild   **refill**

Let volunteers tell a sentence that shows the meaning relationship between **build, rebuild; fill, refill**.

Have students use **painter, planter, miner**, and **timer** to spell other words that end with **er**, meaning person or thing. Give them help to spell the root word if needed. Point out the spelling change—drop **e**—if necessary.

leader   **driver**

Let volunteers tell a sentence that shows the meaning relationship between **lead, leader**; **drive, driver**.

We hope these sample lessons have helped you see how Making Words lessons can provide Guided Discovery opportunities for older students to learn how prefixes and suffixes affect the meanings of root words and how combining word parts will help them to spell lots of other words. Including words with rhyming patterns, spelling changes, and homophones provides additional practice for older students who still need to consolidate their strategies for decoding and spelling short words.

Summary

Making Words is a lesson format that older children enjoy as much as younger ones. Through this hands-on, manipulative activity, your students discover how changing just a letter or two creates a new word. As they sort the words, they discover the rhyming and morphemic patterns that make up our English spelling system. In the Transfer step of the lesson, they learn how words they made and sorted can help them spell and read lots of other words. Making Words lessons always begin with small words and work up to bigger words and finally the secret word, which can be made with all the letters. Because of the variety of words made and patterns sorted for, Making Words lessons have a lot of scope. Students at all different levels can increase their understanding of phonics patterns and how they help us read and spell words.

chapter 13

Phonics Assessment and Interventions

In two earlier chapters in this book, assessment was defined as collecting and analyzing data to make decisions about how children are performing and growing (Caldwell, 2009). The four steps in assessment are:

1. Identify what you want to assess
2. Collect evidence
3. Analyze that evidence
4. Make a decision and act on that decision

When assessing your students' phonics skills, you want to know how well they can use their letter–sound knowledge to figure out words when reading and spell unfamiliar words when writing. To collect that evidence in a valid way, students have to be reading or writing something. Testing their phonics knowledge in a way that is isolated from reading or writing simply tells you what they know about letters and sounds. You still don't know what they do when confronted with an unfamiliar word in their reading or a new word they are trying to spell. This chapter will suggest ways to collect evidence about what phonics knowledge your students can actually use when they are reading and writing.

Observing Word Strategies in Reading

By observing children's reading, you can look at the errors your students make and determine what word identification strategies they are using. Good readers self-correct many of their errors. This usually indicates that they are using context to check that what they are reading makes sense. Successful self-correction is an excellent indicator that the reader is using all three cueing systems—meaning (semantic), sounding like language (syntactic), and letter–sound knowledge (graphophonic). Some readers tend to overuse context—their errors make sense but don't have most of the letter–sound relationships of the original word. Others overuse letter–sound knowledge. Their errors look and sound a lot like the original words but they don't make any sense. By observing your students' reading, you can determine what strategies they are using and what kind of instructional activities you might provide for them.

There are many opportunities throughout the day to make these observations. As your students are engaged in independent reading, ask them to read aloud a page or two. As they read, listen for how fluently they read, how automatically they identify common words, and how they use patterns, context, and other cues to figure out unknown words. When children are reading in partners, circulate to the different partnerships and ask them to read a page to you. Again, note how they use what you are teaching them about words as they actually read text. Another opportunity to observe their sight word, word identification, and fluency behaviors is when you meet with small reading groups.

In Chapter 8, I suggested that you extend the common fluency measures to measure word-identification accuracy. Instead of just checking words read correctly, you make a record of how each child reads, using a simple system to note substitutions, mispronunciations, omissions, hesitations, and self-corrections.

Put a check mark over each word read correctly.

If the child misreads a word (**grows** for **growls**), write the error above it.

If the child leaves a word out, strike through that word.

If the child hesitates on a word but correctly pronounces that word, write *H* above the word. Words a reader hesitates on but correctly identifies are not counted as errors.

If the child self-corrects, write *SC* above it. *SC* words are not counted as errors.

If the child makes the same error more than once, only count it one time.

Whenever you have the opportunity to observe the oral reading of a student, make a record of his or her word-identification accuracy so that you can then analyze errors, hesitations, and self-corrections to determine what word strategies the student is actually using while reading. After listening to Erin read, her teacher concluded that Erin was monitoring her reading well and probably using context to self-correct. Because hesitating or mispronouncing common words can really interfere with fluency, the teacher created a personal word wall for Erin and provided practice with the high-frequency words she was mispronouncing or hesitating on. She decided that Erin and the rest of her third-graders could profit from some instruction on big words and provided that instruction to everyone.

Word-Identification Analysis for Oral Reading				
Name_Erin				
Date	High-Frequency Words	Analysis	Lower-Frequency words	Analysis
10/17	them (pronounced they, self-corrected)	Self-correcting based on context	performing (hesitated, decoded correctly)	Needs more work with big word parts
	could (pronounced cold, self-corrected)		numerous "numer"	
	although (hesitated, pronounced correctly)		popular (hesitated, decoded correctly)	
			traditional "tradi"	
11/24				

Observing Word Strategies in Writing

Writing samples also show growth in word knowledge. Because writing results in a visible, external product, it is easier to determine what skills your students are actually using. By looking at two or three writing samples done a month or more apart, progress in word development is easy to determine.

To examine a writing sample to gain knowledge about phonics knowledge, record all words misspelled and how the word was spelled. Analyze the errors and see if there is a pattern to the types of errors made. Look at your students' spelling of high-frequency words. Remember that many common words do not follow spelling patterns and students just have to learn how to spell them. Look at their attempts at spelling less frequent words. Do their invented spellings indicate that they can hear sounds in words and know what letters usually represent those sounds? Are the letters in the correct order? Are they spelling by pattern rather than just putting down one letter for each sound? Are they adding endings correctly and applying spelling changes when needed?

Looking at Toby's errors, we can conclude that he misspells many common words, including confusing common homophones. If other students have similar misspellings of high-frequency words, these words could be gradually added to the class word wall. If Toby's errors are unique, you might want to create a personal word wall for him, as described in Chapter 8. His misspellings of less frequent words indicate that he is primarily spelling words by putting down a letter for each sound he hears. That spelling strategy works in Spanish where letters almost always represent the same sound, but in English words are spelled by pattern. Lessons such as What Looks Right? described in Chapter 10 and learning how prefixes and suffixes work in big words as described in Chapter 12 should help Toby move forward in using patterns to decode and spell words.

Spelling Errors in Writing Sample

Name Toby

Date	High-Frequency Words	Analysis	Lower-Frequency Words	Analysis
9/7	thay (they)	Misspells many common words, including common homophones	sumer (summer)	Spells one letter=one sound Needs work with prefixes, suffixes, spelling changes
	to (too)		vacashun (vacation)	
	frend (friend)		speshul (special)	
	there (their)		complan (complain)	
	were (where)		hotest (hottest)	
	accept (except)		swiming (swimming)	
			flots (floats)	
			eckspensive (expensive)	
			crouded (crowded)	
10/25				

The Names Test

Another possibility you may want to consider to help you assess your students' use of phonics skills is the Names Test. I developed the Names Test several years ago when working with a group of older remedial readers. These boys were good context users, and it was quite difficult to determine what they knew about letter–sound patterns when they were reading contextually because they were such good context users. I wanted a measure of their word-identification ability that was not confounded by context but that was not just a list of words. Reading a list of words is a rather unnatural act, and choosing the words is quite difficult. If you choose words most children have in their listening vocabularies, you run the risk of also choosing words they know as sight words and thus don't have to decode, and you could overestimate their letter–sound knowledge. If you choose very obscure words, the children probably don't have the words in their listening vocabularies and thus can't use the "sounds right" clue to check their probable pronunciation. If you use nonsense words, many readers will try to turn them into real words.

Imagine that you want to know whether a child can decode words with the common sound for the vowel **a**. If you have the child pronounce common words such as **clay**, **back**, and **star** to determine her ability to decode words with the vowel **a** and she correctly pronounces them, you don't know whether she decoded those words or if these were sight words learned from her previous reading. For this reason, some tests use nonsense words to test decoding skills. The child might be asked to pronounce made-up words such as **glay**, **dack**, and **smar**. Nonsense words solve the problem of the child's knowing the words as sight words, but nonsense words have another problem. While reading, good readers ask themselves questions such as "Did that make sense?" and "Did that sound right?" Asking these questions is a very important reading strategy because it allows the readers to self-correct errors and to constantly check their decoding with the context of what they are reading. Reading nonsense words violates this self-checking strategy good readers use, and many good readers will mispronounce the nonsense words by making them into real words they have heard of. **Glay** might be pronounced as **gray** or **glad**. **Dack** might be **back** or **deck**. **Smar** might be pronounced **smart**. Because children tend to want to make nonsense words into "words they have heard of," tests that use nonsense words often result in children showing less phonics ability than they actually have.

There is one type of word, however, that children hear often—and thus have in their listening vocabularies—but that they don't read often and thus are not apt to have already learned as sight words. Names are heard all over the place. Names are a big part of every TV and radio program, and usually these names are heard but not seen. Names are one type of word that most children have a lot more of in their listening vocabularies than in their sight vocabularies; thus, names can be used to measure decoding ability not confounded by context. If you gave the Names Test to a struggling reader and he correctly pronounced the names **Jay, Blake, Shaw, Slade, Swain, Dale, Yale, Wade, Clark, Zane, Jake**, and the syllables containing an **a** in Con**way**, **Samp**son, **Stan**ley, Ber**nard**, **Aus**tin, Yolan**da**, **Pat**rick, **An**derson, and **Bateman**, you could be pretty certain that he knew the common sounds for the vowel **a**.

In addition to their more-often-heard-than-read quality, names have another advantage for a word-reading test. Teachers and others often "call the roll" (read lists of names). Thus, reading a list is a somewhat more natural real-reading task than most other word-list reading tasks. The Names Test (Cunningham, 1990; Duffelmeyer et al., 1994) was developed to help teachers reliably assess decoding ability using a real-life reading task.

To administer the Names Test, print the names on index cards or copy the reproducible list. Make another list on which you can record responses. Ask the child to pretend that he or she is a teacher and that this is the list of names of the students in the class. Have the child read the list, as if he or she is taking attendance.

Use a check to indicate correct responses and write the phonetic spelling for any incorrect responses given by the child. If the child does not attempt a name, write "no" next to that name and encourage him or her to continue. For polysyllabic words, consider the word correct regardless of where the child places the accent on the word.

Analyze the child's responses, looking for patterns indicative of decoding strengths and weaknesses. Keep a record of each child's responses and give the test again after several weeks or months of instruction as an indicator of growth in the ability to decode words.

Coaching Students to Use What They Know

If you have a typical class of students, you probably have children who know a lot more about letters, sounds, and spelling patterns than they actually use when reading and writing. A basic principle of *Phonics They Use* is that the work we do with words is useful and worthwhile only if children actually use what they know while reading and writing. In all word activities, the focus is on *transfer* to reading and writing. In Guess the Covered Word activities, emphasis is on helping children verbalize how using meaning, all the beginning letters, and word length helps them make a very good guess. By ending each and every Making Words and Rounding Up the Rhymes lesson with a few transfer words that the rhyming words will help children read and spell, you are constantly reminding them how and when to use their word strategies. Children write using words they have explored in Reading/Writing Rhymes and What Looks Right? lessons. All the activities in the big-words chapters focus children on how looking for familiar chunks, roots, prefixes, and suffixes helps them decode, spell, and build meaning for big words.

figure 13.1 **Reproducible List of Names for the Names Test**

Jay Conway	Chuck Hoke
Kimberly Blake	Homer Preston
Cindy Sampson	Ginger Yale
Stanley Shaw	Glen Spencer
Flo Thornton	Grace Brewster
Ron Smitherman	Vance Middleton
Bernard Pendergraph	Floyd Sheldon
Austin Sheperd	Neal Wade
Joan Brooks	Thelma Rinehart
Tim Cornell	Yolanda Clark
Roberta Slade	Gus Quincy
Chester Wright	Patrick Tweed
Wendy Swain	Fred Sherwood
Dee Skidmore	Ned Westmoreland
Troy Whitlock	Zane Anderson
Shane Fletcher	Dean Bateman
Bertha Dale	Jake Murphy
Gene Loomis	

figure 13.2   Names Response Sheet

_____ Jay	_____ Conway
_____ Kimberly	_____ Blake
_____ Cindy	_____ Sampson
_____ Stanley	_____ Shaw
_____ Flo	_____ Thornton
_____ Ron	_____ Smitherman
_____ Bernard	_____ Pendergraph
_____ Austin	_____ Sheperd
_____ Joan	_____ Brooks
_____ Tim	_____ Cornell
_____ Roberta	_____ Slade
_____ Chester	_____ Wright
_____ Wendy	_____ Swain
_____ Dee	_____ Skidmore
_____ Troy	_____ Whitlock
_____ Shane	_____ Fletcher
_____ Bertha	_____ Dale
_____ Gene	_____ Loomis
_____ Chuck	_____ Hoke
_____ Homer	_____ Preston
_____ Ginger	_____ Yale
_____ Glen	_____ Spencer
_____ Grace	_____ Brewster
_____ Vance	_____ Middleton
_____ Floyd	_____ Sheldon
_____ Neal	_____ Wade
_____ Thelma	_____ Rinehart
_____ Yolanda	_____ Clark
_____ Gus	_____ Quincy
_____ Patrick	_____ Tweed
_____ Fred	_____ Sherwood
_____ Ned	_____ Westmoreland
_____ Zane	_____ Anderson
_____ Dean	_____ Bateman
_____ Jake	_____ Murphy

In spite of all this concerted effort to include transfer in all phonics lessons, there are some children who "just don't get it!" They participate, enjoy, and even seem to understand the word activities but when they read and write, they don't use what they know! To help children use whatever phonics they know, you must seize opportunities to coach them during writing conferences and meet with students one-on-one or in small groups and coach them to use what they know to figure out new words.

✻ Coaching during Writing

Writing conferences—when you are helping students revise, edit, and fix their spelling on a piece they are going to publish—provide an opportunity to coach children to use what they have learned about spelling. There are some words that children use in their writing that they can't be expected to know how to spell and, when conferencing with these children, you can simply acknowledge the good efforts shown in their attempts at spelling and then write the correct spelling of the words. But at other times, the writing conference can be used as a teachable moment to nudge students forward in their use of spelling patterns. Imagine that you are editing with a child and the child has written the word **trade** as **trd**. Ask that child:

> "Where's your vowel? Every word needs at least one vowel. Remember in Making Words we always use at least one red letter in every word. Stretch out the word **trade** and listen for the vowel you hear."

The child will probably hear the **a**. Then help him decide where to put it. Add the **e** on the end and tell him that you can't hear the **e** but that if you say **trade** slowly, you can hear the **a** and that when he is trying to spell a word to remember that every word needs at least one vowel.

Now imagine that another child comes to you with **trade** spelled **trad**. You might say something like:

> "That was a good try on **trade**. You wrote down every sound you heard. But let's look at the spelling pattern **a-d**. We know some **a-d** words: **b-a-d** spells **bad**; **m-a-d** spells **mad**; **d-a-d** spells **dad**. Can you think of a word that rhymes with **trade** and uses that spelling pattern?"

If **made** is on the word wall, the child will probably realize that **trade** should be spelled with the same pattern. It is also possible (but not likely) that he will think of **paid** and want to spell **trade** as **t-r-a-i-d**. In this case, acknowledge that **trade** does rhyme with **paid** and could be spelled like **paid** but point out the other pattern in words like **made** and **grade**.

Here is another common example. A child has written **invitation** spelled **invitashun**. You compliment the child for listening for all the sounds in the word but then remind her that big words often have chunks that are spelled differently.

If you have a **tion** word on the word wall—such as **question** or **vacation**—call the child's attention to that word and help her use the last chunk to spell **invitation** correctly. If you don't have a **tion** word on the word wall, try to think of a **tion** word the child might be able to spell—perhaps **nation** or **motion**. If other children make similar errors in spelling, consider adding a **tion** word to the word wall and doing on-the-back activities in which the children use the **tion** word-wall word to spell simple two-syllable words such as **nation**, **motion**, **lotion**, **mention**, and **caption**.

Writing conferences are a great opportunity to individualize what you teach children. For some words, you may simply praise their correct spelling of word-wall words, encourage their invented spelling efforts, and fix the spelling. For other words—words they should be spelling by pattern—you can use the opportunity to point out things about letters, sounds, and spelling patterns that they know but are not applying as they are writing.

✳ Coaching during Reading

To coach children to use what they know while reading, do some short (5 to 10 minutes) individual or very small group coaching sessions in which you coach students to use what they know at the exact moment they need to use it. Use a text that they haven't read before and that contains some words they need to figure out. Before reading, don't introduce any vocabulary. Explain that they will come to words they haven't learned yet and that the purpose of these lessons is to practice how good readers figure out words they don't know.

Imagine that Sean is reading and when he comes to an unknown word he stops and looks at you for help. Instead of telling him the word or asking him to sound it out, say:

> "Put your finger on the word and say all the letters."

Good readers look at all the letters in each word. Children who are struggling with reading tend to look quickly at the word and, if they don't instantly recognize it, they stop and wait for someone to tell them the word. Asking them to say all the letters forces them to look at all the letters. (Note that you are not giving the sounds of letters but rather naming the letters.) Sometimes, after saying all the letters, they correctly pronounce the word! This is proof that they aren't in the habit of looking at all the letters. Let them know what they have done by saying something like:

> "That's right. There are lots of words we see when we are reading that we don't recognize right away but, when we look at all the letters, we can sometimes figure them out. Good job! Continue reading."

If, after saying the letters, Sean does not say the word, you have four possible cues to point out. First look to see if the word has a rhyming pattern Sean should know. If so point that out by saying something like:

"Let's see, you just said the letters in the word **s-t-r-i-n-g**. I bet you know some other words that end in **i-n-g**. What does **t-h-i-n-g** spell?"

If you have been doing some of the rhyming on-the-back activities and the transfer steps of Rounding Up the Rhymes, Making Words lessons, or Using Words You Know lessons, Sean will probably quickly pronounce "string." Let him know what he has done to pronounce the word by saying something like:

"Right. When you see a word you don't know, remember to think of other words that are spelled the same and might rhyme."

If the word is a longer word and made up of chunks Sean should know, ask him if he recognizes any familiar chunks.

"Do you recognize a root word or other chunk you know in that word?"

If he needs further help, use your fingers to cover all but the first chunk and then the other chunks and have him pronounce each. Once he gets the word correctly pronounced, be sure to tell him what he did so that he can begin to use the strategies when you are not with him.

"When you come to a big word, look for parts you know and put all the chunks together to figure out the word."

Sometimes the word does not follow any of the patterns the student should know and does not have recognizable chunks. When that happens, coach the child to use picture clues or context clues to decode the word. If there is a good picture clue (which Sean has ignored!), you could say,

"What animal do you see in the picture that begins with **cr**?"

If Sean has the word **crocodile** in his listening-meaning vocabulary, he will probably quickly say, "crocodile." Again, be sure to tell him the strategy he used so he can learn to use picture clues when he is reading on his own.

If the word does not follow a pattern, has no familiar chunks, and is not cued by the picture, cue Sean to use the letters he knows and the context to figure out the word. Say:

"Keep your finger on that word and finish the sentence."

It may seem foolish to have the child keep his finger there, but many children's print tracking skills are not nearly as good as those of adults. These children can't use the context of the sentence and the letters in the unknown word to figure out a word because once they get to the end of the sentence they can't quickly look back and find the troublesome word. Keeping one finger on the word allows the child to quickly track back. If, after finishing the sentence, the child correctly pronounces the word, say something like:

> "Right. You can figure out lots of words you don't know if you use your finger to keep track of where the word is, finish the sentence, and then do like we do in Guess the Covered Word and guess a word that makes sense, begins with all the right letters, and is the right length. Continue reading."

This explanation of how to coach a child to use what he knows makes coaching sound much longer and more complicated than it actually is. When coaching a child to use what he knows (but isn't using), choose text in which the child is going to come to an unknown word every second or third sentence. When the child stops at a word, go through the following steps:

1. Have the child name all the letters.

2. If after naming the letters, the child correctly pronounces the word, tell him explicitly how he figured out the word.

    "When you say all the letters in a word, you can often put the letters together to figure out the word."

3. If after naming the letters the child does not correctly say the word, decide which of four strategies he should use and cue him to that strategy:

"Let's see. The word is spelled__. We can spell__. Can you make this rhyme with__?"

Or:

"Do you see any root words or other familiar chunks you know?"

Or:

"I see something in the picture that begins with the letters in that word."

4. Finally, if the word does not have a rhyming pattern cue, a chunking cue, or a picture cue, have the child put his finger on the word, finish the sentence, and use letter sounds and context together to figure out the word.

When your students figure out a word after any of your cueing, congratulate them and point out what strategy they used that helped them figure out the word. If students mispronounce a word (instead of the usual struggling reader strategy of stopping on the word and waiting to be told), wait for them to finish the sentence, repeat the sentence as it was read, point out that it didn't make sense, and then cue them to use an appropriate strategy for that word.

Not all your students need the kind of one-on-one or very small group coaching described here, but for those who do, short coaching sessions held a few times each week make a world of difference in their ability to use what they know when they need to use it!

Interventions for Older Struggling Readers

Most upper-grade students who have not learned basic decoding skills are resistant to any kind of "babyish" instruction. They still need to learn the rhyming patterns we use to decode and spell short words and the morphemic patterns we use to decode and spell longer words. Teachers of older children (and adults) have had good success with three game-like teaching strategies: Brand Name Phonics, The Wheel, and Mystery Word Match.

✳ Brand Name Phonics

Brand Name Phonics is based on the Using Words You Know lesson format described in Chapter 10. Instead of using "boring" words, students learn how the products, places, and signs in their environment can be the keys to unlocking the pronunciation and spelling of thousands of words.

Ideally, you would bring the actual box, can, ad, sign, etc. into the classroom for use in the lessons. Some teachers download photos from a company's website and use these to trigger students' interest and awareness that they do indeed see and read these words in their everyday world. You may want to use a combination of real containers, advertisements, and photos depending on the words you are using. After doing each lesson, it is helpful to display the containers, advertisements, photos, etc., on a board somewhere in the room so that students will have these words constantly available for use when they need a word to help them decode or spell a similar word.

For the first lesson, use three products whose names rhyme: Snack Pack, Slim Jim, and Shake 'N Bake. By starting with these rhyming products, you can immediately make the point to students that words with the same spelling pattern usually rhyme. Here is an outline of how this first lesson might go.

1. Begin by displaying the products and letting students talk about them. Do they recognize them, eat them, like them, etc.?

2. Have students identify the names and write these names to head three columns on the board or chart. Once they are all written, help students notice that they rhyme and then underline the spelling pattern: **ack**, **im**, **ake**.

Snack Pack	Slim Jim	Shake 'N Bake

Point out to students that many rhyming words have the same spelling pattern. The spelling pattern begins with the first vowel and goes to the end of the syllable.

3. Have students divide a piece of paper into three columns and head these with Snack Pack, Slim Jim, and Shake 'N Bake, underlining the spelling pattern in each.

4. Tell students that you are going to show them some words and that they should write them under the product with the same spelling pattern. Show them words that you have written on index cards. Let different students go to the board and write the words there as everyone is writing them on their paper. Do not let the students pronounce the words until they are written on the board. Help the students pronounce the words by making them rhyme. Here are some words to use:

back	dim	cake	take	rack
trim	track	Kim	Tim	snake

Once all the words are written, have students verbalize the strategy they used to read the words:

"If s-n-a-c-k is snack, then t-r-a-c-k must be track. If b-a-k-e is bake, s-n-a-k-e is snake."

5. Explain to students that thinking of rhyming words can help them spell also. This time you will not show them the words, but you will say words and they will have to decide which product they rhyme with and use the spelling pattern to spell them. Say some words but do not show them to your students. Have your students write the words under the product word that will help them spell them. Have a student write each word on the chart or board. Here are some words you might pronounce and have them spell:

black	swim	lake	flake	smack
skim	shack	quack	quake	brim

Again, help them verbalize their strategy by leading them to explain,

"If slim is spelled s-l-i-m, brim is probably spelled b-r-i-m. If shake is spelled s-h-a-k-e, quake is probably spelled q-u-a-k-e."

6. End this part of the lesson by helping students verbalize that in English, words that rhyme often have the same spelling pattern and that good readers and spellers don't sound out every letter; rather, they try to think of a rhyming word and read or spell the word using the pattern in the rhyming word.

7. Explain to the students that using the rhyme to help them read and spell words works with longer words too. Show students these words written on index cards and have them write them under the appropriate product. Once the word is written on the board or chart, have them pronounce the word making the last syllable rhyme with the product:

victim	shortcake	paperback	horseback	retake
flashback	denim	soundtrack	drawback	feedback

8. Now say these words and have students decide which product the last syllable rhymes with and use that spelling pattern to spell it. Give help with the spelling of the first part if needed.

handshake	outback	blackjack	remake	Muslim
unpack	bookrack	snowflake	hijack	racetrack

9. Again, end the lesson by helping students notice how helpful it is to think of a rhyming word they know how to spell when trying to read or spell a strange word.

The steps for a Brand Name Phonics lesson are:

1. Display and talk about the products.
2. Identify the spelling patterns.
3. Make as many columns as needed on the board and on student papers. Head these with the product name and underline the spelling pattern.
4. Show the students one-syllable words written on index cards, have them write the words under the product with the same pattern, and then have them use the rhyme to pronounce the words.
5. Say one-syllable words and have your students decide how to spell them by deciding which product they rhyme with.
6. Repeat the above procedure with longer words.
7. Help students verbalize how words they know how to spell help them read and spell lots of other words, including longer words.

For some products that have lots of rhyming words, this lesson might take two days. For other products, the lesson might be completed in one session. It is best to spend no more than 15 to20 minutes in any one session with a lesson because student attention will waver.

For English Language Learners

Products, stores, restaurant names, and signs are some of the first words new arrivals learn when they come to the United States. When English language learners can use brand names they recognize to help them learn how our complex English spelling system works, they will feel empowered and gain the confidence that they can learn to read!

Here are some other lessons your students might enjoy as they learn how lots of words they know will help them decode and spell other words:

Key Words: **Sprite   Coke   Grape**

One-syllable words to read: **ape, bite, poke, scrape, tape, quite, stroke, white, choke**

One-syllable words to spell: **kite, spite, broke, smoke, spoke, shape, drape, joke, cape**

Longer words to read: **ignite, provoke, escape, shipshape, unite, invite**

Longer words to spell: **reunite, landscape, polite, impolite, campsite, reshape, revoke**

Key Words: **Taco Bell   Burger King   Pizza Hut**

One-syllable words to read: **fell, part, shut, bring, yell, sting, string, shell, sell, rut, fling**

One-syllable words to spell: **ring, spring, swell, wing, swing, smell, strut, glut, spell, well**

Longer words to read: **haircut, misspell, first, string, darling, inning, peanut, outsmart**

Longer words to spell: **shortcut, seashell, something, hamstring, upswing, undercut**

Key Words: **Wal Mart   Dollar Store   First Bank (Substitute your local places with mart, store, and bank in their names)**

One-syllable words to read: **thank, tank, tore, prank, part, art, yank, snore, chore, chart**

One-syllable words to spell: **core, smart, rank, crank, start, blank, plank, shore, score**

Longer words to read: **seashore, outflank, ignore, apart adore, anymore, explore**

Longer words to spell: **depart, offshore, outsmart, outrank, restore, drugstore, bookstore**

Key Words: **Bold   Shout   Cheer**

One-syllable words to read: **sold, scout, told, deer, mold, shout, clout, trout, peer, steer**

One-syllable words to spell: **gold, pout, spout, sprout, jeer, sneer, cold, scold, stout, fold**

Longer words to read: **checkout, reindeer, blackout, blindfold, scaffold, uphold, dropout**

Longer words to spell: **cookout, without, handout, unfold, fallout, withhold, volunteer**

Key Words: **ice cream   Cool Whip**

One-syllable words to read: **nice, team, steam, stream, slice, school, vice, skip, beam, spice**

One-syllable words to spell: **gleam, twice, dream, clip, price, pool, spool, scream, grip**

Longer words to read: **mainstream, equip, downstream, gossip, preschool, whirlpool**

Longer words to spell: **upstream, overprice, sunbeam, carpool, friendship, spaceship**

Key Words: **Kit Kat   Goldfish**

One-syllable words to read: **spit, split that grit, flat, dish, bold, spat, mold, rat**

One-syllable words to spell: **slit, old, hold, wish, swish, quit, chat, hat, hit, brat**

Longer words to read: **admit, profit, wildcat, credit, democrat, selfish, unselfish, acrobat, blindfold**

Longer words to spell: **permit, visit, combat, outfit, nonfat, catfish, starfish, doormat**

It is very important for Brand Name Phonics lessons that you choose the rhyming words for the students to read and spell rather than ask them for rhyming words. (There are many good rhyming dictionaries, including some on-line, to help you quickly plan the lessons.) In English, there are often two spelling patterns for the same rhyme. If you ask your students what rhymes with cream or cool, they may come up with words with the **e-e-m** pattern, such as **seem**, and words with the **u-l-e** pattern, such as **rule**. If you ask them for rhyming words and they come up with a word that does rhyme but has a different spelling pattern, they may ignore your instruction teaching them to use patterns from words they know to read and spell other words. Once you have them decoding and spelling by pattern, you can use the What Looks Right? lesson format (Chapter 10) to help them develop their visual checking sense and learn how to use a dictionary to check the spelling of a word.

❋ The Wheel

The popular game show *Wheel of Fortune* is premised on the idea that meaning and some letters allow you to figure out many words. In this game, meaning is provided by the category to which the words belong. A variation of this game can be used to introduce polysyllabic words and teach students to use meaning and all the letters they know. Here is how to play The Wheel.

Possible Brand Names and Rhyming Patterns

A patterns

ace	<u>Ace</u> Hardware
ack	Sn<u>ack</u> P<u>ack</u>
ade	lemon<u>ade</u>
aid	B<u>a</u>nd-<u>Aid</u>; Kool-<u>Aid</u>
ail	n<u>ail</u> polish R<u>ail</u>road Crossing
ain	White R<u>ain</u>
air	h<u>air</u> spray
ake	Sh<u>ake</u> 'N B<u>ake</u>
ale	ginger <u>ale</u>
all	<u>All</u>
am	P<u>am</u>
an	B<u>an</u>
and	B<u>and</u>-Aid
ane	candy c<u>ane</u>s
ank	--- B<u>ank</u>
ap	ginger sn<u>ap</u>s
ape	gr<u>ape</u>
are	Ace Hardw<u>are</u>
ark	No P<u>ark</u>ing
art	Walm<u>art</u>
at	f<u>at</u> free; Kit K<u>at</u>
ate	Colg<u>ate</u>
ay	hair spr<u>ay</u>; Ocean Spr<u>ay</u>

E Patterns

each	<u>Reach</u>
eam	ice cr<u>eam</u>
ean	jelly b<u>ean</u>s
ear	Goody<u>ear</u>
eat	Wh<u>eat</u> Thins; m<u>eat</u>
ee	fat fr<u>ee</u>
eed	Sp<u>eed</u> Stick, sp<u>eed</u> limit
een	Gr<u>een</u> Giant
eer	Ch<u>eer</u> D<u>eer</u> Crossing
eet	Sw<u>eet</u>'N Low
ell	Taco B<u>ell</u>
est	Cr<u>est</u> R<u>est</u> Stop
ew	Mountain D<u>ew</u>

I Patterns

ice	<u>ice</u> cream
ick	Speed St<u>ick</u>
ide	T<u>ide</u>
ield	Y<u>ield</u>
ight	R<u>ight</u> Guard
im	Sl<u>im</u> J<u>im</u>
ime	lemon l<u>ime</u>
in	Wheat Th<u>in</u>s
ine	P<u>ine</u>-Sol
ing	Burger K<u>ing</u>
ip	Cool Wh<u>ip</u>
ipe	Fudge Str<u>ipe</u>s
ish	Goldf<u>ish</u>
it	K<u>it</u> Kat
ite	Spr<u>ite</u>; Wh<u>ite</u> Rain

O Patterns

oad	Railr<u>oad</u> Crossing
og	d<u>og</u> chow
oke	C<u>oke</u>
oil	<u>oil</u>
old	B<u>old</u>
one	Coppert<u>one</u>
ood	G<u>oo</u>dyear
ool	C<u>ool</u> Whip; K<u>ool</u>-Aid
oot	r<u>oot</u> beer
op	p<u>op</u>corn, ST<u>OP</u>
ope	Sc<u>ope</u>
ore	dollar st<u>ore</u>
orn	popc<u>orn</u>
oss	Railroad Cr<u>oss</u>ing
ound	M<u>ound</u>s
out	Sh<u>out</u>
ow	dog ch<u>ow</u>
ow	Ivory Sn<u>ow</u>; Sweet'N L<u>ow</u>
oy	Almond J<u>oy</u>

U Patterns

un	Capri S<u>un</u>
ut	Pizza H<u>ut</u>

Remind students that many words can be figured out, even when they can't decode all the chunks, if they think about what makes sense and whether it has the parts they do know in the right places. Ask students who have watched *Wheel of Fortune* to explain how it is played. Then explain, step by step, how your version of The Wheel will be different:

1. Contestants guess all letters without considering if they are consonants or vowels.

2. They must have all letters filled in before they can say the word. (This is to encourage them to learn to spell.)

3. They will win paper clips instead of great prizes.

4. Vanna will not be there to turn letters!

Write the category for the game on the board and draw blanks for each letter in the first word.

Have a student begin by asking,

"Is there a . . . ?"

If the student guesses a correct letter, fill that letter in. Give that student one paper clip for each time that letter occurs. Let the student continue to guess letters until he or she gets a "No." When a student asks for a letter that is not there, write the letter above the puzzle and go on to the next student.

Make sure that all letters are filled in before anyone is allowed to guess. (This really shows them the importance of spelling and attending to common spelling patterns.) Give the person who correctly guesses the word five bonus paper clips. Just as in other games, if someone says the answer out of turn, immediately award the bonus paper clips to the person whose turn it was. The student having the most paper clips at the end is the winner. Here is an example:

The teacher draws nine blanks on the board and says, "The category is sports. Our first word has nine letters. Al, guess a letter."

_ _ _ _ _ _ _ _ _

Al asks for a **t**. There is no **t**, so the teacher moves on to David, who asks for an **r**. There is no **r** either. Nor is there an **o**, which Carol asks for. But Jon asks for and gets an **a**.

_ _ _ _ _ _ _ a _

Jon goes again and asks for an **s**.

s _ _ _ _ _ _ a _

Next, he asks for an **e**.

s e _ _ _ _ _ a _

Next, he asks for a **d**. There is no **d**, so the turn passes to Paula, who asks for an **n**.

<u>s</u> <u>e</u> _ _ _ _ <u>n</u> <u>a</u> _

Next, Paula asks for an **m**.

<u>s</u> <u>e</u> <u>m</u> _ _ _ <u>n</u> <u>a</u> _

Then she asks for an **i**.

<u>s</u> <u>e</u> <u>m</u> <u>i</u> _ <u>i</u> <u>n</u> <u>a</u>

The light dawns in Paula's eyes. She quickly asks for an **f** and **l** and wins by correctly spelling and pronouncing **semifinal**!

❋ Mystery Word Match

Mystery Word Match is a game I developed to help children learn to look for familiar chunks in unfamiliar big words. To begin the game, the teacher has a polysyllabic word in mind. This big word is the "mystery word." The teacher first draws the number of short blanks to indicate the number of letters in the mystery word. He then writes three clue words under these letter blanks or spaces.

tech tips

Mystery Word Match was in the early editions of *Phonics They Use*. I dropped it out of the third edition, however, because it was so hard for teachers to make up good clue words. The first chunk was easy—you could simply look in the dictionary. But the middle and end chunks were much harder. Before a book is revised, it goes out to reviewers who make suggestions. One of the reviewers bemoaned "the mysterious disappearance of Mystery Word Match." I wished I had a way to tell him or her that I gave up on it because teachers needed to be able use mystery words that fit their curriculum, and it was just too hard to do. Then I thought about the Internet. Surely, there was a site that would match parts of words. I put my husband (who is much better at searching the Web than I) to work, and, in no time at all, he had found several sites. The one I use is www.onelook.com; you put asterisks around the letters you are looking to match and instantly get lots of matches. (Be sure the match has the same pronunciation.) A special thanks to the reviewer whose comment is responsible for the return of this fun and educational big-word game!

Each clue word has a chunk of the mystery word in the same position in the word and with the same pronunciation. Sometimes the chunks are syllables, and sometimes they are larger than syllables. It is important that students not only focus on the syllables because when they are decoding a big word, they access from their word store the words with the largest chunks. For the word **entertainment**, for example, students might have recognized three chunks— **enter**, **tain**, and **ment**. Sometimes the chunks are roots, prefixes, and suffixes, but sometimes they are just familiar parts.

As each clue word is written, the teacher and students pronounce it and put it in a meaningful sentence. Before guessing which part of which clue word is in the mystery word, the students should pronounce the words again to assure that everyone can easily pronounce the clue words.

Sample Mystery Word Match Round   The teacher draws eight short lines on the board and says, "Our mystery word has eight letters." The teacher then writes the three clue words under the lines. The students and teacher pronounce each and put each in a sentence. Before beginning play, all three clue words are once more pronounced by everybody.

_ _ _ _ _ _ _ _

testimony

celebrate

direction

A student is chosen and begins by asking if the mystery word begins like, has a middle like, or ends like one of the clues. If the answer is "yes," the teacher writes these letters on the correct lines and the student continues to ask. If the answer is "no," the turn goes to the next student.

Carl: Does the mystery word begin like **direction**?

Teacher: No, I am sorry. It is Terry's turn.

Terry: Does the mystery word end like **direction**?

Teacher: No, I am sorry. It is Jared's turn.

Jared: Does the mystery word have a middle like **direction**?

Teacher: Yes, it does.

Teacher writes **re** on the appropriate letter lines:

_ _ r e _ _ _ _

Teacher: Jared, you may ask another question.

Jared: Does the mystery word begin like **celebrate**?

Teacher: Yes, it does.

Teacher writes **ce** on appropriate lines:

c e r e _ _ _ _

Teacher: Jared, you may ask another question.

Jared: Does the mystery word end like **testimony**?

Teacher writes **mony**.

c e r e m o n y

Jared pronounces the word **ceremony** and wins this round of Mystery Word Match.

Mystery Word Match is a simple game, but students of all ages love playing it. A few cautions, however. The child who finishes putting the word in the letter blanks must also pronounce the word. If she cannot, play passes to the next person. If you enforce this rule and if you and your students have pronounced the clue words several times before beginning, even your struggling readers will pay attention to the pronunciation of the parts of the clue words. Another issue is students who "call out the answer" when it is not their turn. If that happens, the student whose turn it was is immediately declared the winner and awarded the points. Many teachers have the mystery word worth 10 points to begin with and subtract 1 point for every "no." Under these rules, Jared would have won 8 points for figuring out and pronouncing the mystery word.

You need to use the big words that are part of your curriculum for Mystery Word Match games, but here are some to get you started.

General Vocabulary

mysterious	**expectation**	**destination**
bacterial	respectable	dessert
mystified	limitation	assassination
continuous	explorer	article
transportation	**resolution**	**argument**
reporter	recipe	regulate
transferred	pollution	statement
mutation	insolent	artistic
resistance	**conversation**	**contestant**
insisting	conference	constitution
reformer	overthrow	informant
inheritance	sensation	pretested

Math Vocabulary

multiplication	**geometry**	**perpendicular**
amplify	geography	circular
multimedia	chemistry	expenditures
dedication	thermometer	perfection

denominator	**numerator**	**circumference**
terminator	nucleus	interference
monogram	alligator	incumbent
democracy	commercial	circuitry

equivalent	**equilateral**	**intersection**
turbulent	equivalent	consecutive
cavalry	funeral	international
equitable	gelatin	position

Science Vocabulary

experiment	**microorganism**	**photosynthesis**
nonperishable	microphone	hypothesis
extravagant	disorganized	idiosyncrasy
management	terrorism	photographer

metamorphic	**sedimentary**	**atmosphere**
humorless	secluded	thermostat
metabolic	elementary	attention
geographic	editor	hemisphere

constellation	**precipitation**	**conservation**
interstellar	recipient	consistently
creation	confrontation	casserole
concentrate	prefabricated	innovation

Social Studies Vocabulary

independence	**democracy**	**exploration**
undependable	demolition	deplorable
innocent	literacy	invitation
audience	sacrament	extension

revolution	**constitution**	**communities**
advocate	container	immunize
solution	substituted	compassion
rebellious	attention	activities

population	**republican**	**continent**
accumulated	pelican	constitution
intention	reevaluate	permanent
popularity	unpublished	testify

Summary

Assessment is a part of everything we do. To make any kind of decision, we collect and analyze evidence and then act on that evidence. In assessing children's phonics and spelling knowledge, teachers must be sure to focus more on what the children use than what they know. This chapter has shared a variety of ways to observe children's reading and writing behaviors and to determine what phonics knowledge they have and how they use that knowledge. Recording and analyzing your findings will allow you to pick and choose from the activities described throughout this book and modify them as necessary for the children you teach.

Phonics is helpful to children only if they use it when they need it—to figure out how to spell words while writing and decode words while reading. Many children will learn how to use what they know if you make sure to do the transfer parts of all the activities in this book. Some children need additional help to use what they know. Coaching children during writing conferences and in small groups or one-on-one sessions will ensure that phonics accomplishes its purpose with all the children you teach.

Older students who still struggle with decoding and spelling need instruction that doesn't look like the instruction they have already failed with. Brand Name Phonics, Mystery Word Match, and The Wheel are activities they enjoy and will help them develop the decoding and spelling skills they missed out on.

part four

Research and Terminology

Everything in *Phonics They Use* is grounded in the research literature, and the pertinent research is summarized in Chapter 14. The final chapter summarizes some of the phonics terminology teachers are expected to know. You should try to not use too much of this jargon with your children because it tends to confuse them and take their attention away from what you are really trying to teach them. Teachers, however, are expected to know this terminology, and the final chapter provides you with a handy reference.

chapter 14

The Theory and the Research—The Why Underlying the How

The question of instruction in phonics has aroused a lot of controversy. Some educators have held to the proposition that phonetic training is not only futile and wasteful but also harmful to the best interests of a reading program. Others believe that since the child must have some means of attacking strange words, instruction in phonics is imperative. There have been disputes also relative to the amount of phonics to be taught, the time when the teaching should take place and the methods to be used. In fact, the writer knows of no problem around which more disputes have centered.

PAUL MCKEE (1934, p. 191)

Clearly, the phonics question has been plaguing the field of reading for a long time. In this chapter, I will share with you my own history as a student, a teacher, and a researcher with the phonics dilemma; review the major research findings of the past 40 years; and explain the relationship between the research and the type of phonics instruction found in this book.

 ## *My Personal Phonics History*

My fate was probably sealed in 1949 when I was a first-grader at High Street School in Westerly, Rhode Island. In the morning, we were divided into reading groups and read about the adventures of Sally, Dick, Jane, Puff, and Spot. After lunch each day, we all pulled out bright blue phonics books and sounded out words. Little did I know that at five years old, I was thrust right into the middle of the sight word/phonics controversy.

The year 1965 found me teaching first grade in Key West, Florida. I taught the phonics in my basal manual, and most children learned to distinguish short vowels from long vowels. The children in my top group even developed the ability to "sound out" new words, although even then I didn't quite believe that what they did when they came to a new word was in any way related to what I was teaching them about phonics. One day I overheard a boy remark to a friend,

"The short vowels are pretty short but the long ones look pretty short, too."

His friend then proceeded to explain it to him.

"It's simple. The little ones are the short ones and the capital ones are the long ones!"

Although I continued to teach first grade and the vowel rules for several years, my faith in those rules was badly shaken!

I got my master's degree in reading from Florida State in 1968. *Linguistics* was the buzzword at that time, and I thought that "linguistic readers" were going to solve the decoding problems of our poor readers. I got a chance to try this out with a fourth-grade class of poor readers. Armed with the Merrill Linguistic Readers and the SRA Basic Reading Series, I abandoned phonics rules for linguistic patterns. Things went pretty well for the first month. The students learned all the short **a** patterns and read about Dan in his tan van. As we moved on, however, they began to confuse the previously learned patterns with the new ones. Worse yet, I realized that the children had stopped trying to make sense of what they were reading and were simply sounding out the patterns!

By 1970, context was the only remaining tool in my decoding arsenal. "Say 'blank' and read the rest of the sentence and then go back and think about what would make sense," was my 1970 brand of decoding instruction. In 1971, I found myself in Terre Haute, Indiana, as the special reading teacher at the Indiana State University Laboratory School. All day I worked with poor readers. Mostly, I tried to get these students to enjoy reading and to talk about what they read. I did almost no phonics instruction, but it did worry me that almost all the poor readers had little ability to decode an unfamiliar word.

My "real challenges" arrived after lunch each day. Rod and Eric were sixth-graders of normal intelligence who had been in remedial reading since second grade and who read at the second-grade level. Both boys were fluent with all the high-frequency words and were excellent users of picture and context clues. They could understand anything they could read and most of what you read to them. They had been scheduled for 45 minutes alone with me each day because they were to go on to junior high the next year and their parents were very worried that, after all these years, they still hadn't "caught on to reading."

For both Rod and Eric, the problem was clear-cut. They knew what reading was and that they were to make meaning from it. They enjoyed being read to and even enjoyed reading the high-interest, low-vocabulary books I could find that they could read themselves. They simply had not learned to decode! For the first semester, I taught Rod and Eric "word families." They were very competitive, and I made Go Fish, Old Maid, and Concentration games, which they could win by matching and saying rhyming words. We also made charts of rhyming words and wrote jingles and riddles, which were awful but appealed to their sixth-grade silliness. In addition to rhyming games and writing rhymes, each day we read together and I reminded them of the one strategy I had taught them. Both boys knew that when you came to a short word you didn't know, you should look to see if it would rhyme with a word you did know. When they couldn't think of a rhyming word, I prompted them with one. They used this strategy when they were reading and were amazed to discover that they could figure out even unusual names—**Tran**, **Clark**, **Kurt**.

Unfortunately, their newfound decoding ability did not transfer to bigger words. I taught them a few simple syllable-division rules, and they could sometimes figure out a two-syllable word, the syllables of which were familiar rhyming patterns—**zinger**, **target**, **pastor**. If a word had more than six letters, however, they couldn't even begin to do anything with it and would just skip it and go on!

By March, the boys were reading at a strong third-grade level—sometimes fourth—if they knew a lot about the topic. I knew that their inability and unwillingness to decode long words was the remaining hurdle, but I didn't know how to teach them to figure them out. I taught them some prefixes and suffixes and this helped with some words. I would drive home in the afternoons and see a big word on a billboard and ask myself,

"How did I figure out that word?"

I knew that I had not applied syllabication rules and then sounded out each syllable, but I didn't know what I had done.

We were at six weeks before the end of sixth grade, and Rod and Eric had begun the countdown to summer and junior high! In desperation, I searched the *Education Index* for "polysyllabic word instruction." I didn't find much, and discounted most of what I did find. Context was what Rod and Eric were currently using. Syllabication rules weren't working (and research confirmed that!). They had learned many of the common prefixes and suffixes, but they didn't seem to use them. Finally, one article suggested teaching students to use the dictionary respelling key (the pronunciation guide found at the bottom of the page in most dictionaries).

"Well, that's something I haven't tried," I thought. "But no one is ever going to stop reading and find the word in the dictionary and use the respelling key," I argued with myself.

But I decided to do it. What did I have to lose? We had to do something useful for the last six weeks, and at least they would know how to use the respelling key to pronounce a word if they would take the time to do it. For two weeks, I taught them how to use the key to figure out the pronunciation of unknown words. Then, when they understood how to do it, I gave them each a different list of five "really long" words (**conscientious**, **filibuster**, **mannequin**, **Phoenician**, **sporadically**) each day. Before we could go on to do anything interesting, they each had to find their words and use the key to figure them out and pronounce them for me.

They hated it but "it was good for them," and I was determined that they would have a big-word tool to take with them to junior high, so each day, they came in and picked up their list and their dictionaries and went to work. Ten days before the end of school, Rod walked in and picked up his list of five "humongous" words and his dictionary. He began to look up the first word, then he stopped, looked at the word, and then looked at me. "What if I already know this word? Do I still have to look it up?" he asked.

"Well, no," I responded. "I'm trying to give you a tool so that you can always pronounce any big word you ever come to, but if you know the word, you don't need the respelling key, do you?"

Rod looked again at the first word, studying the letters. He then correctly pronounced "spontaneous"! "That's right!" I exclaimed. "Now, you only have four to look up!" "Not if I know some of the others," Rod asserted. He was able to pronounce two of the other four words and only had to look up and use the key for two of the five big words. Meanwhile, Eric was studying his five words and he managed to pronounce two of his, only having to look up three. I was astonished! "Where had they learned those words?" I wondered. For the remaining nine days of school, Rod and Eric competed to see how many words they could figure out and not have to look up. To my amazement, by the last day of school they had gotten quite good at figuring out words of four or more syllables. The respelling key, which I had taught them to use as a tool, had taught them a system for independently figuring out big words. At the time I didn't understand how this miracle had occurred, but I sent Rod and Eric off to junior high more confident of their success than I had ever thought possible.

In 1972, I arrived at the University of Georgia to work on my doctorate in reading. I took my first seminar, and Dr. Ira Aaron led us to do some initial thinking about a dissertation topic. I already knew what I wanted to find out: "How do we decode an unknown word and particularly an unknown big word?" After much reading, thinking, and discussions with other doctoral students and Dr. George Mason, my advisor, I became convinced that decoding took place in what I called a compare/contrast way. Later this would be called "decoding by analogy." In addition to my dissertation (later published as Cunningham, 1975–76), I did quite a bit of research into analogic decoding (Cunningham, 1979, 1980; Cunningham & Guthrie, 1982; Gaskins et al., 1988), which confirmed for me that decoding was neither a letter-by-letter sounding process nor a rule-based, jargon-filled process. My observations of the children I had taught as well as the research I carried out convinced me that when readers come to unfamiliar words they do a fast search through their cognitive word stores for similar words with the same letters in the same places. They then use these analogs to come up with a possible pronunciation that they try out and cross-check with meaning.

I understood finally that when I complained that my first-graders knew the rules but didn't use them, I was probably right! The rules describe the system. The brain, however, is not a rule applier but a pattern detector. I also understood why teaching children linguistic patterns or "word families" was a powerful strategy if you could get them to use these spelling patterns to write and read words in meaningful texts.

By 1982, 10 years after Rod and Eric had learned to read, I had figured out how they did it. Combining word-family instruction with reading and writing in which they were encouraged to use rhyming words to figure out how to pronounce or spell unknown words taught them to look for patterns in words and, most importantly, that there were patterns to be found when they looked. Looking up big words in the dictionary respelling key forced them to look carefully at all the letters in the words (so that they could find them in the dictionary) and the analogs contained in the respelling key convinced them that there were patterns to be found in big words, too!

What We Know about How Good Readers Read Words

We know a great deal more about how word recognition occurs than can be explained in this section. The theory that explains the incredibly fast ability of the brain to recognize words and associate them with meaning is called *parallel distributed processing*. This theory is complex, but its most important tenets are easily understood. Information about a word is gained from its spelling (orthography), its pronunciation (phonology), its meaning (semantics), and the context in which the word occurs. The brain processes these sources of information in parallel, or simultaneously. The brain functions in word recognition, as it does in all other areas, as a pattern detector. Discussion of parallel distributed processing and its implications for word identification can be found in McClelland and Rumelhart (1986) Rumelhart and McClelland (1986) and Seidenberg and McClelland (1989). The theory is translated and explained simply and elegantly in Adams (1990). Beyond the fact that the brain responds to many sources of information in parallel and that it functions as a pattern detector, the following specific facts seem particularly pertinent to the question of what kind of phonics instruction we should have.

Readers Look at Virtually All of the Words and Almost All the Letters in Those Words   (McConkie, Kerr, Reddix, & Zola, 1987; Rayner & Pollatsek, 1989). For many years, it was generally believed that sophisticated readers sampled text. Based on predictions about what words and letters they would see, readers were thought to look at the words and letters just enough to see if their predictions were confirmed. Eye-movement research carried out with

computerized tracking has proven that, in reality, readers look at every word and almost every letter of each word. The amount of time spent processing each letter is incredibly small, only a few hundredths of a second. The astonishingly fast letter recognition for letters within familiar words and patterns is explained by the fact that our brains expect certain letters to occur in sequence with other letters.

Readers Usually Recode Printed Words into Sound   (McCutchen, Bell, France, & Perfetti, 1991; Tannenhaus, Flanigan, & Seidenberg, 1980). Although it is possible to read without any internal speech, we rarely do. Most of the time, as we read, we think the words in our mind. This phonological information is then checked with the information we received visually by analyzing the word for familiar spelling patterns. Saying the words aloud or thinking the words also seems to perform an important function in holding the words in auditory memory until enough words are read to create meaning.

Readers Recognize Most Words Immediately and Automatically without Using Context   (LaBerge & Samuels, 1974; Nicholson, 1991; Stanovich, 1991). Good readers use context to see if what they are reading makes sense. Context is also important for disambiguating the meaning of some words (for example, "I had a **ball** throwing the **ball** at the **ball**"). Occasionally, readers use context to figure out what the word is. Most of the time, however, words are identified based on their familiar spelling and the association of that spelling with a pronunciation. Context comes into play after, not before, the word is identified based on the brain's processing of the letter-by-letter information it receives. Several studies have found that poor readers rely more on context than good readers.

Readers Accurately and Quickly Pronounce Infrequent, Phonetically Regular Words   (Hogaboam & Perfetti, 1978). When presented with unfamiliar but phonetically regular words, good readers immediately and seemingly effortlessly assign them a pronunciation. The ability to quickly and accurately pronounce phonetically regular words that are not sight words is a task that consistently discriminates between good and poor readers.

Readers Use Spelling Patterns and Analogy to Decode Words   (Adams, 1990; Goswami & Bryant, 1990; Moustafa, 1997). The brain is primarily a pattern detector. Successfully decoding a word occurs when the brain recognizes a familiar spelling pattern or, if the pattern itself is not familiar, the brain searches through its store of words with similar patterns.

To decode the unfamiliar word **knob**, for example, the child who knew many words that began with **kn** would immediately assign to the **kn** the **n** sound. The initial **kn** was probably stored in the brain as a spelling pattern. If the child knew only a few other words with **kn** and hadn't read these words very often, that child would probably not have **kn** as a known spelling pattern and, thus, would have to do a quick search for known words that began with **kn**. If the child found the words **know** and **knew** and then tried this same sound on the unknown word **knob**, that child would have used the analogy strategy. Likewise, the child might know the pronunciation for **ob** because of having correctly read so many words containing the **ob** spelling pattern or might have had to access some words with **ob** to use them to come up with the pronunciation. The child who had no stored spelling patterns for **kn** or **ob** and no known words to access and compare to would be unlikely to successfully pronounce the unknown word **knob**.

Many people believe that when children are just beginning to read, they are not sensitive to patterns—only to individual letters. Cassar and Treiman (1997) investigated this by showing kindergartners and first graders pairs of nonwords (e.g., **baff** vs. **bbaf** and **pess** vs. **ppes**) and asking them which one could be a word. Results indicated that children were sensitive earlier than expected. Even the kindergartners could select which of the two doubled consonants could be a word. Wright and Ehri (2007) replicated these results and concluded that beginning readers in English begin to process units larger than single letters and that very early English readers understand that relationships between letters and sounds must also be sought in multiletter patterns.

Readers Divide Big Words as They See Them Based on Interletter Frequencies

(Mewhort & Campbell, 1981; Seidenberg, 1987). The research on syllabication rules show that it is quite possible to know the rules and still be unable to quickly and accurately pronounce novel polysyllabic words and equally possible to be able to pronounce them and not know the rules. Good readers "chunk" or divide words into manageable units. They do this based on the brain's incredible knowledge of which letters usually go together in words. If you did not recognize the word **midnight** in print, you would divide it between the **d** and the **n**. For the word **Madrid**, however, you would divide after the **a**, leaving the **dr** together. Interletter frequency theory explains this neatly by pointing out that the letters **dr** often occur together in syllables in words you know (**drop**, **dry**, **Dracula**). Words with the letters **dn** in the same syllable are almost nonexistent. This also explains why beginners might pronounce **f-a-t-h-e-r** as "fat her" but children who have some words from which the brain can generate interletter frequencies will leave the **th** together and pronounce "fa-ther."

Although summarizing what the brain does to identify words runs the risk of oversimplification, it seems necessary before considering what we know about instruction. As we read, we look very quickly at almost all letters of each word. For most words, this visual information is recognized as a familiar pattern with which a spoken word is identified and pronounced. Words we have read before are instantly recognized as we see them. Words we have not read before are almost instantly pronounced based on spelling patterns the brain has seen in other words. If the word is a big word, the brain uses its interletter frequency knowledge (based on all the words it knows) to chunk the word into parts whose letter patterns can then be compared. Meaning is accessed through visual word recognition, but the sound of the word supports the visual information and helps to hold the word in memory.

What We Know about How Children Learn to Read Words

At present, we know more about how the word identification process works than we do about how children learn to do it. Here are some research-based findings that should have an impact on instruction.

Children from Literate Homes Have Over 1,000 Hours of Informal Reading and Writing Encounters before Coming to School (Adams, 1990). We have always known that children who were read to came to school more ready, willing, and able to learn to read. Findings from emergent literacy research have made it clear that the reading/writing encounters many children have include more than just a bedtime story. Estimates are that children from literate homes experience almost an hour each day of informal reading and writing encounters—being read to, trying to read a favorite book, watching someone write a thank-you letter, trying to write, manipulating magnetic letters, talking with someone about environmental print such as grocery/restaurant labels and signs, and so forth. From these encounters, the children learn a tremendous amount of critical information. They know what reading and writing are really for and that you use words and letters. They know that you have to write these words and letters in a particular way, from top to bottom and left to right (though they often don't know this jargon). They also learn some words—important words like their name and the name of their pet dog and favorite fast-food restaurant. They learn the names of many of the letters of the alphabet and write these letters, usually in capital form. In addition to learning that words are made up of letters, which they can see, they somehow figure out that words are also made up of sounds, which they can't see.

Phonemic Awareness Is Important to Success in Beginning Reading   (Bryant, Bradley, Maclean, & Crossland, 1989; Ehri & Nunes, 2002). One of the understandings that many children gain from early reading and writing encounters is the understanding that words are made up of sounds. These sounds are not separate and distinct. In fact, their existence is quite abstract. Phonemic awareness has many levels and includes the ability to hear whether words rhyme, to know what word you would have if you removed a sound, and to blend and segment words (Anthony et al., 2003; Norris & Hoffman, 2002). Phonemic awareness seems to be developed through lots of exposure to nursery rhymes, alphabet books, and books that make words sound fun. Although children may be able to learn some letter sounds before they develop phonemic awareness, phonemic awareness must be present before children can manipulate those sounds as they try to read and write words.

Repeated Reading with Feedback and Assistance Improves Fluency   Fluency is the ability to read accurately, at a reasonable rate, and with expression that makes the reading sound like speaking. When children's oral reading is fluent, they usually have good comprehension of what they are reading. Good readers almost always read fluently. Struggling readers often read in a slow word-by-word fashion with many errors and little expression. Various ways of providing feedback and assistance to students as they reread text have been shown to improve reading fluency. The research on reading fluency is summarized in a chapter in the 2011 *Handbook of Reading Research* (Rasinski, Reutzel, Chard, & Linan-Thompson).

Children Who Can Decode Well Learn Sight Words Better (Ehri, 1991; Jorm & Share, 1983; Stanovich & West, 1989). Research indicates that the sight word versus phonics debate lacks reality when you consider how children learn words. When a new word is encountered for the first time, it is usually decoded. In decoding the word, the child forms phonological access routes for that word into memory. These access routes are built using knowledge of grapheme–phoneme correspondences that connect letters in spelling to phonemes in pronunciations of the words. The letters are processed as visual symbols for the phonemes and the sequence of letters is retained in memory as an alphabetic, phonological representation of the word. When the child encounters that word again, the connections between letters and phonemes are strengthened. Eventually, the spelling is represented in memory and the word is instantly recognized—but that instant recognition was based on some prior phonological processing. So words that were originally decoded come to be recognized as wholes, and words originally taught as wholes must be studied letter by letter in order to be instantly recognized. Ehri (2005) demonstrated that students do not decode words they are familiar with while reading and concluded that "students do not persist in decoding words once the words are practiced and retained in memory" (p. 182). The phonics versus sight word debate should be laid to rest.

The Division of Words into Onset and Rime Is a Psychological Reality (Trieman, 1985). In the 1934 edition of *Reading and Literature in the Elementary School*, Paul McKee discussed activities to help children decode words and indicated that there was mixed opinion as to whether it was best to start with the initial letters and then add the end (**sa**-**t**) or to keep the final letters together and add the beginning (**s**-**at**). Expressing some uncertainty, he did take a stand and recommend the latter. Teachers were encouraged to do word activities in which they took a known word and then changed the initial letters—**hand**, **sand**, **band**, **grand**, **stand**. Amazingly, he recommended that phonics instruction include "other tools such as analogy." For example, when confronted with the strange word **meat**, he suggested that a student may derive its pronunciation by proper associations gathered from the known words **eat** and **met** (p. 189).

McKee's intuitive understanding of the reading process in 1934 led him to recommend what researchers confirmed 50 years later. Syllables are the most distinct sound units in English, and children and adults find it much easier to divide syllables into their onsets (all letters before the vowel) and rimes (the vowel and what follows) than into any other units. Thus, **Sam** is more easily divided into **S-am** than into **Sa-m** or **S-a-m**. It is easier and quicker for people to change **Sam** to **ham** and **jam** than it is to change **Sam** to **sat** and **sad**. The psychological reality of onset and rime confirms the age-old practice of teaching word families and spelling patterns.

Lots of Successful Reading Is Essential for Readers to Develop Automaticity and Rapid Decoding   (Juel, 1990; Samuels, 2002; Stanovich & West, 1989). The major observable variable that separates good readers from poor readers is that good readers read a lot more and, when they are reading, they recognize most of the words instantly and automatically. If you recognize almost all the words, an unfamiliar word gets your immediate attention and you will stop and figure it out. Lots of easy reading in which most words are immediately recognized is essential for both the development of instantly recognized words and the ability and willingness to decode the occasional unfamiliar word. Recently, DeJong and Share (2007) confirmed the importance of lots of reading when they demonstrated that third-graders acquired many new words as a result of their independent reading. Many factors—including topic familiarity, text and picture support, number of unfamiliar words, and teacher support—interact to determine how easy or difficult a particular book is for a particular child.

Children Need to Apply Phonics to Their Reading but Not Necessarily in Highly Decodable Text   (Cunningham & Cunningham, 2002). The first time you encounter an unfamiliar-in-print word, you don't recognize it immediately. You have to figure out what it is. You might decode it or you might hear someone pronounce it. The next time you see that word you might remember having seen it but you might not remember what it is. Again, you could figure it out or you could ask someone, "What's that word?" Depending on how many repetitions you need to learn words (and that varies greatly from child to child) and on how important and distinctive the word is (most children learn **pizza** and **dinosaur** with few repetitions!), you will eventually get to the point where you "just know it." A sight word, like a good friend, is recognized instantly anywhere. Recognizing most of the word instantly—and only having to stop and figure out the occasional word—is what allows us to read quickly and fluently.

Some phonics advocates want to restrict materials beginners read to include only words they can decode and the absolutely necessary sight words. They argue that this will give children lots of practice decoding and require them to use their decoding skills as they read. But there is no research to show that children learn to read better when the text they are reading is restricted to only those words they have been taught to decode. One study suggests that a steady diet of decodable text may have a detrimental effect on reading fluency. Mesmer (2010) compared the accuracy and reading rate of 74 first-graders reading both a highly decodable and a nondecodable text at the beginning, middle, and end of first grade. Results showed that children read the decodable texts with significantly less speed. Even when the first-graders reread very simple decodable texts at the end of the year, when they would clearly be able to decode the words, they were still less fluent.

Children do need to learn to decode words, but there is a danger in having them figure out all—or almost all—the words as they are beginning to learn to read. The danger is that they will get in the habit of "sounding out" every word— and that is not how good readers read.

Children Need Systematic Phonics Instruction but There Is No Best Systematic Approach   (National Reading Panel, 2000; Stahl, Duffy-Hester, & Stahl, 1998). The question of how best to teach phonics is an important one and should not be too difficult to answer. In reality, it is quite difficult. Historically, there are three kinds of approaches to phonics—synthetic, analytic, and analogic.

Synthetic phonics programs teach sounds first, and children read words that contain those sounds. When children have learned the short sound for **a** and the sound for **m**, **t**, and **b**, they read the words **am**, **at**, **mat**, **bat**, **tab**, **tam**, and **bam**. As more sounds are added, more "decodable" words are read. The first "stories" the children read contain only words with the sounds they have been taught and a few necessary high-frequency words such as **the**, **is**, and **on**. "Real" stories are read aloud to the children, but the stories they read are intended primarily to practice decoding. Children also write, but their writing is limited to the words that contain the sounds they have been taught. Decodable text generally plays a large role in synthetic phonics programs.

Analytic programs begin by teaching children some words and then helping children to "analyze" those words and learn phonics rules and generalizations based on those words. The phonics in most basal readers is analytic and children read stories using sight words, context, and prediction as they are learning the phonics rules. Phonics is taught gradually over a longer period of time and children are encouraged to read all kinds of text and write about all kinds of topics. Their reading and writing are not controlled by or limited to the sounds they have been taught.

Analogic phonics is also based on words children have learned to read, but rather than teach children phonics rules, children are taught to notice patterns in words and to use the words they know to figure out other words. In an analogic approach to phonics, children would be taught that if you know how to read and spell **cat**, you can also read and spell **bat**, **rat**, **hat**, **sat**, and other rhyming words. Analogic phonics, like analytic phonics, is taught gradually and children's reading and writing are not restricted just to the patterns that they have been taught.

In addition to synthetic, analytic, and analogic approaches, Stahl, Duffy-Hester, and Stahl (1998) identify and review research on two "contemporary" approaches to phonics—spelling-based approaches and embedded-phonics approaches. Spelling-based approaches included word sorting and making words. They conclude that "both of these approaches seem to be effective as part of overall approaches to teaching reading" (p. 347).

The effectiveness of a spelling approach to decoding was confirmed in a study by Roberts and Meiring (2006). First-graders who participated in a spelling approach to decoding were significantly better at decoding at the end of first grade than a similar group whose phonics instruction was embedded with literature instruction. These differences applied to children with low, average, and high levels of letter–sound knowledge at the beginning of first grade. First-graders in the spelling phonics approach demonstrated superior performance on a comprehension test four years later. Graham, Harris, and Chorzempa (2002) found that second-graders experiencing difficulties in learning to spell and given remedial spelling instruction demonstrated significant growth in spelling, writing fluency, and decoding. Weiser and Mathes (2011) did a meta-analysis of studies in which students constructed words from letters or wrote words during phonics instruction. They concluded that children whose phonics instruction included spelling (encoding) words learned to decode much better than children who had systematic decoding instruction alone.

To explain their conclusion that there is no research-proven, most effective approach to phonics instruction, Stahl, Duffy-Hester, and Stahl (1998) theorized:

> The notion that children construct knowledge about words may explain why the differences among programs are small. As long as one provides early and systematic information about the code, it may not matter very much how one does it. . . . If the information is similar, the learning should be as well. . . . If this information is made available to children, then it may not matter exactly how the instruction occurs. (pp. 350–351)

The National Reading Panel (2000) reached a similar conclusion:

> In teaching phonics explicitly and systematically, several different instructional approaches have been used. These include synthetic phonics, analytic phonics, embedded phonics, analogy phonics, onset-rime phonics, and phonics through spelling. . . . Phonics-through-spelling programs teach children to transform sounds into letters to write words. Phonics in context approaches teach children to use sound–letter correspondences along with context clues to identify unfamiliar words they encounter in text. Analogy phonics programs teach children to use parts of written words they already know to identify new words. The distinctions between systematic phonics approaches are not absolute, however, and some phonics programs combine two or more of these types of instruction. (p. 89)

The National Reading Panel report went on to state that

> specific systematic phonics programs are all more effective than non-phonics programs and they do not appear to differ significantly from each other in their effectiveness. (p. 132)

Using a Variety of Phonics Approaches Seems to Matter Most for Struggling Readers　McCandliss, Beck, Sandak, and Perfetti (2003) investigated the effectiveness of Isabel Beck's instructional strategy, Word Building, with students who had failed to benefit from traditional phonics instruction. (Word Building is very similar to Making Words, Changing a Hen into a Fox, and Reading/Writing Rhymes, three of the phonics instructional activities in this book.) They found that the children who received this word-building instruction demonstrated significantly greater improvements on standardized measures of decoding, reading comprehension, and phonological awareness.

Davis (2000) found that spelling-based decoding instruction was as effective as reading-based decoding instruction for all her students but more effective for the children with poor phonological awareness.

A study by Juel and Minden-Cupp (2000) confirmed the notion that the most effective phonics instruction for struggling readers was not limited to a single approach. They concluded that the most effective teachers they observed of children who entered first grade with few literacy skills combined systematic letter–sound instruction with onset/rime analogy instruction and taught these units to application in both reading and writing.

Phonics Is Not the Problem for Most Older Struggling Readers　Given the emphasis on phonics that has pervaded our schools for the last decade, one could assume that intermediate and middle grade students who read below grade level demonstrate a lack of phonics skills. Looking at the profiles of 108 fourth-graders who scored below grade level in reading at the end of fourth grade, Buly and Valencia (2002) concluded that for more than half of these struggling fourth-grade readers, decoding was their strength. After measuring the ability of these students to read both real words and nonwords, their comprehension, fluency, and meaning/listening vocabulary, the researchers concluded:

> "Mandating phonics instruction . . . for all students who fall below proficiency would miss large numbers of students (more than 50 percent in our sample) whose word identification skills are fairly strong yet who struggle with comprehension, fluency or language. (p. 233)"

Similar results were found by Lesaux and Keiffer (2010) who studied 262 sixth-graders who scored below the 35th percentile on a reading comprehension measure. Scores were then obtained for these poor comprehenders on measures of both general and academic meaning vocabulary, fluency, and pseudoword word-identification accuracy. For 78 percent of these sixth-grade struggling readers, phonics skills as measured by their ability to read pseudowords was their strongest area. The remaining 22 percent of the students were weak in all areas—vocabulary, fluency, and word identification. Although weak, the pseudoword-identification accuracy of this third group was their strongest area. These researchers concluded:

"The findings demonstrate the need for middle schools to identify why students are having comprehension difficulties and to target instruction to meet their specific needs, given the wide variation in the struggling reader population. (abstract)"

The decade in which these students attended school was one in which their reading program placed a lot of emphasis on phonics instruction. It appears that the phonics instruction they were given was successful because identifying nonwords was the strength of most of these low-achieving readers. The results of these two studies with older struggling readers remind us that phonics skills are not sufficient for reading comprehension.

Summary: *The Research and Phonics They Use*

The activities described in *Phonics They Use* provide multiple and varied opportunities for children to obtain the information they need to successfully decode and spell words. The activities have a variety of focuses and proceed differently precisely because there is no best way to teach phonics. Also, the activities are multilevel so that children who are at different points in their word knowledge and who need varying amounts of information can all learn something about how words work from the same activity. All activities stress transfer because the only phonics knowledge that matters is the knowledge children actually use when they are reading and writing. There is no research-proven best way to teach phonics, but research does indicate that children who engage in a variety of phonics activities and in lots of reading and writing become fluent readers and writers.

chapter 15

Phonics Terminology for Teachers

In the midst of the current phonics frenzy, various groups have decided we need to test teachers' phonics knowledge. Unfortunately, the items on these phonics knowledge tests have little to do with how readers actually use phonics. The test items test knowledge of terminology and rules. Test items often ask teachers to recognize words with inflected endings, derivational suffixes, bound and free roots, and open and closed syllables. You may be asked to count syllables, speech sounds, and morphemes. Syllables are easy to count, but your answer might be wrong depending on your dialect. Dialect makes a difference for speech sounds, too.

While some studies have reported that many teachers fail such tests of phonics knowledge, there are no studies that demonstrate that teachers who pass such tests actually can and do teach more effectively or even teach phonics more effectively. If you have to take the test, this chapter will help you learn the terminology needed to pass it. The activities in this book will help you teach phonics in a way that all children can learn to decode and spell.

affixes   A term that includes both prefixes and suffixes. *Un* and *ible* are both affixes.

base word   (sometimes called *root* or *root word*) A word to which prefixes and/or suffixes can be added.

blending   Putting phonemes together to form a word. /h/ /a/ /t/ when blended make the word *hat*.

breve   A diacritic mark (ˇ) put over a vowel to indicate it has the "short" sound.

closed syllable   Syllable that ends in a consonant sound, such as the second syllable in *ho-tel*.

compound words   Combinations of two words.

consonant   A letter that is not a vowel. *Y* can be a consonant (*yes*) or vowel (*my, Danny*).

consonant blends   Two or more consonants in which you can hear both sounds blended. The word *blend* begins and ends with a consonant blend. *Squall* and *scrub* begin with blends. *Burst* ends with one. The words *comb* and *down* have two consonants at the end but they are not blends because you only hear one of them.

consonant clusters   Another term for *consonant blends*.

consonant digraph   Two consonant letters with a single sound different from that of either of the letters: *sh, ch, wh, th, ph.* (*Digraph* ends with the digraph *ph.*) The tricky part here is that silent letters don't count. *Write, knock,* and *gnu* do not begin with digraphs. I don't know what you call *wr, kn,* and *gn,* but I am sure it doesn't matter if you can produce the right sound when you see them (rarely) in a word.

consonant *le* syllables   Syllables that end in consonant *le* as in *table.*

decode   To "figure out the pronunciation" of a word.

derivational suffix   A suffix that changes the word meaning. The new word has a separate dictionary entry. The most common of these derivational suffixes include *less, ful,* and *er* (person or thing).

diphthong   Two vowel letters that produce a "gliding" sound. *Oi, oy, ou, ow* (except the *ou* in *soul* and *ow* in *tow*) are not diphthongs because each has a single sound.

encode   To write or spell a word.

homographs   Words with the same spelling but different pronunciations and meanings as in "She did not shed a *tear* when she saw the *tear* in her new dress."

homophones   (also called *homonyms*) Words with different spellings and meanings that are pronounced the same as in "It was *too* late *to* get *to* the *two*-o'clock show on time."

inflected endings   (sometimes called *inflectional suffixes*) Endings added to words to change where in sentences they are used. The most common inflected endings are *s, ing, ed, ly,* and *er/est* (comparative). It may help you to remember that the phrase *inflected endings* has three of them—the *ed* in *inflected* and the *ing* and *s* on *endings.*

long vowels   Vowels that "say their names." They can be spelled in lots of ways. If you are asked to think of all the ways you could spell a vowel such as "long *a*," think of words you know such as *rain, base, they, tray, eight, break,* and *vacation.* Remember that other vowels can spell the sound you are aiming for, as in *they* and *weigh,* and think of polysyllabic words as in *vacation.*

macron   A diacritic mark (—) put over a vowel to indicate it has the "long" sound.

morphemes   Meaning-bearing units in a word, usually roots, prefixes, and suffixes. Many words have multiple morphemes. *Believe* has one morpheme (the *be* in *believe* is not a morpheme): *believer* = 2; *believers* = 3; *unbelievers* = 4.

onsets   All the beginning letters up to the vowel: *sp*end; *kn*ow; *str*ing; *b*and.

open syllable   Syllable that ends in a vowel sound, such as the first syllable in *ho-tel*.

phonemes   (also called *speech sounds*) The smallest units of speech. *Bad* has three phonemes. *Good* has three phonemes—but four letters. To count phonemes, say the words and pretend you are Brian Williams or Katie Couric. In my New England dialect, *park* has only three speech sounds (New Englanders don't do *r*'s!), whereas Jim (husband) insists it has four. Use the "pretend you're a TV anchor" strategy and Jim is right. To determine phonemes, ignore letters and talk anchorese and count (and pray!). Here are a few examples: *ax* = 3; *sing* = 3; *think* = 4; *brought* = 4; *shine* = 3; *through* = 3; *spacious* = 6.

phonemic awareness   The ability to manipulate the sounds in words.

phonograms   Rimes in printed words.

phonological awareness   The awareness that spoken language is composed of separate words that make up sentences and that words are made up of syllables.

phonology   The study of speech sounds.

prefix   Something before a root word that usually changes meaning. The prefix in *unhappy* is *un*. In *uniform*, the prefix is *uni*. In *endure*, the prefix is *en*—but *en* is not a prefix in *end* or *enemy*.

r-controlled vowels   Vowels in which the vowel sound is affected by the *r* as in *car*, *her*, *girl*, *working*, and *urgent*.

rimes   (also called *phonograms* and *word families*) The vowel and following consonants within a syllable.

roots   (sometimes called *base words*) Roots are often of Latin or Greek origin. Roots are *bound* if they are not words by themselves. They are *free* when they are words by themselves. The word *telegraph* has a bound root—*tele* and a free root—*graph*.

schwa   The vowel in an unaccented syllable, sounds kind of like "uh." The schwa sound is underlined in these words: *alone*, *harmony*, *extra*, *celebrate*, *vacation*.

segmenting   The ability to separate the phonemes in a word. Hat is /h/ /a/ /t/

sight word   Another term for a high-frequency word.

silent e syllables   Syllables that end in silent *e* as in *decide*.

soft c and g   *C* and *g* are sometimes pronounced like *s* and *j* when followed by *e*, *i*, or *y* as in *cent*, *city*, *cyclone*, *gentle*, *gist*, and *gym*. These are sometimes called "soft" sounds.

speech sounds   Phonemes.

stem   Root or base word.

structural analysis   Identifying word parts such as compound words, affixes, roots, and syllables.

suffix   Something added to the end of a base or root word. Some suffixes are inflectional and some are derivational.

syllables   Units of sound that contain a vowel and may be preceded or followed by one or more consonants. *Pat* has one syllable; *Alice* has two. *Cunningham* has three. Open syllables end in a vowel and often have a long vowel sound—the *ti* in *tiger*. Closed syllables end in a consonant and often have a short vowel sound—the *Tig* in *Tigger*. If you have to explain why there is a double *m* in *comma*, explain that the first *m* closes the syllable, thus assuring its short vowel sound. With only one *m*, it would have the long sound as in *coma*.

vowel digraphs   Two vowel letters that make one sound. *Coat*, *yield*, *tie*, and *soul* have vowel digraphs.

vowels   Letters that are not consonants: *a, e, i, o, u*, and sometimes *y*.

vowel team syllables   Syllables that have two vowels with one sound (vowel digraphs).

references

Adams, M. J. (1990). *Beginning to read: Thinking and learning about print.* Cambridge, MA: MIT Press.

Allington, R. L. (2009). *What really matters in response to intervention.* Allyn & Bacon.

Anthony, J. L., Lonigan, C. J., Driscoll, K., Phillips, B. M., & Burgess, S. R. (2003). Phonological sensitivity: A quasi-parallel progression of word structure units and cognitive operations. *Reading Research Quarterly, 38,* 470–487.

August, D., & Shanahan, T. (2006). *Developing literacy in second language learners.* Mahwah, NJ: Erlbaum.

Bryant, P. E., Bradley, L., Maclean, M., & Crossland, I. (1989). Nursery rhymes, phonological skills, and reading. *Journal of Child Language, 16,* 407–428.

Buly, M. R., & Valencia, S. W. (2002). Below the bar: Profiles of students who fail state reading assessments. *Educational Evaluation and Policy Analysis, 24,* 219–239.

Caldwell, J. (2009). *Reading assessment: A primer for teachers and tutors* (2nd ed.). New York: Guilford.

Cassar, M., & Treiman, R. (1997). The beginnings of orthographic knowledge: Children's knowledge of double letters in words. *Journal of Educational Psychology, 89,* 631–644.

Clarke, L. K. (1988). Invented versus traditional spelling in first graders' writings: Effects on learning to spell and read. *Research in the Teaching of English, 22,* 281–309.

Clay, M. M. (1985). *The early detection of reading difficulties* (3rd ed.). Portsmouth, NH: Heinemann.

Cunningham, P. M. (1975–76). Investigating a synthesized theory of mediated word identification. *Reading Research Quarterly, 11,* 127–143.

Cunningham, P. M. (1979). A compare/contrast theory of mediated word identification. *The Reading Teacher, 32,* 774–778.

Cunningham, P. M. (1980). Applying a compare/contrast process to identifying polysyllabic words. *Journal of Reading Behavior, 12,* 213–223.

Cunningham, P. M. (1990). The Names Test: A quick assessment of decoding ability. *The Reading Teacher, 44,* 124–129.

Cunningham, P. M., & Allington, R. L. (2011). *Classrooms that work: They can all read and write* (5th ed.). New York: Longman.

Cunningham, P. M., & Cunningham, J. W. (1992). Making Words: Enhancing the invented spelling–decoding connection. *The Reading Teacher, 46,* 106–107.

Cunningham, P. M., & Cunningham, J. W. (2002). What we know about how to teach phonics. In A. E. Farstrup & S. J. Samuels (Eds.), *What research has to say about reading instruction* (3rd ed., pp. 87–109). Newark, DE: International Reading Association.

Cunningham, P. M., & Guthrie, F. M. (1982). Teaching decoding skills to educable mentally handicapped children. *The Reading Teacher, 35,* 554–559.

Cunningham, P. M., & Hall, D. P. (2009). *Making Words first grade: 100 hands-on lessons for phonemic awareness, phonics, and spelling.* Boston: Allyn & Bacon.

Cunningham, P. M., & Hall, D. P. (2009). *Making Words second grade: 100 hands-on lessons for phonemic awareness, phonics, and spelling.* Boston: Allyn & Bacon.

Cunningham, P. M., & Hall, D. P. (2009). *Making Words third grade: 70 hands-on lessons for teaching prefixes, suffixes, and homophones.* Boston: Allyn & Bacon.

Cunningham, P. M., & Hall, D. P. (2009). *Making Words fourth grade: 50 hands-on lessons for teaching prefixes, suffixes, and roots.* Boston: Allyn & Bacon.

Cunningham, P. M., & Hall, D. P. (2009). *Making Words fifth grade: 50 hands-on lessons for teaching prefixes, suffixes, and roots.* Boston: Allyn & Bacon.

Dale, E., & O'Rourke, J. (1981). *The living word vocabulary.* Chicago: Worldbook.

Davis, L. H. (2000). The effects of rime-based analogy training on word reading and spelling of first-grade children with good and poor phonological awareness (Doctoral dissertation, Northwestern University, 2000). *Dissertation Abstracts International, 61,* 2253A.

DeJong, P. F., & Share, D. L. (2007). Orthographic learning during oral and silent reading. *Scientific Studies of Reading, 11,* 55–71.

Duffelmeyer, F. A., Kruse, A. E., Merkley, D. J., & Fyfe, S. A. (1994). Further validation and enhancement of the Names Test. *The Reading Teacher, 48,* 118–128.

Ehri, L. C. (1991). Development of the ability to read words. In R. Barr, M. L. Kamil, P. B. Mosenthal, & P. D. Pearson, *Handbook of reading research* (Vol. 2, pp. 383–417). White Plains, NY: Longman.

Ehri, L. C. (2005). Learning to read words: Theories, findings, and issues. *Scientific Studies of Reading, 9,* 167–188.

Ehri, L. C., & Nunes, S. R. (2002). The role of phonemic awareness in learning to read. In A. E. Farstrup & S. J. Samuels (Eds.), *What research has to say about reading instruction* (3rd ed., pp. 110–139). Newark, DE: International Reading Association.

Elkonin, D. B. (1973). Reading in the USSR. In J. Downing (Ed.), *Comparative reading* (pp. 551–579). New York: Macmillan.

Fielding, L., & Roller, C. (1992). Making difficult books accessible and easy books acceptable. *The Reading Teacher, 45,* 678–685.

Fry, E., Fountoukidis, D. L., & Polk, J. K. (1985). *The new reading teacher's book of lists.* Englewood Cliffs, NJ: Prentice-Hall.

Gaskins I. W., Downer, M. A., Anderson, R. C., Cunningham, P. M., Gaskins, R. W., Schommer, M., & Teachers of the Benchmark School. (1988). A metacognitive approach to phonics: Using what you know to decode what you don't know. *Remedial and Special Education, 9,* 36–41.

Good, R. & Kaminski, R. (2002). *Dynamic indicators of basic early literacy skills* (6th ed.). Eugene, OR: Institute for the Development of Educational Achievement.

Goswami, U., & Bryant, P. (1990). *Phonological skills and learning to read.* East Sussex, UK: Erlbaum Associates.

Graham, S., Harris, K. R., & Chorzempa, B. F. (2002). Contribution of spelling instruction to the spelling, writing and reading of poor spellers. *Journal of Educational Psychology, 94,* 669–686.

Hall, D. P., & Cunningham, P. M. (2009). *Making Words kindergarten: 50 interactive lessons that build phonemic awareness, phonics, and spelling skills.* Boston: Allyn & Bacon.

Hogaboam, T., & Perfetti, C. A. (1978). Reading skill and the role of verbal experience in decoding. *Journal of Verbal Learning and Verbal Behavior, 70,* 717–729.

Johns, J. L., & Berglund, B. L. (2010). *Fluency: Differentiated interventions and progress-monitoring assessments* (4th ed.). Dubuque, IA: Kendall Hunt.

Jorm, A. F., & Share, D. L. (1983). Phonological recoding and reading acquisition. *Applied Psycholinguistics, 4,* 103–147.

Juel, C. (1990). Effects of reading group assignment on reading development in first and second grade. *Journal of Reading Behavior, 22,* 233–254.

Juel, C., & Minden-Cupp, C. (2000). Learning to read words: Linguistic units and instructional strategies. *Reading Research Quarterly, 35,* 458–492.

Kuhn, M. R., Schwanenflugel, P. J., Morris, R. D., Morrow, L., Woo, D. G., Meisinger, E. B., Sevcik, R. P., Bradley, B. A., & Stahl, S. A. (2006). Teaching children to become fluent and automatic readers. *Journal of Literacy Research, 38* (4), 357–387.

LaBerge, D., & Samuels, S. J. (1974). Toward a theory of automatic information processing in reading. *Cognitive Psychology, 6,* 293–323.

Lesaux, N. K., & Kieffer, M. J. (2010). Exploring sources of reading comprehension difficulties among language minority learners and their classmates in early adolescence. *American Educational Research Journal, 47,* 596–632. DOI: 10.3102/0002831209355469

McCandliss, B., Beck, I. L., Sandak, R., & Perfetti, C. (2003). Focusing attention on decoding for children with poor reading skills: Design and preliminary tests of the Word Building intervention. *Scientific Studies of Reading, 7,* 75–104.

McClelland, J. L., & Rumelhart, D. E. (Eds.) (1986). *Parallel distributed processing, Vol. 2: Psychological and biological models.* Cambridge, MA: MIT Press.

McConkie, G. W., Kerr, P. W., Reddix, M. D., & Zola, D. (1987). *Eye movement control during reading: The location of initial eye fixations on words* (Technical Report No. 406). Champaign, IL: Center for the Study of Reading, University of Illinois.

McCutchen, D., Bell, L. C., France, I. M., & Perfetti, C. A. (1991). Phoneme-specific interference in reading: The tongue-twister effect revisited. *Reading Research Quarterly, 26,* 87–103.

McKee, P. (1934). Reading and literature in the elementary school. Boston: Houghton Mifflin.

Mesmer, H. E. (2010). Textual scaffolds for developing fluency in beginning readers: Accuracy and reading rate in qualitatively leveled and decodable text. *Literacy Research and Instruction, 49*(1), 20–39.

Mewhort, D. J. K., & Campbell, A. J. (1981). Toward a model of skilled reading: An analysis of performance in tachistoscoptic tasks. In G. E. MacKinnon & T. G. Walker (Eds.), *Reading Research: Advances in Theory and Practice* (Vol. 3, 39–118). New York: Academic Press.

Moustafa, M. (1997). *Beyond traditional phonics.* Portsmouth, NH: Heinemann.

National Reading Panel. (2000). *Teaching children to read: An evidence-based assessment of the scientific research literature on reading and its implications for reading instruction: Reports of the subgroups* (National Institute of Health Pub. No. 00-4754). Washington, DC: National Institute of Child Health and Human Development.

Nicholson, T. (1991). Do children read words better in context or in lists? A classic study revisited. *Journal of Educational Psychology, 83,* 444–450.

Norris, J. A., & Hoffman, P. R. (2002). Phonemic awareness: A complex developmental process. *Topics in Language Disorders, 22,* 1–34.

Pearson, P. D. (1993). Teaching and learning reading: A research perspective. *Language Arts, 70,* 502–511.

Perfetti, C. A. (1991). The psychology, pedagogy, and politics of reading. *Psychological Science, 2,* 70, 71–76.

Pinnell, G. S & Fountais, I. *Word Matters.* Heinemann.

Rasinski, T. V. (2010). *The fluent reader* (2nd ed.). New York: Scholastic.

Rasinski, T. V., & Padak, N. D. (1998). How elementary students referred for compensatory reading instruction perform on school-based measures of word recognition, fluency and comprehension. *Reading Psychology, 19,* 185–216.

Rasinski, T. V., & Padak, N. D. (2008). *From phonics to fluency: Effective teaching of decoding and reading fluency in the elementary school* (2nd ed., pp. 216–217). Boston: Allyn & Bacon.

Rasinski, T. V., Reutzel, D. R., Chard, D., & Linan-Thompson, S. (2011). Reading fluency. In M. L. Kamil, P. D. Pearson, E. B. Moje, & P. P. Afflerbach (Eds.), *Handbook of reading research* (Vol. 4, pp. 286–319). New York: Routledge.

Rayner, K., & Pollatsek, A. (1989). *The psychology of reading.* Englewood Cliffs, NJ: Prentice Hall.

Roberts, T. A., & Meiring, A. (2006). Teaching phonics in the context of children's literature or spelling: Influences on first-grade reading, spelling, and writing and fifth-grade comprehension. *Journal of Educational Psychology, 98,* 690–713.

Rumelhart, D. E., & McClelland, J. L. (Eds.). (1986). *Parallel distributed processing, Vol. 1: Psychological and biological models.* Cambridge, MA: MIT Press.

Samuels, S. J. (2002). Reading fluency: Its development and assessment. In A. E. Farstrup & S. J. Samuels (Eds.), *What research has to say about reading instruction* (3rd ed., pp. 166–183). Newark, DE: International Reading Association.

Samuels, S. J. (2007). The DIBELS tests: Is speed of barking at print what we really mean by reading fluency? *Reading Research Quarterly, 42*(4), 563–566.

Seidenberg, M. S. (1987). Sublexical structures in visual word recognition: Access units or orthographic redundancy. In M. Coltheart (Ed.), *Attention and performance XII: The psychology of reading* (pp. 245–263). Hillsdale, NJ: Erlbaum Associates.

Seidenberg, M. S., & McClelland, J. L. (1989). A distributed, developmental model of word recognition and naming. *Psychological Review, 96,* 523–568.

Stahl, S. A., Duffy-Hester, A. M., & Stahl, K. A. (1998). Everything you wanted to know about phonics (but were afraid to ask). *Reading Research Quarterly, 33,* 338–355.

Stahl, S. A., & Heubach, K. M. (2005). Fluency-oriented reading instruction. *Journal of Literacy Research, 37*(1), 25–60.

Stanovich, K. E. (1991). Word recognition: Changing perspectives. In R. Barr, M. L. Kamil, P. B. Mosenthal, & P. D. Pearson (Eds.), *Handbook of reading research* (Vol. 2, pp. 418–452). White Plains, NY: Longman.

Stanovich, K. E., & West, R. F. (1989). Exposure to print and orthographic processing. *Reading Research Quarterly, 24,* 402–433.

Sulzby, E., Teale, W. H., & Kamberelis, G. (1989). Emergent writing in the classroom: Home and school connections. In D. S. Strickland & L. M. Morrow (Eds.), *Emerging literacy: Young children learn to read and write.* Newark, DE: International Reading Association.

Tannenhaus, M. K., Flanigan, H., & Seidenberg, M. S. (1980). Orthographic and phonological code activation in auditory and visual word recognition. *Memory and Cognition, 8,* 513–520.

Teale, W. H., & Sulzby, E. (1991). Emergent literacy. In R. Barr, M. Kamil, P. Mosenthal, & P. D. Pearson (Eds.), *Handbook of reading research* (Vol. 2, pp. 418–452). New York: Longman.

Trieman, R. (1985). Onsets and rimes as units of spoken syllables: Evidence from children. *Journal of Experimental Child Psychology, 39,* 161–181.

White, T., Sowell, J., & Yanagihara, A. (1989). Teaching elementary students to use word-part clues. *The Reading Teacher, 42,* 302–308.

Wright, D., & Ehri, L. C. (2007). Beginners remember orthography when they learn to read words: The case of doubled letters. *Applied Psycholinguistics, 28,* 115–133.

Wylie, R. E., & Durrell, D. D. (1970). Teaching vowels through phonograms. *Elementary English, 47,* 787–791.

Young, Sue. (1997). *The Scholastic rhyming dictionary.* New York: Scholastic.

Children's Books Cited

All about Arthur—An Absolutely Absurd Ape by Eric Carle (Franklin Watts, 1974)

Alphabet Starters (Rigby, 1996)

Are You My Mother? by P. D. Eastman (Random House, 1960)

Brown Bear, Brown Bear, What Do You See? by Bill Martin Jr. (Holt, 1983)

The Cat in the Hat by Dr. Seuss (Random House, 1957)

Dr. Seuss's ABC by Dr. Seuss (Random House, 1960)

Goodnight Moon by Margaret Wise Brown (Scholastic, 1989)

I Wish That I Had Duck Feet by Dr. Seuss (Random House, 1972)

In a People House by Dr. Seuss (Random House, 1972)

One Fish, Two Fish, Red Fish, Blue Fish by Dr. Seuss (Random House, 1960)

Ten Apples up on Top by Dr. Seuss (Random House, 1961)

There's a Wocket in My Pocket by Dr. Seuss (Random House, 1996)

index